TRIUMPHS IN SOCIETY

A Reader Celebrating Real Lives and Real Victories

TRIUMPHS IN SOCIETY

A Reader Celebrating Real Lives and Real Victories

JOHN SHERIDAN BIAYS
Broward Community College

CAROL WERSHOVEN
Palm Beach Community College

Prentice Hall

Upper Saddle River, New Jersey 07458

Library of Congress Cataloging-in-Publication Data

Triumphs in society : a reader celebrating real lives & real victories / [compiled by] John Sheridan Biays, Carol Wershoven.
    p.   cm.
    Includes bibliographical references.
    ISBN 0-13-012216-5
    1. Readers—Biography   2. English language—Rhetoric—Problems, exercises, etc.   3.
Report writing—Problems, exercises, etc.   4. College readers.   I. Biays, John Sheridan.
II. Wershoven, Carol

PE1127.B53 T75   2003
808'.0427—dc21   2002030772

Editor in Chief: Leah Jewell
Senior Acquisitions Editor: Craig Campanella
Editorial Assistant: Joan Polk
Assistant Editor: Karen Schultz
Production Editor: Maureen Benicasa
Production Assistants: Elizabeth Best and Marlene Gassler
Copyeditor: Krystyna Budd
Prepress and Manufacturing Buyer: Ben Smith
Marketing Manager: Rachel Falk
Marketing Assistant: Christine Moodie
Text Permissions Specialist: Robyn Renahan
Interior Image Specialist: Beth Boyd-Brenzel
Image Permissions Coordinator: Carolyn Gauntt
Cover Image Specialist: Karen Sanatar
Cover Director: Jayne Conte
Cover Designer: Bruce Kenselaar
Cover Art: Getty Images, Inc./PhotoDisc, Inc.; Pearson Education/PHCollege;
CORBIS; AP/WideWorld Photos; Guide Dogs for the Blind, Inc.; PhotoEdit

This book was set in 11/13 ITC Bookman by Interactive
Composition Corporation and was printed and bound by
Courier Companies, Inc. The cover was printed by Phoenix Color Corp.

For permission to use copyrighted material, grateful
acknowledgment is made to the copyright holders
on pages 339–343, which are considered an extension
of this copyright page.

Printed in the United States of America
10   9   8   7   6   5   4   3   2   1

ISBN 0-13-012216-5

Pearson Education LTD., London
Pearson Education Australia PTY, Limited, Sydney
Pearson Education Singapore, Pte. Ltd
Pearson Education North Asia Ltd, Hong Kong
Pearson Education Canada, Ltd., Toronto
Pearson Educación de Mexico, S.A. de C.V.
Pearson Education—Japan, Tokyo
Pearson Education Malaysia, Pte. Ltd
Pearson Education, Upper Saddle River, New Jersey

CONTENTS

*Sammy Sosa, Chicago Cubs superstar, breaks major
league records with ease, but his greatest gift is
using his fame and fortune to provide heartfelt relief
for hurricane victims in his native Dominican
Republic.*

SECTION 2: READING SELECTIONS GROUPED THEMATICALLY

Chapter 4: Everyday Heroes

In these profiles of compassionate individuals from all walks of life, People magazine describes how these "ordinary Americans make themselves unassuming symbols of the spirit of charity."

SELECTIONS BY RHETORICAL CONTENTS

NARRATION

DESCRIPTION

ILLUSTRATION

DIVISION AND CLASSIFICATION

COMPARISON AND CONTRAST

ARGUMENT

PREFACE

Triumphs in Society: A Reader Celebrating Real Lives and Real Victories is designed to provide writing instructors with an alternative to a traditional reader. Over the years, we became especially frustrated when searching for a suitable and accessible reader for our beginning writing students. So-called "reality-based" readers did a fine job of reflecting problems in society and patterns in popular culture, but their heavy reliance on the controversial issues of the day (with no resolution), along with their attempts to cover a multitude of societal ills, made us long for some well-written selections with universal appeal. We gradually started to understand what our students meant when they asked, "Are we going to read anything that's not so depressing?" They weren't actually expecting rose-colored, happily-ever-after vignettes; they merely wanted an uplifting change of pace. Thus, *Triumphs in Society* was born.

Initially, we collected over four hundred reading selections from a variety of journals and periodicals, and forty-six made our final cut. Aside from meeting our criteria for relevance, accessibility, and positive themes, each selection contains a clear premise, well-organized supporting paragraphs, specific details, and descriptive phrasing. We have grouped the readings thematically and have included an alternate table of contents for instructors interested in the rhetorical patterns of writing. In our table of contents, we have provided a brief overview of each reading for easy scanning and reference as you plan your assignments.

On a personal note, we were in the middle of developing *Triumphs in Society* when the tragedies of 9/11 shocked our nation and the world, and we certainly had doubts about continuing the project. Somehow, the uplifting nature of the book seemed less serious than readers filled with political and socioeconomic analysis, and a nation in mourning seemed far from triumphant. Soon, however, numerous stories started surfacing about extraordinary acts of selflessness and courage on the part of everyday heroes; we became more convinced than ever that our multicultural nation is indeed a success story in itself, one that we take pride in celebrating.

Triumphs in Society focuses on possibilities and solutions rather than on the severity of social problems and alarming trends. Although some selections have graphic descriptions, their inclusion is based primarily on the merits of good writing. We trust that our blend of writing instruction, positive readings, and suggested writing options will help your students develop their own voices, unique talents, and potential for success.

ACKNOWLEDGMENTS

We are indebted to many individuals whose enthusiasm for this project remained constant through some challenging times. We thank both our former and current editors, Maggie Barbieri and Craig Campanella, respectively, who recognized the need for a fresh approach in composition readers. We were also fortunate to work with Maureen Benicasa, production editor, who somehow kept track of all the chapters through several permutations; Krystyna Budd, the sole copyeditor for this reader who coded every selection for production; Robyn Renahan, who patiently tracked down permissions over several months; and Karen Schultz, who coordinated the cover design process and facilitated the photo archive searches. Also, many thanks to Joan Polk, editorial assistant, for answering our many questions and following up on any concerns we had. You fine folks at Prentice Hall are very skilled at calming authors' fears while production deadlines loom; thanks for keeping us on track through your good humor and camaraderie.

We also extend our deep thanks to the various publishers and authors who granted us permission to reprint their fine works. We are especially grateful to Earl Maucker, editor of the *South Florida Sun-Sentinel*, for granting special permission to reprint several articles that appeared in his paper over the past several years.

Thanks as always to our colleagues at Broward Community College and Palm Beach Community College for their ongoing support of our work. Finally, and most importantly, thanks to our students who are a constant source of ideas, inspiration, and purpose. We know you will continue to triumph over any adversity.

John Sheridan Biays
Carol Wershoven

SECTION ONE
READING ACTIVELY
AND WRITING FROM READING

Chapter One

Reading Actively

ATTITUDE

Reading actively involves a certain *attitude*. That attitude involves thinking of what you read as half of a conversation. The writer has opinions and ideas; he or she makes points just as you do when you write or speak. The writer supports his or her points with specific details. If the writer were speaking to you in a conversation, you would respond to his or her opinions or ideas. You might agree, disagree, or question, and you would jump into the conversation, linking or contrasting your ideas with those of the other speaker.

The right attitude toward reading requires that you read the same way you communicate with others: you *become involved*. In doing this, you mentally talk back as you read. Reacting as you read will keep you focused on what you are reading. If you are focused, you will remember more of what you read. With an active, involved attitude, you are ready to begin the steps of active reading.

READING IN STEPS

Active reading is done in three steps:

1. Prereading.
2. Reading.
3. Rereading with a pen or pencil.

PREREADING

Before you actually read an assigned essay, a chapter in a textbook, or an article in a journal, magazine, or newspaper, take a few minutes to look it over, and be ready to answer the questions in the Prereading Checklist.

A Prereading Checklist

✓ How long is this reading?

✓ Will I be able to read it in one sitting, or will I have to schedule several time periods to finish it?

✓ Are there subheadings in this reading? Do they give any hints about the reading?

✓ Are there any charts? Graphs? Boxes with information?

✓ Are there any photographs or illustrations with captions? Do the photographs, illustrations, or captions give any hints about the reading?

✓ Is there any introductory material about the reading or its author? Does the introductory material give me any hints about the reading?

✓ What is the title of the reading? Does the title hint at the point of the reading?

✓ Are any parts of the reading underlined or emphasized in some other way? Do the emphasized parts hint at the point of the reading?

Why Preread?

Prereading takes very little time, but it will help you a great deal. Some students believe it is a waste of time to scan an assignment; they think they should just jump right in and get the reading over with. However, spending just a few minutes on preliminaries can save hours later. Most importantly, prereading helps you become a *focused* reader.

If you scan the length of an assignment, you can pace yourself. In addition, if you know how long a reading is, you can see the overall format. A short reading, for example, makes its main point fairly soon, but a longer essay may take more time to develop its point and may use more details and examples.

Subheadings, charts, graphs, photographs, illustrations, and boxed or other highlighted materials are important enough that the author wants to emphasize them. Looking over that material *before* you read gives you an overview of the important points the reading will contain.

Introductory material or introductory questions will also help you know what to look for as you read. Background on the author or the subject may hint at ideas that will appear in the reading. Sometimes even the title of the reading will give you the main idea.

You should preread so that you can start reading the entire assignment with as much *knowledge* about the writer and the subject as you can gain. When you then read the entire assignment, you will be reading *actively* to gain even more knowledge.

Forming Questions Before You Read

If you want to read with a focus, it helps to ask questions before you read. Form questions by using the information you gain from prereading.

Start by noting the title and turn it into a question. If the title of your assigned reading is "The Worst Flood in U.S. History," you can ask the question, "What was the worst flood in U.S. history?" You can turn subheadings into questions. If you are reading an article about fighting stress, and one subheading is "Exercise," you can ask, "How is exercise related to fighting stress?"

You can also form questions from boxes, graphs, photographs, and illustrations. If a chapter in your music appreciation textbook includes a photograph of Carnegie Hall, you could ask, "What is Carnegie Hall?" or "What does Carnegie Hall have to do with music?" or "Why is Carnegie Hall so important?"

An Example of the Prereading Step

Take a look at the following article. Don't read it; *preread* it.

SAMPLE READING

Finding the Key

Matt Schudel

Matt Schudel, a writer for the South Florida Sun–Sentinel, wrote this article about an outstanding teacher and his exceptional students.

Words That You May Need to Know

ineducable (para. 12)	unable to learn
abstract (12)	not specific or touchable
chromosomes (12)	in a cell, chromosomes are the bodies that carry the genes. A "blind chromosomal chance" would be an accident of birth.
impairment (13)	weakness
autism (14)	a disorder with extreme withdrawal
multiple sclerosis (14)	a nerve disease that affects speech and movement
Down's syndrome (14)	a disorder present at birth that can include many mental and physical problems
unaccountable (14)	not explainable
phenomenal (14)	extraordinary
the norm (17)	typical
conventional (17)	usual, customary
prodigy (20)	someone of extraordinary talent
vocal (21)	related to the voice
vocation (21)	a calling, a strong inclination to follow a particular career

mute (23)	silent
nuances (27)	fine points
coherent (27)	logical, consistent
exults (27)	rejoices
marimba (27)	a musical instrument made of a set of wooden bars, struck with mallets
albeit (29)	although

> *Come to the classroom of Josué Rodriguez. You will hear more than the sound of music from seriously disabled students. You will hear a harmony of hearts.*

"We're going to be doing a medley," the teacher tells his class. "Do you know what a medley is?" 1

"Two songs at once," one of the students answers, eager as he can be. 2

"At least two," the teacher corrects. "Two or more songs, one after the other." 3

The teacher, surrounded by the nine students in this music class, begins to strum his guitar. 4

"You've got to look at me so you can sing nice and pretty," he says. 5

Two of the kids in his class are in motorized wheelchairs and have trouble controlling their limbs. One girl compulsively covers her face with her hands. Others have a hard time sitting still—or can do nothing but sit still. All are students at Bright Horizons School in Pompano Beach, Florida, a special public school for the mentally and physically handicapped. In spite of the obstacles, the teacher, Josué Rodriguez, reaches through the many veils and barriers of disability and opens a window where others had seen only darkness. 6

He asks the students, who are in their mid to late teens, to look at his eyes. He smacks a drumstick on a music stand to show how sharply a note should be sung. 7

"We've got to be very careful to sing soft and pretty," he says. "I've got to see your eyes."

He pauses, never losing the eye contact with his students, which is a kind of triumph in itself.

"Ready? 1-2-3-4. Now!"

All the kids start singing at the same time. They know all the words.

> All I really need is
> A song in my heart
> food in my belly
> love in my family

It may not be the finest music you have ever heard, but it is surely a thing of beauty. Your eyes and ears are witness to the kind of small miracle that is too seldom honored in our world: You see students, once branded "ineducable," grasp something abstract and repeat what they have learned. You see young people deprived by disease, circumstance, and blind chromosomal chance now move beyond the sad, dim place that had seemed their fate. You see smiles on their faces and a light in their eyes. And you understand why the patient, energetic, and sometimes stern man in the middle, Josué Rodriguez, is Broward County's Teacher of the Year.

Bright Horizons is part of the Broward County public school system, but it is hardly a traditional school. It was formed in 1978 to offer help to students many people used to think were beyond help. There are about 210 students, ranging from kindergarten to twelfth grade, and all have a physical or mental impairment. The purpose of Bright Horizons is to show these students—and the world at large—that their lives are not without purpose or hope. And, through a four-year post–high school program, Bright Horizons prepares some of its older students for jobs and helps them build lives of some independence.

You might think it would be depressing to stroll the halls of a school where wheelchairs line the halls, where the students are afflicted by autism, multiple sclerosis, Down's syndrome, or some unaccountable misfiring of impulses in the brain. But it's a bright, airy school, distinguished by a dedicated faculty, each of whom is certified in teaching the mentally handicapped. "All the teachers at Bright Horizons are there because they want to be," says Dolly Rump, whose fifteen-year-old son, Michael, has attended the school for several years. "When you see the dedication and gifts these teachers have, it's just phenomenal."

As you enter room 147, where Josué Rodriguez per- 15 forms his educational miracles, you see a slogan on the wall: "Music is the Universal Language of Mankind." He has taught at Bright Horizons for nine years. "This is a great place to work," he says. "The administration here always recognized the importance of music and the benefit of music in therapy. The parents are very thankful and appreciative."

Something about music, researchers have learned, 16 stimulates receptors in the brain that words and pictures can't reach. Children classified as profoundly retarded, children who can't speak an intelligible word, sometimes respond to the language of melody and rhythm. "I don't look at them or treat them with pity," says Rodriguez. "I feel very comfortable with them." His goal isn't to make his students into musicians. Rather, he wants them to maintain eye contact, to follow directions. Several times a year, his students take the stage for recitals and perform at malls, offices, and in other public settings. After a concert last year, Dolly Rump sent Rodriguez a letter. "As I watched the moving performance with tear-filled eyes," she wrote, "I was amazed and overwhelmed with pride and joy."

"Being Teacher of the Year doesn't define being success- 17 ful," Rodriguez explains. "Having my students do well is success." Teaching is hard under the best of circumstances. To work in a school where unpredictable behavior is the norm, where the students do not learn in conventional ways, is even more of a challenge. Rodriguez and the other teachers at Bright Horizons have an unusual devotion to their calling.

You can't coast in a school like this. It takes someone with strong inner will.

> *"Even if I won the lottery, I would still do this."*

At thirty-seven, Rodriguez has been a professional musician for more than twenty years. His grandfather in his home town of San Juan, Puerto Rico, taught him to play guitar when he was ten. His father is a draftsman by trade but writes songs on the side. By the time Josué (pronounced ho-SWAY) was sixteen, he was playing trumpet in dance bands. He attended a fine arts high school in San Juan, then went to college to study business. The call of music couldn't be denied, though, and after two years he transferred to the Puerto Rican Conservatory of Music and earned his degree. "I don't consider myself musically talented," he says—even though he plays trumpet in professional Latin bands and can play guitar, keyboards, and percussion instruments. "This is not being modest. I'm being sincere. But I truly believe this: I like music so much that it just goes to the students."

Another early influence on his life was the presence of neighbors and relatives with handicaps of various kinds. Young Josué was moved by their struggles and the gentleness of their spirit. He received a master's in music education for the handicapped at Ohio State University and became certified as a music therapist at Florida State University. "I've always loved teaching, all my life," he says. "I'm first a musician, then an educator, then a music educator for the handicapped, then a music therapist."

He is also a coach, helping direct a Little League team. He and his wife, Grace, have a five-year-old son, Daniel, who is already playing tunes by ear on piano. Josué almost hopes his son won't turn out to be a prodigy—he would rather have him get a solid education rather than turn exclusively to music early in life.

In his classes at Bright Horizons, Rodriguez uses some basic techniques of music education—breathing, vocal exercises, how to understand musical lines. But there's so much more to his teaching than music. He has to be firm with his students, reminding them to sit up, to watch him, to pay attention, to keep their hands at their sides. Beyond music and discipline, he has to form a bond that touches the human spirit. "I have always wanted to work with the mentally handicapped," he says. "It's something I call vocation. Even if I won the lottery, I would still do this."

"You can see the gift and the glow," says Dolly Rump, 22 the mother of one of Rodriguez's students. "It's beautiful what he can do with these kids."

At one time or another during the week, most of Bright 23 Horizons' 210 students will pass through Rodriguez's room. Some remain lost in a mute world of their own, but others are reaching beyond the narrow limits that they had known all their lives. Seated in a semicircle, they tap their feet in rhythm. "I'm trying to see if they have the concept of continuity, form, and structure," says Rodriguez. "I try to get them to pick up cues, to recognize a song." He punctuates the rhythmic strumming of his guitar with an occasional thump of his thumb against the wooden case. "You know why I'm playing like this?" he asks his class. "So you can feel the rhythm."

On his own time, Rodriguez has recorded several songs, 24 in which he plays all the musical parts on a computerized keyboard. He can add or remove any of the musical parts—percussion, bass, string effects—with the flip of a switch. Each four-to-five-minute tape takes four to eight hours to make. "You keep exploring, you keep growing, you keep learning," he says. "You do better things here"—he points at his head—"and you will demand better things from the students."

The kids hold bell-like chimes in their hands, each of a 25 different pitch. They receive their instructions: "You cannot scratch your head or scratch your nose or close your eyes. You must watch me closely, or the music will not be complete." Rodriguez begins the tape he has recorded, then points to each student at the right intervals in the song,

"Manha de Carnaval" by Luis Bonfa. When they keep up with their teacher, when they can strike their instruments on cue, the reward is the sound of music. It's a lovely thing to hear—and to see.

"There you go!" Rodriguez encourages. "I'm happy now. Beautiful."

In another class, the kids are singing, some with a real feeling for the nuances of music. Rodriguez is playing the Richie Valens hit "La Bamba" on his guitar, and one student sings, "Bye, La Bamba, Bye, La Bamba." "Go, boy!" Rodriguez calls out. Later he explains that this student cannot speak in any coherent sense. Yet, when words are matched with music, he can repeat the lyrics—and remember them from one class to the next. "To me, that's great," Rodriguez exults. "It's the power of music. He's capable of putting groups of words and phrases together when it's with music." A girl in another class plays the marimba with flair, and a boy sings with strength and a touching grace in his voice. "When you see kids with that ability, it's wow, great," says Rodriguez.

"I've made unannounced appearances in class, just to see what's going on," adds parent Dolly Rump. "I'm so amazed at what he can get these kids to do. Each kid is so in tune with him." His fellow teachers at Bright Horizons, equally amazed, nominated him for Teacher of the Year, the highest honor a classroom teacher can receive. "Everybody who meets Josué is not surprised," notes Arlene Klaasen, the assistant principal. "He's taken his music into the classroom, but he looks at the total child. He embraces everything we are doing here at Bright Horizons."

Rodriguez did not expect the award, "especially since this is not my first language." His English is perfectly fluent, albeit with a strong accent. But his most eloquent language is music—and the ways he can make it resound with students who have known too little harmony in their lives. "Sometimes there are things I cannot explain," he says. "This is my life. You have no choice but to open your heart."

Prereading Results

By prereading the article, you might notice the following:

- The title is "Finding the Key."
- The author is a writer in Florida.
- There are many vocabulary words.
- The essay is about a teacher and his students.
- There is something in italics about Josué Rodriguez's classroom, music, and disabled students.
- There is a box with a statement about winning the lottery and still doing something.

Prereading Questions

You can make questions out of the information you gathered by prereading. Then you can begin reading the article with these questions in mind:

- What is the key? What is the key to?
- What is special about this teacher and students? Who is Josué Rodriguez?
- What does music have to do with him or his students?
- Who would keep doing something if he or she won the lottery?
- What would he or she keep doing?

READING

The first time you read, *try to get a sense of the whole piece* you are reading. Reading with questions in mind can help you do this. If you find that you are confused by a certain part of the reading selection, go back and reread that part. If you do not know the meaning of a word, check the vocabulary list to see if it is defined for you. If it is not defined, try to figure out the meaning from the way the word is used in the sentence.

If you find that you have to read more slowly than usual, do not worry. People vary their reading speed according to what they read and why they are reading it. If you are reading for entertainment, for example, you can read quickly; if you are reading a chapter in a textbook, you must read more slowly. The more complicated the reading selection, the more slowly you will read it.

An Example of the Reading Step

Now read "Finding the Key." When you've completed your first reading, you will probably have some answers to the prereading questions that you formed.

Answers to the Prereading Questions

Here are the answers to the prereading questions formed earlier:

- The key in the title can be a key in music, or it can be the key to open students' minds.
- This teacher is a Teacher of the Year.
- Josué Rodriguez is his name.
- He teaches music to disabled students.
- He says he would keep teaching music to the handicappped even if he won the lottery.

These answers provide you with a great deal of information about the ideas in this reading selection. Now you are ready to reread, for a closer look at the essay.

REREADING WITH PEN OR PENCIL

The second reading is the crucial one. At this point, you begin to think on paper as you read. In this step, you make notes or write about what you read. Some students are reluctant to do this, for they are not sure what to note or write. Think of *making these notes as a way of learning, thinking, reviewing, and reacting.* Reading with a pen or pencil in your hand keeps you alert. With that pen or pencil, you can do any of the following:

- Mark the main point of the reading.
- Mark other points.

- Define words you don't know.
- Question points of the reading you are not sure of.
- Evaluate the writer's ideas.
- React to the writer's opinions or examples.
- Add ideas, opinions, or examples of your own.

There is no single system for marking or writing as you read. Some readers like to underline the main idea with two lines and to underline other important ideas with one line. Some students like to put an asterisk, a star, next to important ideas; others like to circle key words.

Some people use the margins to write comments such as "I agree!" or "Not true!" or "That has happened to me." Sometimes readers put questions in the margin; sometimes they summarize a point in the margin, next to its location in the essay. Some people make notes in the white space above the reading and list important points; others use the space at the end of the reading. Every writer who writes as he or she reads has a personal system; what these systems share is an attitude. *If you write as you read, you concentrate on the reading selection, get to know the writer's ideas, and develop ideas of your own.*

As you reread and write notes, do not worry too much about noticing the "right" ideas. Think of rereading as the time to jump into a *conversation* with the writer.

An Example of Rereading with a Pen or Pencil

For "Finding the Key," your marked article might look like the following:

Finding the Key

Matt Schudel

Come to the classroom of Josué Rodriguez. You will hear more than the sound of music from seriously disabled students. You will hear a harmony of hearts.

"We're going to be doing a medley," the teacher tells his class. "Do you know what a medley is?"

"Two songs at once," one of the students answers, eager as he can be.

"At least two," the teacher corrects. "Two or more songs, one after the other."

The teacher, surrounded by the nine students in this music class, begins to strum his guitar.

"You've got to look at me so you can sing nice and pretty," he says.

Two of the kids in his class are in motorized wheelchairs and have trouble controlling their limbs. One girl compulsively covers her face with her hands. Others have a hard time sitting still—or can do nothing but sit still. All are students at Bright Horizons School in Pompano Beach, Florida, a special public school for the mentally and physically handicapped. In spite of the obstacles, the teacher, Josué Rodriguez, reaches through the many veils and barriers of disability and <u>opens a window where others had seen only darkness</u>.

He asks the students, who are in their mid to late teens, to look at his eyes. He smacks a drumstick on a music stand to show how sharply a note should be sung.

"We've got to be very careful to sing soft and pretty," he says. "I've got to see your eyes."

He pauses, never losing the eye contact with his students, which is a kind of triumph in itself.

"Ready? 1-2-3-4. Now!"

All the kids start singing at the same time. They know all the words.

All I really need is
A song in my heart
food in my belly
love in my family

It may not be the finest music you have ever heard, but it is surely a thing of beauty. Your eyes and ears are witness to the kind of small miracle that is too seldom honored in our world: You see students, once branded "in-educable," grasp something abstract and repeat what they have learned. You see young people deprived by disease, circumstance, and blind chromosomal chance now move beyond the sad, dim place that had seemed their fate. You see smiles on their faces and a light in their eyes. And you understand why the patient, energetic, and sometimes stern man in the middle, Josué Rodriguez, is Broward County's Teacher of the Year.

Bright Horizons is part of the Broward County public school system, but it is hardly a traditional school. It was formed in 1978 to offer help to students many people used to think were beyond help. There are about 210 students, ranging from kindergarten to twelfth grade, and all have a physical or mental impairment. The purpose of Bright Horizons is to show these students—and the world at large—that their lives are not without purpose or hope. And, through a four-year post-high school program, Bright Horizons prepares some of its older students for jobs and helps them build lives of some independence.

You might think it would be depressing to stroll the halls of a school where wheelchairs line the halls, where the students are afflicted by autism, multiple sclerosis, Down's syndrome, or some unaccountable misfiring of impulses in the brain. But it's a bright, airy school, distinguished by a dedicated faculty, each of whom is certified in teaching the mentally handicapped. "All the teachers at Bright Horizons are there because they want to be," says Dolly Rump, whose fifteen-year-old son, Michael, has attended the school for several years. "When you see the dedication and gifts these teachers have, it's just phenomenal."

As you enter room 147, where Josué Rodriguez performs his educational miracles, you see a slogan on the wall: "Music is the Universal Language of Mankind." He has taught at Bright Horizons for nine years. "This is a great place to work," he says. "The administration here always recognized the importance of music and the benefit of music in therapy. The parents are very thankful and appreciative."

Something about music, researchers have learned, stimulates receptors in the brain that words and pictures can't reach. Children classified as profoundly retarded, children who can't speak an intelligible word, sometimes respond to the language of melody and rhythm. "I don't look at them or treat them with pity," says Rodriguez. "I feel very comfortable with them." His goal isn't to make his students into musicians. Rather, he wants them to maintain

that's true!

likes his work

able to be understood

attitude to students

eye contact, to follow directions. Several times a year, his students take the stage for recitals and perform at malls, offices, and in other public settings. After a concert last year, Dolly Rump sent Rodriguez a letter. "As I watched the moving performance with tear-filled eyes," she wrote, "I was amazed and overwhelmed with pride and joy."

"Being Teacher of the Year doesn't define being successful," Rodriguez explains. "Having my students do well is success." Teaching is hard under the best of circumstances. To work in a school where unpredictable behavior is the norm, where the students do not learn in conventional ways, is even more of a challenge. Rodriguez and the other teachers at Bright Horizons have an unusual devotion to their calling. You can't coast in a school like this. It takes someone with strong inner will.

wants students to succeed

"Even if I won the lottery, I would still do this."

At thirty-seven, Rodriguez has been a professional musician for more than twenty years. His grandfather in his home town of San Juan, Puerto Rico, taught him to play guitar when he was ten. His father is a draftsman by trade but writes songs on the side. By the time Josué (pronounced ho-SWAY) was sixteen, he was playing trumpet in dance bands. He attended a fine arts high school in San Juan, then went to college to study business. The call of music couldn't be denied, though, and after two years he transferred to the Puerto Rican Conservatory of Music and earned his degree. "I don't consider myself musically talented," he

music background

says—even though he plays trumpet in professional Latin bands and can play guitar, keyboards, and percussion instruments. "This is not being modest. I'm being sincere. But I truly believe this: I like music so much that it just goes to the students."

Another early influence on his life was the presence of neighbors and relatives with handicaps of various kinds. Young Josué was moved by their struggles and the gentleness of their spirit. He received a master's in music education for the handicapped at Ohio State University and became certified as a music therapist at Florida State University. "I've always loved teaching, all my life," he says. "I'm first a musician, then an educator, then a music educator for the handicapped, then a music therapist."

the handicapped in his life

loves teaching

He is also a coach, helping direct a Little League team. He and his wife, Grace, have a five-year-old son, Daniel, who is already playing tunes by ear on piano. Josué almost hopes his son won't turn out to be a prodigy—he would rather have him get a solid education rather than turn exclusively to music early in life.

In his classes at Bright Horizons, Rodriguez uses some basic techniques of music education—breathing, vocal exercises, how to understand musical lines. But there's so much more to his teaching than music. He has to be firm with his students, reminding them to sit up, to watch him, to pay attention, to keep their hands at their sides. Beyond music and discipline, he has to form a bond that touches the human spirit. "I have always wanted to

forms a bond

work with the mentally handicapped," he says. "It's something I call vocation. <u>Even if I won the lottery, I would still do this.</u>"

wouldn't quit if he were rich

"You can see the gift and the glow," says Dolly Rump, the mother of one of Rodriguez's students. "It's beautiful what he can do with these kids."

At one time or another during the week, most of Bright Horizons' 210 students will pass through Rodriguez's room. Some remain lost in a mute world of their own, but others are reaching beyond the narrow limits that they had known all their lives. Seated in a semicircle, they tap their feet in rhythm. "I'm trying to see if they have the concept of continuity, form, and structure," says Rodriguez. "I try to get them to pick up cues, to recognize a song." He punctuates the rhythmic strumming of his guitar with an occasional thump of his thumb against the wooden case. "You know why I'm playing like this?" he asks his class. "So you can feel the rhythm."

<u>On his own time, Rodriguez has recorded several songs</u>, in which he plays all the musical parts on a computerized keyboard. He can add or remove any of the musical parts— percussion, bass, string effects—with the flip of a switch. <u>Each four-to-five-minute tape takes four to eight hours to make.</u> "You keep exploring, you keep growing, you keep learning." he says. "You do better things here"—he points at his head—"and you will demand better things from the students."

makes special tapes

The kids hold bell-like chimes in their hands, each of a different pitch. They receive their instructions: "You cannot scratch your head or scratch your nose or close your eyes. You must watch me closely, or the music will not be complete." Rodriguez begins the tape he has recorded, then points to each student at the right intervals in the song, "Manha de Carnaval" by Luis Bonfa. When they keep up with their teacher, when they can strike their instruments on cue, the reward is the sound of music. It's a lovely thing to hear—and to see.

"There you go!" Rodriguez encourages. "I'm happy now. Beautiful."

In another class, the kids are singing, some with a real feeling for the nuances of music. Rodriguez is playing the Richie Valens hit "La Bamba" on his guitar, and one student sings, "Bye, La Bamba, Bye, La Bamba." "Go, boy!" Rodriguez calls out. Later he explains that this student cannot speak in any coherent sense. Yet, when words are matched with music, he can repeat the lyrics— and remember them from one class to the next. "To me, that's great," Rodriguez exults. "It's the power of music. He's capable of putting groups of words and phrases together when it's with music." A girl in another class plays the marimba with flair, and a boy sings with strength and a touching grace in his voice. "When you see kids with that ability, it's wow, great," says Rodriguez.

"I've made unannounced appearances in class, just to see what's going on, adds parent Dolly Rump. "I'm so amazed at what he can get these kids to do. Each kid is so in tune with him." His fellow teachers at Bright Horizons, equally amazed, nominated him for Teacher of the Year, the highest honor a classroom teacher can receive. "Everybody who meets

Josué is not surprised," notes Arlene Klaasen, the assistant principal. "He's taken his music into the classroom, but he looks at the total child. He embraces everything we are doing here at Bright Horizons."

Rodriguez did not expect the award, "especially since this is not my first language." His English is perfectly fluent, albeit with a strong accent. But his most eloquent language is music—and the ways he can make it resound with students who have known too little harmony in their lives. "Sometimes there are things I cannot explain," he says. "This is my life. You have no choice but to open your heart."   *

What the Notes and Markings Mean

In the marked article, "Finding the Key," the underlining indicates sentences or phrases that seem important. The words in the margin are often summaries of what is underlined. The words "attitude to students," "music background," and "makes special tapes," for example, are like subtitles or labels in the margins. The asterisks refer to very important ideas.

Sometimes words in the margin are reactions. The words "That's true!" in the margin next to "Music is the Universal Language of Mankind" express the reader's agreement with the slogan. One word in the margin is a definition. The word "intelligible" in the essay is defined as "able to be understood" in the margin.

Why Marking and Making Notes Is Important

The marked-up article is a flexible tool. You can go back and mark it further. You may change your mind about your notes and comments and find other, better, or more important points in the article.

You write as you read to involve yourself in the reading process. Marking what you read can help you in other ways, too. If you are to be tested on the reading selection or asked to discuss it, you can scan your markings and notations at a later time for a quick review. If you are required to write a summary of the reading selection or to react to it by writing on a related topic, marking is the first step to your own successful writing.

Chapter Two
Writing a Summary of a Reading

THE READING STEPS

Before you can begin to write a summary of an article or essay, you must work through the reading steps:

1. **Prereading:** Survey the reading selection, noting its title, length, introductory information, boxes, charts, subtitles, photographs, or illustrations. Form questions about the information you gathered by surveying.
2. **Reading:** Read the entire selection, looking for answers to the questions you formed.
3. **Rereading with Pen or Pencil:** Carefully reread the selection, marking it and noting important points, examples, and your reactions.

PLANNING A SUMMARY

A summary of a reading tells the important ideas in brief form. It includes

1. the writer's main idea,
2. the ideas used to explain the main idea, and
3. some examples used to support the main idea.

When you make notes on a reading selection, you have already begun the planning stage for a summary. Review the marked article, "Finding the Key," on pages 14–21. The marked article reveals your first thoughts about a reading selection.

Marking a List of Ideas

To think further about the article, you can *list the points* (words, phrases, sentences) you've already marked on the reading selection. To find the main idea for your summary and the ideas and examples connected to the main idea, you can *mark related items on your list.* Four letters are used to mark the following:

G	descriptions of Josué Rodriguez's **gift**
M	his love for **music**
S	his love for his **students**
W	his love for his **work**

Items without a mark do not fit any of the categories.

A List of Ideas for a Summary of "Finding the Key"

G	opens a window for students
G	students who were lost are learning
S	patient, energetic
	Teacher of the Year
	Music is the Universal Language
W	a great place to work
S	feels comfortable with students
S	wants them to succeed
M	professional musician for more than twenty years
M	degree in music
	relatives and neighbors with handicaps
S	degree in music education for the handicapped
W	loves teaching
G	he forms a bond
W	would still teach if he won the lottery
W	makes special tapes
G	you have to open your heart

The marked list could then be organized into categories, like this:

Descriptions of Josué Rodriguez's Gift

opens a window for students
students who were lost are learning
he forms a bond
you have to open your heart

His Love for Music

> professional musician for more than twenty years
> degree in music

His Love for His Work

> a great place to work
> loves teaching
> would still teach if he won the lottery
> makes special tapes

His Love for His Students

> patient, energetic
> feels comfortable with students
> wants them to succeed
> degree in music education for the handicapped

Selecting a Main Idea

The next step is to select the idea you think is the writer's main point. From reading and thinking about this article, you know that it is about a teacher who won an award as Teacher of the Year. The article tells about the teacher, Josué Rodriguez. It tells about his background, his attitudes, and his behavior in the classroom. But it seems to focus on Josué Rodriguez's gift. He has a gift for teaching. You have several ideas about his gift in one part of your list. You decide part of your main point will be about his gift. Then you think about *why* he is so gifted, and you look at the categories on your list: love for music, love for work, love for students. You decide on this main idea:

Josué Rodriguez is a gifted teacher because he loves music, his work, and his students.

Once you have a main idea, you can move to the next stage of writing a summary.

WRITING A SUMMARY PARAGRAPH

The Outline of a Summary Paragraph

With your main idea and your categories, you can write an outline. In the following outline, your main idea has become the topic sentence of the outline, and the ideas in the other categories are the support.

An Outline for a Summary Paragraph of "Finding the Key"

topic sentence: Josué Rodriguez is a gifted teacher because he loves music, his work, and his students.

love for music
- He has a college degree in music.
- He has been a professional musician for more than twenty years.

love for his work
- He says his school is a great place to work.
- He loves teaching.
- He would still teach if he won the lottery
- He makes special tapes for his students.

love for his students
- He is patient and energetic.
- He got a degree in music education for the handicapped.
- He feels comfortable with handicapped students.
- He wants his students to succeed.

In the outline, the order of some points has been changed from what it was in the categories. You can do this kind of rearranging in planning a summary.

Writing the Draft of a Summary Paragraph

The first draft of your summary paragraph is your first try at combining all the material into one paragraph. This draft is much like the draft of any other paragraph, with one exception: *When you summarize another person's ideas, be sure to say whose ideas you are writing.* That is, *attribute* the ideas to the writer. Let the reader of your paragraph know

1. the author of the article you are summarizing
2. the title of the article you are summarizing

You may want to do this by giving your summary paragraph a title, such as

A Summary of "Finding the Key" by Matt Schudel

(**Note** that you put the title of Schudel's article in quotation marks.)

You may want to *put the title and the author into the paragraph itself.* Following is a draft version of a summary paragraph of "Finding the Key" with the title and author incorporated into the paragraph. As you read it, you'll notice the title and author are part of an introductory sentence.

A Draft for a Summary Paragraph of "Finding the Key"

"Finding the Key" by Matt Schudel is about Josué Rodriguez, a man chosen as Broward County, Florida's Teacher of the Year. Rodriguez is a gifted teacher because he loves music, his work, and his students. He has a college degree in music. Rodriguez has been a professional musician for more than twenty years. He says his school is a great place to work. He loves teaching. He says he would still teach if he won the lottery. He makes special tapes for his students. He feels comfortable with handicapped students. He got a degree in music education for the handicapped. He is patient and energetic in the classroom. He wants his students to succeed.

When you look this draft over and read it aloud, you may notice a few problems:

- The sentences are choppy; some could be combined.
- The paragraph needs transitions.
- More specific details are needed.
- The information that Josué Rodriguez teaches music to handicapped students should come early in the paragraph.
- The paragraph needs a conclusion.

(**Note** that when you refer to a person in your summary, use the person's first and last name the first time you make a reference. For example, you write "Josué Rodriguez" the first time you refer to him. Later in the paragraph, if you want to refer to him again, use only the last name. Thus, your second reference would be to "Rodriguez.")

A Final Version of a Summary Paragraph of "Finding the Key"

(Changes from the draft are underlined.)

information added	"Finding the Key" by Matt Schudel is about Josué Rodriguez, <u>a music teacher of handicapped children</u> and Broward County, Florida's Teacher of the Year. Rodriguez is a gifted teacher because he loves music, his
sentences combined	work, and his students. <u>Rodriguez has a college degree in music and has been a professional musician</u>
details added	<u>for more than twenty years. He plays trumpet in a Latin band and can play other instruments.</u> <u>In</u>
transition added	<u>addition to loving music,</u> Rodriguez
details added	loves to teach it. He says <u>Bright Horizons School</u> is a great place to work. He claims that he loves teaching so much he would still

transition added	teach if he won the lottery. He <u>even</u> <u>spends his free time making special</u>
details added	<u>music tapes on a computerized key-</u> <u>board, so that his students can</u> <u>become more involved in music.</u>
transition added	<u>Rodriguez's devotion to his work is</u> <u>linked to</u> his devotion to his
sentences combined	students. <u>He has a degree in music</u> <u>education for the handicapped and</u> <u>feels comfortable with these special</u> <u>students.</u> In the classroom, he wants
conclusion added	his students to succeed. <u>Because of</u> <u>Rodriguez's gift of caring, students</u> <u>who were lost are learning.</u>

WRITING A SUMMARY ESSAY

If you are asked to write a summary in essay form, you begin the same way you would begin to write a summary paragraph: by following the steps of active reading, by listing and grouping ideas, and by identifying the main idea and including supporting ideas and examples.

   Look again at the original list of ideas and categories for a summary paragraph of "Finding the Key."

A List of Ideas and Categories for a Summary Essay of "Finding the Key"

Descriptions of Josué Rodriguez's Gift

   opens a window for students
   students who were lost are learning
   he forms a bond
   you have to open your heart

His Love for Music

   professional musician for more than twenty years
   degree in music

His Love for His Work

> a great place to work
> loves teaching
> would still teach if he won the lottery
> makes special tapes

His Love for His Students

> patient, energetic
> feels comfortable with students
> wants them to succeed
> degree in music education for the handicapped

Selecting a Main Idea

To write a summary essay, you could work with the same main idea that you could work with in a summary paragraph:

Josué Rodriguez is a gifted teacher because he loves music, his work, and his students.

The main idea would be the same whether you write a paragraph or an essay to explain it. The article is about Josué Rodriguez's gift, and it focuses on describing his gift and why he is so gifted. Your sentence links the gift and the reasons for it.

The Outline for a Summary Essay

You know that a summary essay must be longer than a summary paragraph, but you may not know that it does not have to include more points. That is, it can use the same main point and use the same subpoints (taken from the categories) to explain the main point, as a summary paragraph. But *the ideas need to be developed with more examples and details.* Following is an outline for a summary essay of "Finding the Key." Read it; then compare it to the outline for a summary paragraph of the same article.

Outline for a Summary Essay
of "Finding the Key"

Thesis sentence

I. Josué Rodriguez is a gifted teacher because he loves music, his work, and his students.

Topic sentence

II. Rodriguez's life has always been full of music.

Details

   A. He learned to play guitar when he was ten.
   B. He has a college degree in music.
   C. He has been a professional musician for more than twenty years.
   D. He plays several instruments.
   E. A sign in his office calls music a universal language.

Topic sentence

III. Rodriguez loves to teach music.

Details

   A. He says his school is a great place to work.
   B. He says he would still teach if he won the lottery.
   C. He says he likes music so much his enthusiasm goes to the students.
   D. He makes special tapes for the students.
   E. He says he keeps learning himself, to help students learn.

Topic sentence

IV. Rodriguez cares deeply for his students.

Details

   A. He got a degree in music education for the handicapped.

> B. He feels comfortable with
>   handicapped students.
> C. He is patient and energetic.
> D. He wants his students to
>   succeed.
> E. The mother of one of his
>   students praises him.
>
> **Topic**   V. In his classroom, Rodriguez
> **sentence**   combines three talents:
>
> **Conclusion**   a talent for music, a talent
>   for teaching, and a talent for
>   opening his heart.

If you compare the paragraph outline to the essay outline, you notice these similarities and differences:

- The topic sentence of the paragraph outline is the thesis of the essay outline.
- The three categories of the paragraph outline—love of music, love of work, love of students—are changed into topic sentences for the body paragraphs in the essay outline.
- There are more details in the essay outline.

Writing the Draft of a Summary Essay

The first draft of your summary essay is your first try at combining all the material of your outline into an essay. It is the place where you can add more supporting details and examples and where you write a lead-in (introduction) to your thesis and a short concluding paragraph.

In this draft, you also need to attribute the ideas of the summary essay to the author of the article you are writing about. You do this by one of the following strategies:

1. using the title and author of the article in the title of your essay, or
2. including the title and author of the article in your first paragraph.

Following is a draft of a summary essay on "Finding the Key."

Draft for a Summary Essay on "Finding the Key"

lead-in   "Finding the Key" by Matt Schudel is about Josué Rodriguez, a music teacher of handicapped children. Rodriguez was selected as Broward County, Florida's Teacher of the Year because of his extraordinary ability to open windows for students who were believed to be

thesis sentence   unable to learn. Josué Rodriguez is a gifted teacher because he loves music, his work, and his students.

topic sentence   Rodriguez's life has always been full of music. He learned to play

body paragraph on love for music   guitar when he was ten. He has a degree in music from the Puerto Rican Conservatory of Music. He has been a professional musician for more than twenty years. He plays several instruments. A sign in his office calls music a universal language.

topic sentence   Rodriguez loves to teach music. He says Bright Horizons School is a

body paragraph on love for work   great place to work. He says he would still teach even if he won the lottery. He says he likes music so much his enthusiasm goes to his students. He makes special tapes for his students. He says he keeps learning himself, to help students learn.

topic sentence   Rodriguez cares deeply for his students. He got a degree in music

body paragraph on love for students	education for the handicapped. He feels comfortable with handicapped students. He is patient and energetic. He wants his students to succeed. The mother of one of his students praises him.
topic sentence	In his classroom, Rodriguez combines three talents: a talent for music, a talent for teaching, and a
conclusion	talent for opening his heart. His gift helps lost students to learn.

When you look over this draft and read it aloud, you notice a few problems:

- Too many sentences start with "He." In one paragraph, four sentences start with "He says."
- The essay could use a few more specific details.
- Some choppy sentences could be combined.
- In some places, transitions are needed.
- In some places, the word choice could be improved.
- The conclusion is too short.

Revising the draft would mean eliminating the repetitive use of "He" at the beginning of sentences, adding details and transitions, improving the word choice, combining sentences, and improving the conclusion.

(**Note** that when you refer to a person in your writing, you use his or her first and last name (like Josué Rodriguez) the first time you make a reference, and his or her last name (Rodriguez) in further references. But in this essay, the thesis sentence, which is not the first reference to Josué Rodriguez, uses his full name. It does so to emphasize the full name of this person in the thesis, the main point of the essay.)

A Final Version of a Summary Essay

Look carefully at the revised, final version of the summary essay. Notice how details have been added, and how transitions link ideas more smoothly. Notice also how sentence combining has made some sections less choppy and how the word choice has been improved. Finally, note that a sentence has been added to the conclusion.

A Final Version of a Summary Essay of "Finding the Key"

(Changes from the draft are underlined.)

"Finding the Key" by Matt Schudel is about Josué Rodriguez, a music teacher of handicapped children. Rodriguez was selected as Broward County, Florida's Teacher of the Year because of his extraordinary ability to open windows for

word choice   students who were <u>considered ineducable.</u> Josué Rodriguez is a gifted teacher because he loves music, his work, and his students.

Rodriguez's life has always been

details added   full of music. When he was ten, <u>his grandfather in Puerto Rico taught</u>

transition added   <u>him</u> to play guitar. <u>Years later,</u> he earned a degree in music from the Puerto Rican Conservatory of Music.

sentences combined, details added   <u>A professional musician for more than twenty years, he plays the trumpet, keyboards, and percussion</u>

---

instruments as well as guitar. A
sign in his office shows how much he
values music; it says, "MUSIC IS THE
UNIVERSAL LANGUAGE OF MANKIND."

transition
details added

transition
sentences
combined,
word choice

Rodriguez not only loves music,
he loves to teach it. He says Bright
Horizons School is a great place
to work and claims he would still
teach even if he won the lottery.

word choice
word choice
details added

Rodriguez believes he loves music so
much that his students catch his enthusiasm. On his own time, he spends
hours making special tapes for his

details added

students so they can play special
musical parts along with the tape.
He says he keeps learning himself,
to help students learn.

transition

Rodriguez works so hard at
teaching because he cares deeply for
his students. He got a degree in
music education for the handicapped.
He feels comfortable with handi-

transition,
sentences
combined

capped students. In the classroom,
Rodriguez is patient and energetic,
devoted to his students' success.
The mother of one of his students

details added

praises him, saying, "You can see
the gift and the glow" when he works
with his class.

In his classroom, Rodriguez combines three talents: a talent for
music, a talent for teaching, and a
talent for opening his heart. His
gift helps lost students to learn.

sentence
added

He has found a key to their minds
and hearts.

Writing summaries is good writing practice, and it also helps you develop your reading skills. Even if your instructor does not require you to turn in a polished summary of an assigned reading, you may find it helpful to summarize what you have read. In many classes, midterms or other exams cover several assigned readings. If you make a short summary of each assigned reading, you will have a helpful collection of focused, organized material to review.

Chapter Three
Writing a Reaction Paper

THE READING STEPS

In a writing class, your instructor may ask you to write a *reaction paper* in which you write about some idea related to a reading selection. That idea usually comes from an assigned topic. Before you can begin to write a reaction paper, you must work through the reading steps:

1. **Prereading:** Survey the article, noting its title, length, introductory information, boxes, charts, subtitles, photographs, or illustrations. Form questions about the information you gathered through prereading.
2. **Reading:** Read the entire article, looking for answers to the questions you've formed.
3. **Rereading with Pen or Pencil:** Carefully reread the article, marking it and noting important points, examples, and your reactions.

THE READING SELECTION

Following is a sample reading selection. Work through the reading steps so that you are familiar with the ideas in the article.

Sammy Sosa:
Homerun Hitter with Heart

Robert Huer

This baseball superstar covers all bases, whether breaking major league records or providing relief to hurricane victims in his native Dominican Republic.

Words You May Need to Know

assessors (para. 2)	people who estimate the value of something
catapulted (3)	hurled
fabled (3)	legendary, famous
schtick (4)	amusing trick, routine
homering (4)	hitting a homerun
funky (4)	clever, cute
hustle (5)	earn money by aggressive or illegal tactics
custom-free zone (5)	a part of the city where buyers do not have to pay special fees (duties) on imported items
evolved (5)	gradually developed
philanthropist (6)	a person who donates large sums of money
auspices (6)	support, sponsorship
ham (7)	an actor who overacts
deferred (8)	yielded or submitted
antics (8)	playful behavior or tactics
compadres (8)	friends
inner sanctum (9)	a holy place
conduit (10)	channel or pipeline
largess (10)	generous gifts

leveraging (11)   using the power of

rookie (12)   first season on a professional team

norm (13)   standard

accommodating (13)   helpful, obliging

subsequent (14)   following, later

Jackie Robinson (13)   an African–American baseball hero

strident (14)   harsh and loud

pilfering (16)   stealing

stature (17)   status

transcended (17)   rose above

alderman (20)   city councilman

emigre (21)   a person who has left his or her native land

initiated (21)   begun

prefabricated (22)   constructed beforehand and ready for quick assembly

unanimous (22)   completely agreed on

shagging (25)   retrieving and throwing back balls in baseball practice

surreal (28)   fantastic, unbelievable

fathomed (28)   understood

charismatic (29)   powerful, gifted

In the summer of 1997, the Chicago Cubs made their biggest investment ever in a player, signing rightfielder Sammy Sosa to a four-year, $42.5 million contract. A waste of money, critics charged. This twenty-eight-year-old Dominican was an underachieving hotdog. Sure, he'd averaged thirty-four homeruns and one hundred runs-batted-in during five seasons for the Cubs, but Sosa produced when it didn't matter and then, with the game on the line, swung and missed at curve balls in the dirt. His nickname was "Sammy So-so."

Cubs management saw somebody else wearing uniform number 21. They saw a young man maturing physically and emotionally. They saw what assessors of baseball flesh call "a five-tool player"—fast runner, very good outfielder, outstanding arm, good hitter, and power hitter. An outstanding family man with consistent work habits, Sosa was also a personality who could add value to what ultimately is an entertainment business. 2

And entertain he has. In 1998 a record-breaking sixty-six homerun season catapulted Sosa to rock-star status. But—as every baseball fan knows—the Dominican was not alone in his historic quest: He and St. Louis Cardinal Mark McGwire propelled the season into their own private slugfest in pursuit of the most fabled single-season record in all of professional sports. The immortal Babe Ruth hit sixty homeruns in 1927, a feat that was supposed to last forever but endured only thirty-four years until Roger Maris hit sixty-one in 1961. Thirty-seven years later, on September 8, McGwire slapped number sixty-two barely over the St. Louis Busch Stadium fence. Five days later, Sosa hit numbers sixty-one and sixty-two—rifle shots that seared over the left-field wall at Wrigley Field and landed near a streetlight where a Dominican flag fluttered in the breeze. Two weeks later, he smashed number sixty-six, a record tied within one hour by McGwire who, in one last ball-crunching frenzy, hit four homeruns in the season's final three games to reach a season total of seventy. 3

Sosa proved to be a more endearing entertainer than McGwire. Slammin' Sammy's most delightful schtick comes after homering, circling the bases, returning to the dugout, looking into the television camera, making this funky little heart-tapping gesture and then, blowing a kiss . . . to his mother, Lucretia, back home in the Caribbean. 4

One of seven children, Sosa was seven when his father, Bautista Montero, died. His mother eventually remarried, yet it was the death of his father—a tractor operator on a 5

San Pedro de Macoris sugar plantation—that forced the oldest Sosa brothers, Sammy and José, to work. Like so many other Dominican kids, they saw little hope for their immediate future other than trying to hustle coins by shining shoes. Their energy and intelligence impressed U.S. businessman Bill Chase, who had recently arrived with his wife to start a shoe factory in San Pedro's custom-free zone. In the early years, when Chase went to the city park, he'd always get a shoeshine from the Sosa boys, who soon were doing odd jobs around his factory. The friendship evolved, and the Chases and Sosas became like family. (The Chases moved to Florida in 1994 after selling a business which at its peak in the 1980s included three factories employing fifteen hundred people and manufacturing $60 million worth of shoes per year.)

In 1998, the generous Sosa was giving away $500,000 ϵ annually—without taking a philanthropist's usual route of tax protection. Chase worried that one day Sosa might wake up after his playing days were done and discover he was broke. So they set up a foundation to support the ballplayer's charities on the island. Sosa's real estate project—San Pedro's closest thing to a shopping mall—was among the assets put under the auspices of the Sammy Sosa Foundation. Sosa had seen too many kids go to the state-run hospital with an injury like a broken arm and receive no treatment other than aspirin. So he decided that his foundation would focus on health care for kids with the long-range plan of establishing a clinic.

But then, all of a sudden, circumstances jolted Sosa ⁊ into the international limelight. In June, he hit twenty homeruns—a single-month major league record that turned him into a headline-making duo with McGwire. The media herd that had been driving McGwire nuts since spring training jumped all over the Sosa story, too. Soon this natural-born ham was entertaining two-hundred members of the news media in daily news conferences before and after each game, claiming the only pressure he ever felt was being a child trying to support an entire family shining shoes back home in San Pedro.

The ever-grateful Sosa always deferred to the frontrunner, 8 calling McGwire, a red-headed native of Southern California, the man to break the Ruth-Maris record. However, by mid-August McGwire was beginning to lash out at reporters. That's when the Cardinals happened to arrive in Chicago. For once, McGwire didn't feel alone. At their joint news conferences, Sosa's antics lightened McGwire up. The two compadres became the feel-good sports story of the decade.

In late September, 1998, Sosa was slugging his way 9 into baseball's legendary inner sanctum, and also leading the Cubs to a rare post-season appearance, when Hurricane Georges ripped through a dozen Caribbean nations. The Dominican Republic took the storm's brunt. Several hundred people were killed, more than 100,000 were homeless, and property damage was estimated at $2 billion. San Pedro de Marco was badly hit.

Sosa was stunned. He gracefully turned his daily media 10 sessions into a powerful publicity machine to illuminate the plight of the Dominican people. The Cubs' community relations office became the conduit for contributions, receiving over $450,000 in funds on behalf of the Sosa Foundation, including nearly $230,000 in small checks from fans thanking Sosa for a great season. Many included a note that said something like, "God bless you and your countrymen." The largess translated into a steady flow of relief supplies. Cubs' community relations director Rebecca Polihonris explained, "Sammy wants to know that the aid is going directly to the people most in need."

By leveraging his baseball fame to help relieve the 11 suffering of victims of a natural disaster, Sosa is following in the footsteps of his idol, the late great Hall of Famer Roberto Clemente. Playing for the Pittsburgh Pirates from 1955 to 1972, Clemente won four batting titles, the National League's 1966 Most Valuable Player award, twelve Gold Gloves for defensive excellence, and the 1971 World Series Most Valuable Player Award. He was selected to the All-Star Team fifteen times, and his .317 lifetime batting average is among the best of the post–World War II era.

Like Sosa, the Carolina, Puerto Rico, native never forgot his modest origins as the son of a sugar plantation worker, nor his role as a representative of his people. Sosa charms people with a jovial manner; by contrast, Clemente was more serious, reserving his good-natured, kindheartedness for friends and strangers, but not sportswriters. A lifelong battle with the press began his rookie season when he angrily reacted to being called a Puerto Rican Negro rather than a Puerto Rican.

"All the Latins wanted was some respect, and Clemente was responsible," recalled Monte Irvin, a Hall of Fame player who was Clemente's idol, in 1982. Clearly, players like Clemente, Juan Marichal, Luis Aparicio, Orlando Cepeda, Felipe Alou, and Tony Oliva became accepted because they played baseball so well. Clemente challenged the cultural norm by demanding that they also be appreciated and, in the process, created a more accommodating climate for subsequent generations of Spanish-speaking players, Indeed, this Latin American Jackie Robinson did much to make major league club houses more tolerant of the Spanish language than almost any street corner in the country.

In the U.S. and his native Puerto Rico, more than thirty schools and two hospitals are named for Clemente, who used success in the field during an eighteen-year major league career to speak out for social justice. A strident voice for the underdog, he elevated the status of Spanish-speaking ballplayers and—in an act of genuine heroism—died in the crash of a plane carrying supplies to victims of the 1972 Nicaragua earthquake.

Clemente was perhaps too much of a perfectionist to have done well as a manager of professional ballplayers. However, as his career drew to a close, he began talking of building a Sports City in Puerto Rico where children would be taught the skills to become well-rounded human beings. As the 1972 season ended, he became only the eleventh man in baseball history to get three thousand hits—a perfect round number that, oddly enough, turned out to be his last.

That November the thirty-eight-year-old Clemente and 16
his wife, Vera, traveled to Nicaragua to manage a Puerto
Rican all-star team in an international amateur tournament. On December 23, when the earthquake struck the
capital, Managua, killing seven thousand people and leaving
nearly a quarter-million homeless, Clemente, then home in
Puerto Rico, formed a committee to provide aid and put in
fourteen-hour days throughout the holidays. After finding
out that the Somoza army was pilfering relief intended for
the truly needy, Clemente and four others boarded a rickety
and overloaded plane on a rainy New Year's Eve. His
Nicaraguan-bound plane had barely taken off before crash-
ing into the Caribbean.

Four years old at the time, Sosa grew up on the nearby 17
island of Hispaniola admiring Clemente, a Latin American
whose stature transcended his achievements on the field.
Sosa wears number 21 today because that was Clemente's
number.

"Sammy is a very religious person, with boundless en- 18
ergy and determination," his friend Chase explains. "I often
tell him that for some reason God chose him to be a special
person."

On August 31, 1998, a night game in which Sosa hit 19
his fifty-first homerun, my first glimpse of this broad-
shouldered figure with brown skin and white Cub uniform
and the number 21 on his back sent chills down my spine.
Watching Sosa roam around in front of the ivy-covered brick
walls, I thought of Clemente who always dominated Wrigley
Field both in right field and at the plate when the Pirates
were in town. As a ten-year-old, I saw Clemente in what
turned out to be his last season, standing in the same side
of the batter's box as Sosa, foul off maybe a dozen pitches
before blasting a homerun over the left-field fence. Twenty-
five years since his death, it felt like Clemente had come
back to life.

> *At the president's State of the Union message in January 1999,*
> *Sosa stood next to the First Lady and was recognized by the*
> *President as 'a hero in two countries.'*

At season's end, after the Cubs were swept by the Atlanta Braves in the playoffs, Sosa turned his attention to raising money for hurricane victims—going from the Chicago City Council, where he suggested maybe he'd run for alderman someday, to national television talk shows.

October 18, 1998 was "Sammy Sosa Day" in New York City, home to a huge Dominican emigre population. Thousands turned out for a parade in the Canyon of Heroes—a distinction reserved for the likes of Charles Lindbergh, Nelson Mandela, Pope John Paul II and, recently, John Glenn. New York sports champions regularly travel this route but never before an athlete who plays in a different city. Sosa was awarded the first annual Jackie Robinson Empire State Freedom Medal, which had been initiated by the state of New York as part of the fiftieth anniversary honoring Robinson's role as the first African-American major leaguer of the twentieth century. Robinson's widow, Rachel, hailed Sosa as a humble, socially responsible man who "sets a very high standard for this award." That night, Sosa threw out the first pitch of the World Series.

Three days later, Sosa finally managed to make the long-awaited return home to see, among other things, that relief was actually getting to the victims. A jet chartered by Tribune Company (the Chicago-based media conglomerate owners of the Cubs) carried their precious human cargo from Chicago to Santo Domingo. President Leonel Fernandez, who had declared Sosa's homecoming a "national day of celebration," was the official greeter, along with Juan Marichal, the San Francisco Giants' "Dominican dandy," who now heads the national sports ministry. Sosa pledged to do everything in his power to help hurricane victims—including personally unloading supplies shipped in by international relief organizations. Soon he jetted off to Japan and on November 13 celebrated his thirtieth birthday in Tokyo while taking part in an exhibition tour with a team of Major League all-stars. Japan's favorite Dominican hit .500, was the tour's most valuable player, and through his brother José arranged for the Japanese government to donate one thousand units of prefabricated housing to hurricane victims. Days later

Sosa returned to Chicago for the announcement that he was the sportswriters' near-unanimous choice as the National League Most Valuable Player. In the midst of this schedule, when he was even too busy to visit the White House, Hillary Rodham Clinton made time to tour the hurricane-ravaged landscape and pledge staff support in helping the Red Cross get Sosa's medical clinic off the ground. At the president's State of the Union message in January 1999, Sosa stood next to the First Lady and was recognized by the president as "a hero in two countries."

23   Cubs general manager Ed Lynch doesn't sound worried that Sosa might burn himself out only one year into his four-year deal. Their $10-million-a-year man's plan was to focus on the upcoming baseball season starting January 1. "Rebuilding the Dominican Republic is close to his heart, but Sammy knows the 1999 season is as important as 1998," Lynch said.

24   Luis Rodriguez Mayoral, the Texas Rangers' media relations office's liaison for Latin America, got to know Clemente while a young man growing up in Puerto Rico in the 1960s. In 1973 Rodriguez persuaded then commissioner Bowie Kuhn to rename an annual award for sportsmanlike ballplayers in the memory of Clemente. Rodriguez also organized a Latin American Appreciation day and, with the help of an ad hoc committee that included Vera Clemente, singled out a Latin ballplayer to receive an annual Roberto Clemente Memorial Prize. For twenty-five years Rodriguez traveled to different Major League parks and held a modest pregame ceremony to both honor an unsung player and keep alive the Clemente name.

25   The physical resemblance between Sosa and Clemente has been apparent to Rodriguez for years. In 1992 Rodriguez emerged from the clubhouse before a Florida spring training game and, walking toward right field, happened to notice Sosa, then with the Chicago White Sox, shagging fly balls. Seeing the number 21 and a trim body form very much like that of his revered friend, he shouted, "Hey, man, you remind me of Roberto Clemente." Sosa frowned. "Let him go," he said. "He's dead."

Soon thereafter, Sosa was traded across town to the Cubs for fellow macorisano Jorge Bell and again took number 21. Since joining the Cubs, in Rodriguez's view, this itchy kid who couldn't stay still now appears patient and relaxed: "Sammy seems so much more secure than he used to be, you can see the touch of happiness in his face."

Roberto Clemente, Jr., thinks he knows why. Six years old when his father died, the oldest of the three Clemente boys played briefly in the Philadelphia Phillies organization and today does Spanish-language commentary for one hundred New York Yankee games each season. At the All-Star game in Denver in July 1988, he cornered Sosa and offered some unusual advice. "When you pray, ask my dad to help you out. He can help you have a really monster year," he said. "Sammy smiled," Clemente recalls. "He was really happy to hear that." The pair next crossed paths at Yankee Stadium at the first game of the World Series.

That night Clemente had something to say to Sosa that no doubt capped his day of honor in New York. Robert Jr. and his brother Luis Roberto, the president and chief officer of the Sports City complex in Puerto Rico, run a licensing company that promotes their father's name. The Disney Company had the rights to make a feature-length film but is now relinquishing them. While shopping the idea elsewhere, Roberto has been thinking about who would play his father in the movie. He thinks Sosa would be perfect for the role. His features are close enough, especially the eyes. "I told Sammy, 'You're the man who can do this.'" Sosa's eyes lit up in surprise. Not in his wildest dreams, not even in a year as surreal as this one, is it likely that Sosa ever fathomed that his destiny might include getting top billing in telling his idol's life story.

Sosa, of course, doesn't need a contract from Hollywood. This charismatic young man seems to be following the script of Clemente, who once said, "Any time you have the opportunity to accomplish something for somebody who comes behind you and you don't do it, you are wasting your time on this earth."

FROM READING TO WRITING

Once you have completed the reading steps, you are ready to begin writing. Imagine that your instructor has explained that the article you have just read focuses on two athletes who are admirable for their achievements in sports and in society, Sammy Sosa and Roberto Clemente, and on one who broke an important sports record, Mark McGwire. Then you instructor has assigned you this topic:

Write about an athlete that you admire.

Your next step is to think about the topic.

GATHERING IDEAS FOR A REACTION PAPER

One way to think about your topic is to *freewrite*. When you freewrite, you give yourself ten or fifteen minutes to write whatever comes into your mind on your subject. If your mind is a blank, write "My mind is a blank, my mind is a blank," over and over until you think of something else. The main goal of freewriting is to *write without stopping*. Do not stop to tell yourself, "This is stupid," or "I will not be able to use this idea in a paper." Do not stop to correct your spelling. Just write freely by letting your ideas flow.

If you freewrote on the topic of an athlete you admire, your freewriting might look like the following:

Freewriting on the Topic of an Athlete You Admire

Athletes I admire. I don't know. Who? Michael Jordan? Yes. Definitely. Basketball is great. Basketball on television in the spring when it's March Madness. But I like football, too. The Super Bowl. The play-offs. The Olympics, too. Fun to watch on television. A hero? How about Florence Griffith-Joyner? I read about her once and saw some photographs. Then I saw a program on tv and liked her. Those outfits and those nails. Wow! What about Dennis Rodman? What about his outfits and hair?

Reviewing Your Freewriting

When you look over your freewriting, you find that you have three sports figures that you can write about: Michael Jordan, Florence Griffith-Joyner, and Dennis Rodman. You decide you don't really admire Dennis Rodman; you just like to watch his antics. You also decide you don't know much about Michael Jordan. Consequently, you decide to write about Florence Griffith-Joyner.

Brainstorming

Once you have an athlete to write about, you can *brainstorm* to gather more ideas about the athlete. Brainstorming means asking yourself questions about your subject, answering them, and even letting the answers lead you to more questions—and answers. For instance, brainstorming about Florence Griffith-Joyner might look like this:

Brainstorming on the Topic of an Athlete You Admire

Question: What do you admire about Florence Griffith-Joyner?
Answer: She was an Olympic champion.

Question: When?
Answer: In the 1980s.

Question: What else do you admire?
Answer: She had asthma.

Question: Why is that something to admire?
Answer: When a person has asthma, it is difficult to play sports, but she did it.

Question: What sport are you talking about?
Answer: Running track.

Question: So she was a good runner. What else do you admire about her?
Answer: Those clothes.

> **Question:** What about the clothes?
> **Answer:** Her track clothes were wild. Some had only one shoulder, and they were in wild colors. They looked great against her black skin. And her nails were very long. She had style.
>
> **Question:** Is that all you like? Her looks and her winning?
> **Answer:** No. She was a fighter. She came back from her losses.

ORGANIZING YOUR IDEAS

Your freewriting and brainstorming have led you to a topic and some ideas. One way to see what ideas you have and how they might be connected is to list them.

A List of Ideas from Freewriting and Brainstorming

Florence Griffith-Joyner was an Olympic Champion in the 1980s.
She had asthma.
When a person has asthma, it is difficult to play sports, but she did it.
She ran track.
Her track clothes were wild.
Some had only one shoulder.
They were in wild colors.
The colors looked great against her black skin.
Her nails were very long.
She had style.
She was a fighter.
She came back from her losses.

Putting Your Ideas in Categories

When you survey your list, you notice that you have several important ideas about Florence Griffith-Joyner:

> She was an Olympic champion.
> She had style.
> She was a fighter.

One way to work with these ideas is to see if other items on your list can be related to these categories:

She was an Olympic champion.

> She ran track.
> She was a champion in the 1980s.

She had style.

> Her track clothes were wild.
> Some had only one shoulder.
> They were in wild colors.
> The colors looked great against her black skin.
> Her nails were very long.

She was a fighter.

> She had asthma.
> When a person has asthma, it is difficult to play sports, but she did it.
> She came back from her losses.

Selecting a Main Idea

The next step is to survey your categories and decide on a main point. Looking at the categories, you realize that you have ideas about three aspects of Florence Griffith-Joyner: her success, her style, and her ability to fight. Your assigned topic was to write about an athlete you admire, so you combine your ideas with the topic and write this main point:

> **Florence Griffith-Joyner was admirable for her fighting spirit, her athletic victories, and her personal style.**

Now that you have a main point, you are ready to outline your writing.

WRITING A REACTION PARAGRAPH

The Outline for a Reaction Paragraph

With your main idea and your categories, you can write an outline. In the following outline, your main idea has become the topic sentence of the outline, and the ideas in the other categories are your support.

An Outline for a Reaction Paragraph
on an Athlete You Admire

Topic sentence: Florence Griffith-Joyner was
admirable for her fighting
spirit, her athletic victories,
and her personal style.

fighting spirit
- She was a fighter.
- She had asthma.
- When a person has asthma, it is difficult to play sports, but she did it.
- She lost at one Olympics.
- She came back from her losses.

athletic victories
- She was an Olympic champion in the 1980s.
- She ran track.
- She won gold medals.

personal style
- She had style.
- Her track clothes were wild.
- Some had only one shoulder.
- They were in wild colors.
- The colors looked great against her black skin.
- Her nails were very long.

As you read the outline, you notice that some new ideas, that Griffith-Joyner lost at one Olympics and that she won gold medals, have been added. You can add ideas to your outline to develop your points.

WRITING THE DRAFT OF A REACTION PARAGRAPH

The first draft of your reaction paragraph is your first try at blending all the material into one paragraph. In the draft below, you will notice that some of the sentences of the outline have been combined and some new details and transitions have been added.

A Draft for a Reaction Paragraph
on an Athlete You Admire

Florence Griffith-Joyner was admirable for her fighting spirit, her athletic victories, and her personal style. First of all, Griffith-Joyner was a fighter. She had asthma, which makes it difficult to play sports, but she did it anyway. She also lost in one Olympics, but she came back from her losses. She was an Olympic champion in the 1980s. She ran track. She won gold medals. She had style. Her track clothes were wild. Some had only one shoulder, and they were in wild colors. The colors looked great against her black skin. Her nails were long.

After looking over this draft and reading it aloud, you probably noticed a few problems:

- Some sentences are short and choppy. They need to be combined.
- In some places, transitions are needed.
- The paragraph could use a few more specific details.
- In some places, the word choice could be improved.
- The paragraph needs some kind of conclusion.

(**Note** that when you refer to a person in something that you write, you use the first and last name, like Florence Griffith-Joyner, the first time you make a reference, and the last name, like Griffith-Joyner, in further references.)

The Final Version of a Reaction Paragraph

Look carefully at the revised, final version of the reaction paragraph. Notice how sentences have been combined, details and transitions have been added, and word choice has been improved. Notice also that an added, final sentence provides a conclusion.

A Final Version of a Reaction Paragraph on an Athlete You Admire

(Changes from the draft are underlined.)

	Florence Griffith-Joyner was admirable for her fighting spirit, her athletic victories, and her personal style. First of all, Griffith-Joyner was a fighter. She had asthma, which makes it difficult to play sports, but she did it anyway. She also lost in one Olympics, but she came back
sentences combined, detail added transition added	from her losses. <u>In the 1980s, Griffith-Joyner won three gold medals for track.</u> <u>She had victories, and she also</u> had style. Her track clothes were wild. Some had only one
word choice detail added	shoulder, and they were in <u>neon</u> colors <u>like lime green or shocking pink.</u> The colors looked great
transition added detail added conclusion added	against her black skin. <u>In addition</u>, she had long, <u>perfectly manicured</u> nails. <u>Florence Griffith-Joyner looked great, ran like a champion, and kept her fighting spirit.</u>

Giving Your Reaction Paragraph a Title

When you prepare a final copy of your reaction paragraph, you may be asked to give it a title. The title should be short and should fit the subject of the paragraph. For an example, an appropriate title for the paragraph on Florence Griffith-Joyner might be, "An Athlete to Admire," or "A Woman Who Fought and Won." Check with your instructor to see if your paragraph needs a title.

WRITING A REACTION ESSAY

If you are asked to write a reaction essay, you begin the same way you would begin to write a reaction paper: by following the steps of active reading, by freewriting and/or brainstorming, by listing and grouping ideas, and by identifying the main idea and enough supporting ideas and examples.

Look again at the original list of ideas and categories for a reaction paragraph on an athlete you admire.

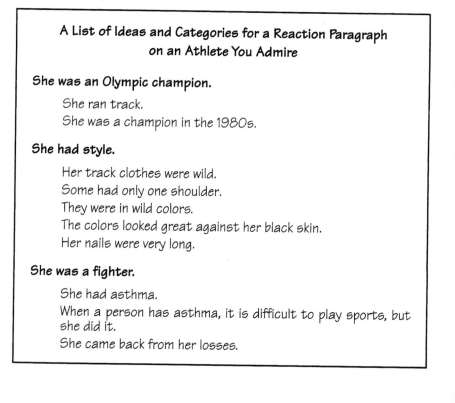

A List of Ideas and Categories for a Reaction Paragraph on an Athlete You Admire

She was an Olympic champion.

> She ran track.
> She was a champion in the 1980s.

She had style.

> Her track clothes were wild.
> Some had only one shoulder.
> They were in wild colors.
> The colors looked great against her black skin.
> Her nails were very long.

She was a fighter.

> She had asthma.
> When a person has asthma, it is difficult to play sports, but she did it.
> She came back from her losses.

Selecting a Main Idea

To write a reaction essay, you could work with the same main idea that would work in a summary paragraph:

Florence Griffith-Joyner was admirable for her fighting spirit, her athletic victories, and her personal style.

The main idea would be the same whether you write a paragraph or an essay to explain it. Your point is about an athlete you admire and what made her admirable. It would work in both a paragraph or an essay. The difference would be in how you develop the main point.

The Outline

You know that a reaction essay must be longer than a reaction paragraph, but you may not know that it does not need to include more points. That is, it can use the same main point (and use the same subpoints to explain the main point) as a reaction paragraph. However, *the main idea has to be developed with more examples and details.* Following is an outline for a reaction essay on an athlete you admire. Read it; then compare it to the outline for a reaction paragraph on the same topic.

Outline for a Reaction Essay on an Athlete You Admire

thesis sentence	I. Florence Griffith-Joyner was admirable for her fighting spirit, her athletic victories, and her personal style.
topic sentence for body paragraph	II. Griffith-Joyner had to fight against the odds.
	A. She had asthma.
details	B. When a person has asthma, it is difficult to play sports, but she did it.

     C. She lost at one Olympics.
     D. For a while, she gave up and stopped training.
     E. Eventually, she came back from her losses.

topic sentence for body paragraph

III. She had great triumphs.
  A. She was an Olympic champion in the 1980s.

details

  B. She ran track.
  C. She won gold medals.
  D. She was called "Flo-Jo."
  E. She was called the fastest woman in the world.

topic sentence for body paragraph

IV. Griffith-Joyner had her own style.
  A. Her clothes were wild.

details

  B. Some had only one shoulder.
  C. They were in wild colors.
  D. The colors looked great against her black skin.
  E. Her nails were very long.

topic sentence for conclusion

V. Griffith-Joyner brought strength, talent, and glamour to sports.

When you compare the outline for a reaction paragraph and the outline for a reaction essay, you notice these similarities and differences:

- The topic sentence of the paragraph outline is the thesis sentence of the essay outline.
- The three categories of the paragraph outline (fighting spirit, athletic victories, and style) are changed into the topic sentences for the body paragraphs of the essay outline.
- There are more details in the essay outline.

Writing the Draft of a Reaction Essay

The first draft of your reaction essay is your first try at combining all the material of your outline. It is the place where you can add more supporting details and examples and where you write a *lead-in* (introduction) to your thesis and a short concluding paragraph. Following is a draft of a reaction essay on an athlete you admire.

A Draft of a Reaction Essay
on an Athlete You Admire

lead-in

Fans praise some athletes for the athletes' ability to win and praise other athletes for their courage in overcoming hardships. One athlete, a black woman who ran track, was known for several

thesis sentence

outstanding qualities. Florence Griffith-Joyner was admirable for her fighting spirit, her athletic victories, and her personal style.

topic sentence

Griffith-Joyner had to fight against the odds. She had asthma.

body paragraph on fighting spirit

When a person has asthma, it is difficult to play sports, but she did it. She also lost at one Olympics. For a while, she gave up and stopped training. Eventually, she came back from her losses and began to train again.

topic sentence

She had great triumphs. She was an Olympic champion in the 1980s. She won gold medals for running track.

body paragraph on triumphs

She was called "Flo-Jo." She was called the fastest woman in the world.

`topic sentence`	Griffith-Joyner had her own style. Her track clothes were wild. Some of
`body paragraph on style`	them had only one shoulder. They were in wild colors. The colors were great against her black skin. Her nails were very long and perfectly manicured.
`topic sentence for conclusion`	Griffith-Joyner brought strength, talent, and glamour to sports.

When you look this draft over and read it aloud, you notice a few problems:

- In some places, transitions are needed.
- In some places, additional details would develop a paragraph or improve choppy sentences.
- In some places, the word choice could be improved.
- Some sentences need to be combined.
- The conclusion is too short. In an essay, the conclusion should be more than one sentence long.

(**Note** that when you refer to a person in something that you write, you use his or her first and last name, like Florence Griffith-Joyner, the first time you make a reference, and his or her last name, like Griffith-Joyner, in further references.)

Revising the draft means rewriting it to add transitions (smooth links between paragraphs and between sentences in the same paragraph). It means examining the sentences to see if some choppy, short ones need to be developed or combined, and it means considering the choice of words and amount of specific detail. Also, it means developing a longer conclusion around the one-sentence conclusion in the draft.

The Final Version of a Reaction Essay

Look carefully at the revised, final version of the reaction essay. Notice the added transitions and details. Notice how some short sentences have been developed or combined, and how the conclusion has been expanded. Notice also how a change in word choice has replaced general terms with more specific ones.

A Final Version of a Reaction Essay on an Athlete You Admire

(Changes from the draft are underlined.)

Fans praise some athletes for the athletes' ability to win and praise other athletes for their courage in overcoming hardships. One athlete, a black woman who ran track, was known for several outstanding qualities. Florence Griffith-Joyner was admirable for her fighting spirit, her athletic victories, and her personal style.

transition added

Griffith-Joyner had to fight against the odds. <u>One strike against her</u> was her asthma. When a person has asthma, it is difficult to play sports, but she did it. <u>Another obstacle</u> was her loss at the <u>Olympics of 1980.</u> For a while, she gave up and stopped training. <u>She had lost the energy to fight,</u> but eventually she <u>overcame</u> her loss and began to train again.

transition added

detail added

detail added

word choice

<u>Once she returned to the fight,</u> she had great triumphs. <u>She was an Olympic champion in the 1988 Olympics, where she won three gold medals in track.</u> She was so famous she was known everywhere as "Flo-Jo." <u>Her Olympic victories also earned her the title of</u> "The Fastest Woman in the World."

transition added

sentences combined, detail added, more detail added

transition added

transition added	<u>Griffith-Joyner was as striking as she was fast.</u> She had her own style.
sentences combined, detail added,	Her track clothes were wild. <u>Some of them had only one shoulder; they were in neon colors like lime green or shocking pink.</u> The colors were
transition added	great against her black skin. <u>In addition,</u> her nails were very long and
detail added	perfectly manicured. <u>Running on the track, Griffith-Joyner looked like a fashion model—but a model who could run.</u>
conclusion developed	<u>Griffith-Joyner found obstacles, but she did not let them defeat her. She was a winner with a unique beauty.</u> She brought strength, talent, and glamour to sports.

Giving Your Essay a Title

When you prepare the final copy of your reaction essay, you may be asked to give it a title. The title should be short and should fit the subject of the essay. For example, an appropriate title for this essay might be "An Admirable Athlete" or "The Strength and Style of Florence Griffith-Joyner." Check with your instructor to see if your reaction essays need a title.

SECTION TWO
READING SELECTIONS
(GROUPED THEMATICALLY)

Chapter Four

Everyday Heroes

"If you're smart, you gratefully take your heroes where you find them. As it happens, they are everywhere."

Elizabeth Berg

"I know that people are scared that something could happen, but you simply have to look up and say, 'Well, Lord, I'm trying to do a good thing here. Please look out for me.'"

Ron Bond, firefighter

My Heroes

Elizabeth Berg

Elizabeth Berg notes that "those who inspire us most aren't always larger than life." Everyday heroes do not seek recognition; they lead by example.

Words You May Need to Know

mystified (para. 6)	confused, bewildered
wise up (8)	become aware
undeniable (9)	obvious, unquestionable
straight-laced (10)	strict
critical (10)	important
premium (10)	high value
pit (11)	set in opposition
aflame (11)	burning
grossly (11)	extremely
infuriated (11)	made furious
sulked (11)	was silently resentful
bowed (11)	gave in, submitted
legitimate (11)	genuine
ironically (11)	unexpectedly
essence (12)	distinctive characteristic
sophisticated (12)	worldly-wise
astounding (12)	amazing
feat (12)	achievement, extraordinary act
unfailingly (12)	always, endlessly
luxuriating (13)	enjoying, taking great delight
relinquish (15)	give up, quit

My eight-year-old daughter, Jenny, was given a school 1
assignment not too long ago to write about a hero. "So who
did you pick?" I asked her. I was imagining some possibilities: Rosa Parks, Christa McAuliffe, Sara Lee. But Jenny
answered, "Laura."

"Who?" I asked.   2

"Laura," she said again.   3

"You mean your friend from across the street?" I asked. 4

"Yeah!" she said.   5

I was a little mystified. "How come you picked her?" I 6
asked. "Because," Jenny answered in the ultrapatient voice
of Instructor to the Hopeless, "she is my hero."

"Oh," I said. "I see."   7

I must confess that at first I was disappointed. I thought 8
that if her hero was only her friend, she had failed to appreciate the magnificent contributions that real heroes have
made to the world. I thought I'd better go out that afternoon
and buy some books about famous scientists, artists,
athletes, world leaders. That would wise her up. Also, I'd
have a look at what they were teaching in her school—didn't
she have an appreciation for Martin Luther King?

But then I thought about who I would say my heroes 9
are, and I realized that if I told the truth, they wouldn't be
famous, either. For although it is undeniable that there have
been outstanding people in history who have set glorious
examples and inspired me mightily, the people who inspire
me most tend to be those who touch me personally, and in
quiet ways.

For example, I had an eighth-grade English teacher 10
named Mrs. Zinz. She was demanding and rather straight-
laced, I thought, but she taught us certain critical skills for
reading and writing. She was concerned not only with what
we learned but also with what we were becoming: She put a
premium on honesty and tried to get us to understand why
it was important. She insisted that we always do our best,
and in her class, we almost always did. She told me that I
was a terrific creative writer and encouraged my every effort.

As payment for all her good work, I, along with my evil best friend, tortured her. We laughed at her in class, tried to pit our other teachers against her by telling them how unfairly she graded, and once, in a moment of extreme obnoxiousness, called her on the telephone over and over, only to hang up when she answered. Mrs. Zinz was no dummy. She knew who was calling her. In turn she called my mother, who insisted that I call Mrs. Zinz and apologize. With my face aflame, and between clenched teeth, I muttered a grossly insincere "Sorry." She accepted my apology warmly and with a style so graceful that I was infuriated all the more. And though I sulked every day in her class for the rest of the year, she never bowed by reacting to it. I got an A for the term. I moved soon after that and lost track of Mrs. Zinz. I never did apologize in any legitimate way to her. Ironically, she is still an inspiration to me, a lesson in how not to lower yourself to someone else's level, even when that person is doing everything she can to make you crazy. She is, in that way, a hero.

My grandfather, known to me as "Papa," was also a hero of mine. For one thing, he made all of us grandchildren laugh all of the time. He told riddles that were viewed by us as the essence of sophisticated humor. When he greeted us, he shook our hands enthusiastically and at great length, shouting, "How do! How do!" We used to line up to sit on his lap and watch him pop his dentures in and out of his mouth, an astounding feat that thrilled and terrified us—especially before we realized that the teeth were false. He was unfailingly warm and kind and knew how to make a friend out of a stranger; he loved people. I saw him as a man who felt light inside, happy; and feeling that way is no small task in a world that often seems intent on taking back two for every one you get.

Then there is my mother-in-law, Sylvia, who at the age of retirement went back to school to pursue a lifetime dream: getting a college diploma. She bumped her bifocals into microscopes, suffered verbal abuse at the hands of an insensitive computer instructor, got used to being the last one to

finish every exam, and worried about homework on weekends when she could have been luxuriating in the fact that
she had nothing to do. She says that she learned an awful
lot, but if you ask me, it's she who did the teaching. I am
honored that our family has her love of learning to inspire us.

Beyond that, there are people who are heroes to me be- 14
cause of what they do: mail carriers, who, on days when I
stay inside hiding from the cold or heat, subject themselves
to hours of it; nurses, who care for those who can't care for
themselves every second of every day. I admire stay-at-home
mothers for their patience and their creativity in the face of
almost no thanks or recognition, and working mothers for
the way they juggle an awesome load of responsibilities.

There are people with chronic illness, for whom getting 15
through each day is heroic. There are people who have been
married for sixty years, who have lessons to teach us all.
There are those who are strong enough in heart and in spirit
to speak up when something feels wrong to them, to go
against the majority, and oftentimes to risk themselves for
the sake of others. And then there are those whom I admire
most of all: people who seem to have found the secret of
calm and can relinquish the race for the pleasure of seeing
what's around them, right here, right now.

I was thinking about all this when I saw Jenny and 16
Laura come into the house. I wanted to know a little more
about what had precipitated Jenny's calling Laura a hero.
Was it her sharing her brand-new toys? Being there to listen, to soothe, to make better a bad situation in the way that
only good friends can? Well, as it happens, no. Jenny told
me that Laura was her hero because Laura had saved her
from drowning in a creek. "*What*?" I yelled.

Laura rolled her eyes. "Jenny, the water was only about 17
an inch deep." Jenny shrugged and said, "So? You still
saved me."

Laura and I let pass a certain look between us. Then 18
she and Jenny went outside again to play.

If you're smart, I thought, you gratefully take your 19
heroes where you find them. As it happens, they are

everywhere. So what if the water was only an inch deep? Someone was there, caring about Jenny, and showing that she did; a safe hand stretched out to another who was in trouble. This seemed heroic indeed, and later that night when I was tucking her in, I told Jenny that I thought her choice was perfect. "I know," she yawned. "Good night."

DISCUSSION QUESTIONS

1. Why was Jenny's mother initially disappointed by her daughter's choice of a hero?
2. Why does the author state that Mrs. Zinz is "still an inspiration" for her?
3. How did the author's father become one of her heroes?
4. What did Laura do that Jenny felt was heroic?
5. Why did the author feel that Jenny's choice of a hero was "perfect"?

WRITING OPTIONS

Collaborate With Peers

1. Interview a classmate about his or her reasons for a personal hero. Write a brief summary based on your notes.
2. With three or four classmates, brainstorm a list of characteristics that define the term "hero." Based on your notes from this collaboration, write your own paragraph or short essay defining this term.

Connecting With the Author's Ideas

3. The author states that "people who inspire me most tend to be those who touch me personally and in quiet ways." Write a paragraph or short essay describing how someone you know has inspired you to be a better person.
4. One of the author's heroes is her grandfather because of his positive attitude and love of people. Describe the most positive person you know, and include specific examples of how this person's positive behavior affects others.

The Man in the Water

Roger Rosenblatt

On January 14, 1982, Air Florida Flight 90 took off from Washington (D.C.) National Airport, hit a bridge, and crashed into the Potomac River. Millions of television viewers watched as rescuers entered the icy water, trying to save the victims. Roger Rosenblatt was one of the viewers. In this essay, he writes of one of the victims who chose to become a rescuer and a hero.

Words You May Need to Know

roster (para. 1)	list
element (1)	ingredient
clipped (1)	hit the edge of
intersecting (1)	crossing
disrupting (1)	interrupting, causing disorder
chaotic (1)	completely confused
deregulated (1)	disorderly
swoop (1)	sweep down through the air
emblemized (1)	symbolized, represented
aesthetic (1)	artistic
collision (2)	crash, coming together with a violent impact
the elements (2)	the atmospheric forces, like wind, rain, cold
groping (2)	blindly searching
flailing (2)	tossing around
clipped the skids (3)	slid the runners of the helicopter
flotation ring (4)	life preserver
mass casualty (4)	severe accident involving many people

anonymity (4)	lack of a name
invested (4)	gave
Everyman (4)	an ordinary man, everybody
capacity (5)	ability
dutifully (5)	respectfully
stunning (5)	amazing
essential (7)	fundamental
classic (7)	basic
commenced (7)	began
the Potomac (7)	a river in Washington, D.C.
distinctions (7)	recognizing of differences
principles (7)	rules of behavior
peculiar to (8)	limited to
abiding (8)	continuing
wonder (8)	miracle
Emerson (9)	Ralph Waldo Emerson, a famous American writer of the nineteenth century
implacable (9)	inflexible, unbending
impersonal (9)	inhuman

As disasters go, this one was terrible, but not unique, certainly not among the worst on the roster of U.S. air crashes. There was the unusual element of the bridge, of course, and the fact that the plane clipped it at a moment of high traffic, one routine thus intersecting another and disrupting both. Then, too, there was the location of the event: Washington, the city of form and regulations, turned chaotic, deregulated, by a blast of real winter and a single slap of metal on metal. The jets from Washington National Airport that normally swoop around the presidential monuments like rushed gulls are, for the moment, emblemized by the one that fell, so there is that detail. And there was the aesthetic clash as well—blue-and-green Air Florida, the name a flying garden, sunk down among gray chunks in a black river. All that was worth noticing, to be sure. Still, there was nothing very special in any of it, except death, which, while always special, does not necessarily bring millions to tears or attention. Why, then, the shock here?

Perhaps because the nation saw in this disaster some-   2 thing more than a mechanical failure. Perhaps because people saw in it no failure at all, but rather something successful about their makeup. Here, after all, were two forms of nature in collision: the elements and human character. Last Wednesday, the elements, indifferent as ever, brought down Flight 90. And on that same afternoon, human nature—groping and flailing in mysteries of its own—rose to the occasion.

Of the four acknowledged heroes of the event, three are   3 able to account for their behavior. Donald Usher and Eugene Windsor, a park police helicopter team, risked their lives every time they clipped the skids into the water to pick up survivors. On television, side by side in bright blue jumpsuits, they described their courage as all in the line of duty. Lenny Skutnik, a twenty-eight-year-old employee of the Congressional Budget Office, said, "It's something I never thought I would do"—referring to his jumping into the water to drag an injured woman to shore. Skutnik added that "somebody had to go in the water," delivering every hero's line that is no less admirable for its repetitions. In fact, nobody had to go into the water. That somebody actually did so is part of the reason that this particular tragedy sticks in the mind.

But the person most responsible for the emotional im-   4 pact of the disaster is the one known at first simply as "the man in the water." (Balding, probably in his fifties, an extravagant mustache.) He was seen clinging with five other survivors to the tail of the airplane. This man was described by Usher and Windsor as appearing alert and in control. Every time they lowered a lifeline and flotation ring to him, he passed it on to another of the passengers. "In a mass casualty, you'll find people like him," said Windsor. "But I've never seen one with that commitment." When the helicopter came back for him, the man had gone under. His selflessness was one reason the story held national attention, his anonymity another. The fact that he went unidentified invested him with a universal character. For a while he was Everyman, and thus proof (as if one needed it) that no man is ordinary.

Still, he could never have imagined such a capacity in himself. Only minutes before his character was tested, he was sitting in the ordinary plane among the ordinary passengers, dutifully listening to the stewardess telling him to fasten his seat belt and saying something about the "no smoking sign." So our man relaxed with the others, some of whom would owe their lives to him. Perhaps he started to read, or to doze, or to regret some harsh remark made in the office that morning. Then suddenly he knew that the trip would not be ordinary. Like every other person on that flight, he was desperate to live, which makes his final act so stunning.

For at some moment in the water he must have realized that he would not live if he continued to hand over the rope and ring to others. He *had* to know it, no matter how gradual the effect of the cold. In his judgment he had no choice. When the helicopter took off with what was to be the last survivor, he watched everything in the world move away from him, and he deliberately let it happen.

Yet there was something else about the man that kept our thoughts on him, and which keeps our thoughts on him still. He was *there,* in the essential, classic circumstance. Man in nature. The man in the water. For its part, nature cared nothing about the five passengers. Our man, on the other hand, cared totally. So the timeless battle commenced in the Potomac. For as long as that man could last, they went at each other, nature and man; the one making no distinctions of good and evil, acting on no principles, offering no lifelines; the other acting wholly on distinctions, principles, and, one supposes, on faith.

Since it was he who lost the fight, we ought to come 8
again to the conclusion that people are powerless in the
world. In reality, we believe the reverse, and it takes the act
of the man in the water to remind us of our true feelings in
this matter. It is not to say that everyone would have acted
as he did, or as Usher, Windsor, and Skutnik. Yet whatever
moved these men to challenge death on behalf of their fel-
lows is not peculiar to them. Everyone feels the possibility in
himself. That is the abiding wonder of the story. That is why
we would not let go of it. If the man in the water gave a lifeline to the people gasping for survival, he was likewise giving
a lifeline to those who observed him.

The odd thing is that we do not really believe that the 9
man in the water lost his fight. "Everything in Nature contains all the powers of Nature," said Emerson. Exactly. So
the man in the water had his own natural powers. He could
not make ice storms, or freeze the water until it froze the
blood. But he could hand life over to a stranger, and that is
a power of nature, too. The man in the water pitted himself
against an implacable, impersonal enemy; he fought it with
charity; and he held it to a standoff. He was the best we
can do.

DISCUSSION QUESTIONS

1. The crash of Air Florida Flight 90 was tragic, but it also brought
   out the best in human nature. Excluding the anonymous hero,
   who are the other heroes of this tale, and what did they do that
   was so admirable?

2. Why did the story of the anonymous "man in the water" capture
   "national attention"?

3. What do you think is the most descriptive line in this essay? Visu-
   alize the scene. What is the most memorable line about human
   nature? Why?

4. The author states that the "odd thing is that we do not really believe that the man in the water lost his fight." What do you think
   the author means?

WRITING OPTIONS

1. Write a narrative paragraph in which you describe a courageous, unselfish act you have observed or read about.
2. Based on what you know about the anonymous hero of this article, write a creative essay that traces his day, his decisions, and his thoughts.

Beyond the Call

Tamika Simmons

High risks are not unusual, but service beyond the call of duty is often rare. Here is the tale of a Good Samaritan who simply did what he thought was right, a simple decision that was also extraordinary.

Words You May Need to Know

moniker (para. 1)	name, nickname
Good Samaritan (2)	a person who freely gives help to someone in distress
saga (3)	tale
command (4)	skill or knowledge
hefty (6)	heavy

As a child, Boca Raton firefighter Ron Bond was known 1 as "Little Ron" to distinguish him from his father, with whom he shares his name. On Tuesday, Bond received a new moniker—one of Florida's finest.

Bond was commended on Tuesday by Governor Lawton 2 Chiles, who phoned the Boca Raton Fire Department to thank Bond for a Good Samaritan effort that resulted in a new transmission for a Lake Worth woman and a $900 bill for the firefighter.

The saga began last week when Bond saw Elida 3 Martinez stopped in front of him at a stoplight in Lake Worth. When the light turned green, Bond honked his vehicle horn at Martinez, thinking the woman was reading a book. Bond soon discovered that she was stalled. "I looked at the transmission, and I could tell that they had had problems with it before," Bond said. "It was completely burned out."

Bond offered Martinez a ride home. That presented yet 4 another problem. Martinez had little command of English, and Bond said he knew only a few words of Spanish. "She just started pointing out the directions to me. If I got to one corner and had to make a right turn, she'd just point right, and we were able to find the house," Bond said.

His good deeds didn't end there. After Martinez's daughter explained that her mother had lost her job and had no money to repair the car, Bond had the car towed to a mechanic and asked that the $900 repair bill be sent to him.

A little after 4:00 P.M. on Tuesday, Bond received his reward. "I just wanted to tell you how much the state appreciates the help you gave Mrs. Martinez," Chiles said from Tallahassee. "I try to take some time to recognize people who go above and beyond the call of duty, and you certainly did that . . . and got a hefty little bill for your effort. I'm glad we've got people like you in the state of Florida."

Bond said he hopes there are others like him, willing to take some time to help someone else. "Most people live by example, and I would hope that people would hear about what I did and try to do the same thing," Bond said. "I know that people are scared that something could happen, but you simply have to look up and say, 'Well, Lord, I'm trying to do a good thing here. Please look out for me.'"

DISCUSSION QUESTIONS

1. What did Ron Bond do for Elida Martinez that went far beyond his responsibilities as a firefighter?
2. Do you find Bond's behavior surprising? Explain.

WRITING OPTIONS

1. Write a narrative paragraph or short essay describing how you once benefited from the unselfish act(s) of a stranger.
2. Write a paragraph summarizing why and to what extent you once aided a stranger who needed help.

New Yorkers Comfort the Rescuers

Michael Mayo

In the days after the September 11, 2001, terrorist attack on the World Trade Center in Manhattan, residents from all over New York City united to pay tribute and respect to local rescue workers, hundreds of whom lost their lives as they rushed into the Twin Towers shortly before the buildings collapsed. Witnessing the outpouring of public affection for these everyday heroes, Michael Mayo writes, "It's a scene that's uplifting and depressing, the aftershocks of the worst in humanity bringing out the best."

Words You May Need to Know

head shots (para. 2)	photographs of a person's head and shoulders
devastated (3)	overwhelmed with emotion
simultaneously (4)	at the same time
congregating (4)	coming together
poignant (5)	distressing, moving
urging (15)	encouraging, pushing
marathon (15)	a long distance foot race
New York's Finest and Bravest (17)	New York's police and firefighters
invoking (18)	calling on for help

One woman walked up to the firehouse with a case of water and bags of candy, another with a sealed envelope containing a card and cash. "I wanted you guys to have this," she said. 1

Fire Lieutenant Bob Jackson looked out from the truck bay onto Eighth Avenue and 48th Street on Saturday, surveyed the mountain of flowers, the sea of candles, the 2 pictures and letters by children posted on the walls. A steady stream of friends, neighbors, strangers, and tourists stared at the fifteen glossy head shots mounted in a single frame, three rows of five, bordered in black and headlined "Our Brothers."

"This means so much," said Jackson, a fourteen-year veteran and Brooklyn native. "It gets you pumped up to keep going. Then you get somebody's wife walking in here, and you're devastated again."

Four days after the World Trade center massacre, New Yorkers are doing their best to support firefighters, police, and other rescue workers who somehow must work and grieve simultaneously. People are holding up signs, shouting encouragement, applauding, saluting, and cheering as fire trucks roll by. Volunteers hand out water; restaurants offer them free meals. And people are congregating at firehouses across the city, with 350 in a department of 11,550 feared lost.

It's a scene that's uplifting and depressing, the after-shocks of the worst in humanity bringing out the best. It's a scene that's especially poignant at Engine 54, Ladder 4, Battalion 9, which sits on the edge of Manhattan's theater district. "We took a big hit," Jackson said. "A big hit."

Nearly one quarter of the station's sixty firefighters are gone: Al Feinberg, Dave Wooley, Jose Guadalupe, Ed Geraghty, Chris Santora, Joe Angelini, John Tipping, Len Ragaglia, Dan O'Callahan, Mike Haub, Mike Brennan, Mike Lynch, Paul Gill, Sam Oitice. So too is Carl Asaro, who recently transferred from the station to become a driver for a deputy commissioner.

They were among the first at the disaster scene on Tuesday, about three miles south, racing into the burning towers to rescue as many people as they could.

Jackson was lucky. He wasn't on duty when the hijacked planes hit, but he rushed down to the scene when his wife Fran called him on his cellular phone to tell him what had happened.

"I didn't hear from him again until 4 P.M. that day," Fran 9
Jackson said. "I was out of my mind."

Outside the fire station, on its red brick wall, nine-year- 10
old Kevin Velez posted a drawing of a fire truck with the
words: "Dear Enemies: Love and Peace. It hurts. It hurts.
Why????"

"He didn't want to go to school on Friday," said his 11
mother, Carmen Perez. "He was afraid a plane was going to
crash into it."

Next to Velez's picture is another in crayon. It shows a 12
fire truck parked next to a blazing tower, with little stick
figures jumping from the building. "Thank you for saving
people. From Shayna."

There are dozens of letters posted. "Dear Firefighters: 13
Thank you for putting out fires and keeping our city safe.
We love you. From, Second Grade, School of the Blessed
Sacrament."

"Dear Firemen, I am so happy you risked your life to 14
save people. I'm so sad the building collapsed when you
were saving people. You are the best heros I ever wrote to. I
hope you are alrite in heven with god. Love, Zuzu."

The scenes of support throughout the city—people 15
handing out water, people cheering and clapping, people
urging on the exhausted—are scenes you usually see during
the New York Marathon.

Only this is a different New York marathon, one with no 16
finish line in sight. An estimated 500,000 tons of rubble covers the area that used to be the World Trade Center, one bil-
lion pounds. In four days, workers have removed a little over
one percent. At the current excruciating rate, with workers
moving delicately to avoid more casualties and sifting carefully for clues and human remains, the cleanup effort could
stretch over a year.

The police, who fear they have lost seventy-five officers, 17
still have streets to patrol. The firefighters still have fires to
extinguish, although Jackson noted, "It's been very quiet
these last few days. Very quiet." You wonder how New York's

Finest and Bravest are going to make it. "It's going to be a long haul," Jackson said.

He looked out at the thousands of flowers—roses, gladiolas, lilies. He looked at the hundreds of candles—Jewish mourning candles, inscribed with Hebrew words, candles inscribed with prayers invoking Catholic saints. He looked at scores of people gathered, gave thanks and smiled to those who gave donations. This is how they're going to make it.

"This is a community-type firehouse," Jackson said. "People bring their children here all the time, we give them tours of the trucks, let them try on our hats. We're always giving here.

"It looks like they're paying us back."

DISCUSSION QUESTIONS

1. How did the public show its support for the efforts of rescue workers?
2. Fire Lieutenant Bob Jackson's firehouse took what he calls a "big hit." What does he mean by this phrase?
3. What did a nine-year-old boy post outside the fire station? What message was this young boy trying to convey, and what is he confused about?
4. Lieutenant Jackson describes his firehouse as a "community-type" station. What does he mean by this description?

WRITING OPTIONS

Collaborate with Peers

1. Movies and television programs usually depict police or soldiers dealing with life-and-death situations. Yet there are many other professions that must deal with such situations. In a group of three or four, brainstorm about other professions which deal with life and death, but which the public seldom hears about. Based on the ideas you gather through brainstorming, write a paragraph or short essay about a group (other than police or soldiers) that faces life-and-death conflicts often.

Connecting with the Author's Ideas

2. The author writes of the "aftershocks" of the attack on the World Trade Center as a time when "the worst in humanity" brought out "the best." Write about another time when human evil provoked others to do and be their best.

Other Options

3. If a child asks you why some people want to hurt others, how would you answer this youngster's question? Compose a letter that assures the youngster that most people are not evil despite tragedies that we see in our world.

4. In times of tragedy, communities often unite for a common cause. Describe a time when a tragic event in your town (or region) brought ordinary citizens together to help others or solve problems.

A Real Survivor

Ardy Friedberg and Jeremy Milarsky

Trapped in the wreckage of her car for three days, eighty-three-year-old Tillie Tooter triumphed over heat, bugs, and thunderstorms.

Words You May Need to Know

dense (para. 2)	thick
scorching (3)	burning
predicament (3)	dangerous situation
dehydrated (4)	deprived of water
rappelled (5)	moved down a steep incline, supported by a double rope wound around their waists
the Jaws of Life (5)	a rescue device used to pry accident victims out of smashed vehicles
debris (9)	rubbish, fragments of anything broken down or destroyed
feverishly (12)	excitedly, impatiently
billowed (12)	rushed in a swelling wave
teetered (15)	wobbled
ordeal (16)	terrible experience

Tillie Tooter is one tough grandma.   1

First, the eighty-three-year-old Pembroke Pines (FL) 2
widow survived her Toyota Tercel's thirty-two-foot dive off Interstate 595 into a dense grove of mangrove and willow trees.

Then, rescuers said, she endured three days of scorch- 3
ing heat and thunderstorms and three insect-infested nights
in the confinement of her shattered car. Her cell phone, a
ticket out of her predicament, lay just out of reach. She
drank rainwater collected in her steering-wheel cover and
sucked on dew-soaked golf socks.

Finally, on Tuesday morning, rescuers used a fire truck 4
ladder and a wire Stokes basket to lift a bruised and
dehydrated—but fully conscious—Tooter out of her car and
into a waiting ambulance. Asked how the woman could have
survived such an ordeal, Fort Lauderdale fire lieutenant
Michael Hicks said simply: "God."

Tooter made one last request of the sweating rescuers 5
who rappelled over the highway wall, chainsawed a dozen
trees to cut a path through the undergrowth, then used the
Jaws of Life to cut the top off her silver 1995 Toyota: "Could
you please get my pocketbook?"

"We were glad to oblige," said Fort Lauderdale Fire Divi- 6
sion Chief Stephen McInerny. "This lady had it all together.
That may have made a difference between surviving and
dying." Paramedics, escorted by Florida Highway Patrol
Troopers, took Tooter to Broward General Medical Center.
She had bruises and insect bites but no broken bones, and
was listed in serious condition.

Tooter will remain in the hospital for several days, but 7
doctors expect her to make a full recovery. "I'm just so
thankful and relieved she's alive," said a tearful Lori Simms,
Tooter's granddaughter.

The case of the missing grandmother began at 2:45 A.M. 8
Saturday, when Tooter left her Century Village condo-
minium in Pembroke Pines to pick up Simms and her
boyfriend, Steven Poulos, at Fort Lauderdale–Hollywood
International Airport. Their flight from New Jersey had been
delayed for several hours. When she didn't show up at the
airport, Simms called police.

For three days, officers searched canals, lakes, and 9
highways. There was no sign of Tooter until about 9:00 A.M.
Tuesday, when a Department of Transportation worker collecting road debris along I-595 near the New River noticed
something odd: A row of mangrove trees appeared to be bent
over, as if a huge weight had crushed them.

The worker, Justin Vanelli of Deerfield Beach, looked 10
down to see what had happened. "I saw the car first, then I
saw her legs sticking out. I told my dad to call an ambulance."

Justin's father, Chuck Vanelli, called 911. "It went over the top of the bridge wall," he told the dispatcher. "I see a lady down inside moving. The car went straight down." Minutes later, Fort Lauderdale firefighters began to arrive. "We put three medics over the wall immediately," McInerny said.

As a fleet of rescue vehicles arrived, police blocked off eastbound I-595 and traffic backed up to University Drive. Hicks' team found Tooter sprawled on the back seat, her legs propped over the steering and stretched out over a crumpled front seat. "She's conscious," he told his colleagues. "She's talking to us, and this is the missing woman from Pembroke Pines."

They worked feverishly in the swamp below the highway, their boots sucked into the eight-inch-deep ooze. Steam billowed from the standing water. Bugs were everywhere.

"This kind of thing, you don't have time to think about it," McInerny said. "It's got to be done now." As rescue workers labored to cut open the crumpled car, they kept Tooter talking. The first thing she said was, "Can you get me out of here?" said David Bourgouin, a firefighter/paramedic.

Florida Highway Patrol said the accident early Saturday happened when another vehicle struck Tooter's car. "She was definitely struck by some vehicle in the left rear," said Lt. John Bagnardi, a Florida Highway Patrol spokesman. "The back of her car had a lot of damage. There are so many scars and marks on the road and retaining wall that it's difficult to piece things together. She doesn't know if it was a truck or a car, but that she was definitely tagged in the rear."

"The Toyota climbed the wall and rode it for thirty to forty feet," Bagnardi said. It teetered for a moment, then tumbled over, landing on the driver's side. "The trees cushioned the fall, and her seatbelt kept her from being thrown around," he said. "That's why she survived." There are no other leads on the other driver, he said.

For the next three days, with thousands of cars and trucks passing within feet of her car, Tooter hoped for a miracle. "Does anybody hear me? Please," she repeated, according to her granddaughter. During her ordeal, Tooter wrote a good-bye note to her family, just in case. Family members would not share its contents.

When help finally arrived, Tooter told rescuers, "I'm very thirsty." She said she had slept very little. She was covered with ant and mosquito bites. But McInerny said she was extremely sharp in responding to questions from medics trying to determine her condition. "She knew her date of birth, her address, and what flight her granddaughter was expected on," he said. 17

At a news conference on Tuesday afternoon, rescuers and family members praised Tooter's strength and courage. The steering wheel cover Tooter had used to collect water was sticking out of Hicks' back pocket. 18

Hicks and his colleagues took a little over an hour to rescue Tooter. But they say she did the hardest work of all: She stayed alive. 19

DISCUSSION QUESTIONS

1. What are the hardships Tillie Tooter had to endure during the three days she was trapped in her car? How did she stay alive?
2. What steps did the rescuers take to rescue Tooter?
3. One rescuer, Stephen McInerny, states that Tooter "had it all together." What, specifically, did he mean by that comment?
4. Why couldn't Tooter be found easily? Who first spotted her, and what did he do?
5. What probably caused Tooter's car to dive off the highway's bridge wall?

WRITING OPTIONS

Collaborate with Peers

1. Interview a classmate about a close call he or she experienced. Summarize the sequence of events in a well-constructed paragraph.

Connecting with the Author's Ideas

2. According to rescuer Stephen McInerny, the Fire Division chief supervising the paramedics, rescuing Tooter was "the kind of thing you don't have time to think about." Describe a crisis or situation that caused you to act on instinct. Be as specific as possible.

Other Options

3. Write about a close call you experienced.
4. Write a short essay about a frightening experience that taught you something about yourself or others.
5. Tooter can be admired for her ability to think clearly in a crisis. Write a short essay describing someone you admire for surviving an ordeal. Include specific details about how this person behaved admirably under pressure.

Chapter Five
Family Commitment

"The family is one of nature's masterpieces."

George Santayana

The Heroism of Day-to-Day Dads

Susan Straight

Susan Straight writes an account of one father, her friend, Eric Gaines, and the two other fathers who have joined him in a remarkable mission to do what's best for their children.

Words You May Need to Know

trinkets (para. 2)	small items of little value
siblings (3)	brothers and sisters
inseparable (10)	unable to be separated
forlornly (10)	unhappily, miserably
maternal (15)	motherly
orchestrated (17)	arranged
limb (18)	arm or leg
phantom (18)	ghostly
phenomenon (18)	occurrence
collectively (18)	together
pact (19)	agreement
ecological (20)	environmental

1   Marvin Sanders has a tree house in his back yard, made by two boys who are not his sons but who come and stay with him often. They come to visit their sister, who is his daughter, and to be a family again. Sanders is a long-distance truck driver, and at least once a month after returning from a thousand-mile run, he gets back on the freeway with his daughter to drive another two hours so she can see her brothers. He meets up with two other men, all of them working and fathering full time, all of them traveling extra miles to keep four children together.

2   These men are hardly "deadbeat dads." We hear those words all the time in this decade of divorced fathers who

never support or see their children, and who never find the time for even their required weekend visitation. "Disneyland Dad." We hear that phrase, too, describing a divorced father who doesn't do the everyday things for his kids, who only buys them fancy trinkets and takes them to amusement parks to fulfill his role as a playmate.

But what about three fathers who not only have full 3 custody of their children, who do all the daily chores of preparing lunches and helping with homework, but who also travel hundreds of miles every year to make sure the four siblings get a chance to see each other? Three men, all married to the same woman in years past, who laugh and joke and even spend the night in each other's houses so that their kids can hang out together, the way brothers and sisters should? Three men and four children at Knott's Berry Farm amusement park? Not Disneyland Dads, but dads who might go to Disneyland this year if they can arrange it, and to Mexico and San Francisco—or maybe just to the local playground.

Marvin Sanders, DeWitt Cheateam, and Eric Gaines are 4 everyday heroes to me, for their unfailing generosity to their children. I have known Eric since our high school days in Riverside, California. When he married a woman with three children, our kids went to the same day care. Eric soon had a son from that marriage. We both ended up driving dark-green minivans, and we got teased for hauling around loads of children and smiling about it.

Then Eric's marriage broke up, and after a few months, 5 the children's circumstances became increasingly difficult. All four children were taken from their mother by child protective services, and the three fathers were abruptly told that they had full custody. Eric's young son came to live with him in January of 1997.

Marvin Sanders, 40, was called on his cellular phone, in- 6 formed that if he didn't pick up his daughter, Amanda, then 13, she would be placed in foster care. Sanders said, "I'm in Needles, California, right now, headed to Philadelphia!" He made emergency phone calls to find a place for Amanda, and drove all that night and the next day to return and start making a life with her in Fullerton, California, where he has a comfortable home with his fiancée.

7   DeWitt Cheateam, 39, a correctional officer in El Centro, California, 150 miles from Riverside, came to pick up his two sons, DeWitt Jr., then 9, and Matthew, then 7. They settled into a routine of early-morning rising, school buses, and no more double shifts for DeWitt, who turned down extra hours, saying, "I've got two boys getting home from school in half an hour. I have to be there."

8   Eric Gaines, 37, a roofer, moved back in with his parents so he wouldn't have to take his son, Aaron, then 2, to day care at 5:00 A.M., when he has to leave for work. But while trying to create a normal life for Aaron—going with his son to the mall or drugstore after work, buying Pez dispensers his son loves to collect—he realized that Aaron thought the green van seemed empty without his sister and brothers.

9   Before they became full-time dads, all the fathers had visited their children often. Amanda had just spent a month in Detroit with Marvin, getting to know all his relatives, and DeWitt saw his sons frequently in Riverside when they were living there with their mother. He would spend a weekend taking them to a local park. Eric had taken care of Aaron for days at a time after his divorce. So the children seemed to adjust well to their new lives with their fathers—but one thing bothered them: They missed each other terribly.

10   When all four children lived with Eric and their mother, they were inseparable, he said. And now, Aaron kept asking forlornly, "Where do the boys live? Where?"

11   Eric said, "I felt relieved that all the kids were in a better situation, but they wanted to see each other real bad. I'd driven out a few times to pick up Amanda, and she stayed with us. But Aaron wanted to go all the way to El Centro. So I called Marvin and DeWitt, and we started putting together these trips."

12   DeWitt said, "It was kind of unusual, getting all the kids together and we dads not even knowing each other that

well." DeWitt is a native of New York City, Marvin was born in Detroit, and Eric is a lifelong Riverside resident. They had seen each other many times, of course, but how many times do men, all divorced from the same woman, spend an entire weekend laughing together?

Eric and Marvin made the three-hour drive to the desert 13 city of El Centro, near the Mexican border, for Labor Day weekend. The kids played in the house, visited a nearby construction site, and watched TV. When Eric told me about the weekend, I had to laugh, picturing the three fathers playing endless hands of cards and eating pizza. But didn't they talk about their ex-wife? How could they not bring up their common bond? Eric laughed, too, saying they'd each received a recent letter from her, and they discussed it for about five minutes. Then they talked about the kids, work, the world, and the kids again.

They are the day-to-day dads. DeWitt says, "I have so 14 much respect for mothers now—with the laundry, the bruises, the sickness, and the colds. I get up at 3:30 A.M. to make their lunches, get their breakfasts ready and lay out their school clothes. Then I do my own stuff, and the day starts. When we spend the night at Marvin's place, we discuss all the different things he has to deal with by raising a girl."

Marvin stopped doing the cross-country trucking jobs, 15 traveling mostly to San Francisco, Sacramento, Las Vegas, or Phoenix so he could work 24 hours and then be home for 24. "Amanda has a lot of homework," Marvin says, chuckling. "But she had a lot of responsibilities before," he says, "like feeding the boys and taking care of the house. I think she just saw what needed to be done back then. Amanda has a lot of maternal instincts, and when she came to live with me, there weren't any kids around to mother. So I would do whatever it took—letting Aaron stay here for a weekend, driving them to El Centro or taking DeWitt Jr. and Matthew with us for a truck run."

That was a highlight of the summer, when Marvin took 16 the three older kids with him in his truck. "I've got the sleeper, the double bunk, refrigerator, and TV," Marvin chuckles. "It's really funny—the boys washed the windows, and one day when we were in San Leandro, they got out and helped me unload all these cans of crushed pineapple at an ice-cream store. They were great."

17   I saw the kids at Aaron's third birthday, here in Riverside. Eric had rented a jumping cage, hired a clown, and orchestrated a daylong affair. My two older daughters remembered Matthew and DeWitt, but they didn't have a chance to talk to them much because Aaron was following his big brothers around as though they were minor gods, as big brothers often are. He touched them constantly, ran around and then came back as if to make sure they were still there, to make sure they hadn't disappeared.

18   Siblings who are separated must always feel like people missing a limb—the phantom limb phenomenon, in which an arm or leg is missing but still aches. Kids sent to different foster homes are miserable. But these four children have remarkable fathers. Mervin says, "One thing that really got to me was people saying, 'Oh, they shouldn't be separated. Can't their grandmother keep them all?' But the fact remains that they have fathers who collectively care about all of them."

19   "We made a pact," DeWitt says, "to keep them seeing each other. If there's a birthday or holiday, we barbecue somewhere. We take them to their grandmother's house in Riverside once a month, and another weekend I'll drive the four hours to Marvin's and spend the night. It's worth it, to see them all together."

20   Eric took the four kids to a dinosaur-themed ecological park in Riverside one weekend. And last January, a year after the three dads got the kids, they all met at Knott's Berry Farm. DeWitt organized the outing. "For Law Enforcement Day, all the kids were free admissions, so I said, 'Let's do it!' It was good to see them all running around the park. It means something to keep them all together. They need to know they haven't been taken away from each other."

When I spoke with all three fathers, each mentioned 21 something different coming up. Eric knows a roller-skating rink in Riverside, and DeWitt can't wait to take the kids to an amusement park and fishing place right across the Mexican border. They will probably get together for a week this summer.

But every day, Marvin can look into his backyard and 22 see the huge pepper tree with the tree house that Matthew and DeWitt made with Amanda last summer. "It has a wooden floor, and they got a front seat from this old MG I had. They made rope pulleys to lift stuff up to each other. They're still working on it. Amanda came up with the idea, but the boys loved it so much, every time they come over, they find wood and keep adding on to it." Marvin paused, then said, "I know the other kids aren't mine, but I treat them like mine—they're kids, and they all need love."

DISCUSSION QUESTIONS

1. What does the author, Susan Straight, mean when she states that none of the men in the article is a "deadbeat dad" or a "Disneyland Dad"? What is meant by these labels?
2. What is unusual about the background of these men?
3. What specific sacrifices did each of the fathers make to provide a stable environment for their children? (Find specific examples for each father.)
4. Why does Dewitt have such great respect for mothers now?
5. Why do you think the children missed each other so much?

WRITING OPTIONS

Collaborate with Peers

1. Interview a classmate about a time he or she was separated from a sibling for an extended period. Did they miss each other more than they expected? Why? Did they even miss arguing with each other? Based on your notes, write a paragraph about the special bond between brothers and sisters.

Connecting with the Author's Ideas

2. Susan Straight calls the fathers heroes "for their unfailing generosity to their children." Write about a parent you know who is generous to his or her children. The person does not have to be generous with money or gifts but can be giving of time, encouragement, love, and so forth.

Other Options

3. The fathers arranged various trips to enable the siblings to spend time together, and much planning is involved. Write a short essay about how difficult it is to plan a trip involving your entire family.
4. The fathers depicted in this article are not stereotypical single fathers. In a short essay, describe a single father or a single mother you know who does not fit the stereotypical image of a single parent.

Winning for Zora

Collin Perry

Former Chicago Bears and Washington Redskins linesman Chris Zorich seemed destined to go nowhere, but his mother had other plans for him. Chris grew up knowing the pain of feeling different, but he had someone rooting for him, "someone who lifted his hopes and inspired him with her endurance and devotion."

Words You May Need to Know

funneled (para. 1)	poured in
gaggle (1)	group, flock
impaired (3)	damaged, weakened
crucial (4)	important, decisive
taunted (5)	mocked, ridiculed
badgered (7)	harassed
predominantly (8)	mainly
forged (11)	formed, shaped
adversity (11)	trouble, misery
tenement (11)	poor, crowded apartment building
welfare (12)	health and happiness
torturous (13)	painful
tittering (13)	giggling, snickering
hardships (16)	suffering, troubles
razzed (17)	teased
vowed (19)	promised himself
unremitting (20)	constant
diabetes (20)	a disease commonly caused by the inability of the body to use sugar
rummage (21)	search thoroughly

ravenous (22)	extremely hungry
compelled (22)	drove
glimmer (24)	hint, dim perception
discipline (25)	training and rules
rigors (27)	strictness, harshness
mulled (32)	considered
emerging (34)	rising, developing
impoverished (34)	poor
initiative (39)	leading movement

1   As the crowd funneled into the skating rink last February, a thickly muscled man with a bronze, shaved head towered above a gaggle of two dozen kids. The children, who came from Lydia Home Association, had been abused or neglected; some were also handicapped. All were the guests of pro football player Chris Zorich, who in his bow tie and sports jacket, looked like a cross between the Incredible Hulk and Mother Goose.

2   When the show started, a boy with poor vision settled next to Zorich. From time to time the twenty-eight-year-old athlete would gently turn the child's head to help him find the action on ice. Having grown up on Chicago's tough South Side, Zorich knew all too well the pain of feeling different.

3   "As a child, I had four strikes against me," he says. "I was poor, fat, bi-racial, and speech-impaired." Remembering that pain motivates Chris to work with kids of all income levels and social backgrounds to help them do their best.

4   Chris Zorich always knew he had one crucial thing going for him—someone who lifted his hopes and inspired him with her endurance and devotion. If there was one reason he was here today, she was it.

5   "You *better* not cry," taunted the teenager one day, holding eight-year-old Chris off the ground as he tried to shake money from his pockets.

"I ain't c-c-crying," Chris gasped.   6

On other days, a different boy badgered Chris and   7
punched him in the chest. "You honky, you better have
some money for me tomorrow, got that?"

Such incidents often happened as Chris returned home   8
from school in the predominantly black neighborhood on
Chicago's South Side in the late 1970s. To explain his
bruises, he would tell his mother, Zora, that he had tripped.
He never confessed that other kids were beating him up, as
he knew she would demand to know who they were.

One day, however, Chris finally asked her why the other   9
kids had such a problem with his skin color. "I get 'white
boy' and 'honky' from the guys around here," he said. "And
in the white neighborhood they call me n-n-nigger."

Chris already knew that his black father had aban-   10
doned the family before his birth. Now Zora tried to comfort
him. "I'm white. Your father was black. You're bi-racial, and
I love you. And no matter what, always know that I'll be
there for you."

The bond between Chris and his mother was especially   11
tight, having been forged in the shared adversity of inner-
city life. Mice and cockroaches infested the tenement building they lived in; outside, muggings were almost routine.

Chris always turned to his mother for guidance and re-   12
assurance. Zora responded by putting her son's welfare
above everything else. She made ends meet by baby-sitting,
not just for the money but to provide Chris with companions
she could supervise. She read to him, helped with homework,
and made sure his hand-me-down clothes were always clean.

In school, Chris's stuttering proved torturous. When he   13
was ten, he had to read an essay in front of the class. He
stuttered and mumbled along. When he heard his classmates tittering, he quit halfway through and returned to his
seat, his face hot with embarrassment.

That evening, when Chris told Zora about the incident,   14
she said, "Try it out on me. Pretend *I'm* the class."

Chris began reciting his essay and, though still stutter-   15
ing, managed to finish it. That was a good start for Zora, but

not enough. She asked him to read it again and again, and each time his speech improved. "Now show the class what you can do," she insisted. At the end of the year, Chris found the nerve to ask his teacher for another chance. Telling himself it was only his mother in the audience, he got through the reading with few hesitations.

16   Despite their hardships, Chris noticed that his mother was generous to others. Whenever children approached and offered to carry her groceries, hoping to earn a tip, she'd always give them a dime or a piece of candy—even though she'd carry her own packages. Chris was shocked, but he said nothing. Zora believed in treating the world as she would her own family. It was a lesson he never forgot.

17   Zora tried to do everything for Chris that a father would. She'd watch a lot of sports and television with Chris. She would even take him to the park, where she'd chase passes and hit fly balls. Other kids razzed him for playing ball with his mother, but their taunts barely mattered to him. With Zora he felt secure and happy.

18   Chris returned his mother's affection openly. On Zora's birthday he would make her a card and buy her an inexpensive gift. On Mother's Day he would present her with a bouquet of dandelions.

19   Still, their devotion to each other couldn't stop others from being cruel about Chris's mixed-race background. One winter, as Zora and Chris walked home, a group of kids pelted them with snowballs. One hit Zora square in the face, and Chris saw a tear run down her cheek. At that moment, he vowed he would someday get them out of there.

20   The obstacles in their lives seemed unremitting, especially after Zora was told she had severe diabetes. Overweight and unable to stay on her feet for prolonged periods, she was forced to turn to public assistance.

21   The two plunged to their lowest. Food became so short that Chris sometimes went to bed at 6:00 P.M. to sleep through his hunger pains, knowing he'd wake up to a hot breakfast at school. Other times they would rummage

through a supermarket garbage bin for discarded food. "It's fine," Zora would say at the sight of a package of hamburger meat that was well past its "sell by" date. "I'll cut off the bad parts."

Ironically, food became an escape for Chris. His raven- 22 ous appetite and fear of being hungry compelled him to eat every scrap he could get his hands on. By the time he was twelve, his weight had ballooned to 250 pounds.

Chris envied gang members, who had the girls, cars, 23 and clothes—everything a kid wanted. But his mother had been mugged by neighborhood thugs right in front of him as a toddler. Because of this incident, Chris knew he could never join a gang.

Chris's first real glimmer of finding a way out came 24 when he was admitted to Chicago Vocational High School in September 1983. Soon the high school's football coach, John Potocki, noticed the oversized boy. "You playing football?" he asked Chris. "You're big enough to be on the squad."

Chris started going to after-school football practice and 25 discovered, to his delight, he was with people who had some real goals in life. He enjoyed the discipline of it and working with others. Potocki found that the sweet-tempered boy was fast, strong, and determined—indeed, he had a "killer instinct" on the football field.

Zora became the team's biggest fan. Before each game 26 Chris would scan the crowd until he found her in the stands. And he established himself as a standout player. In his junior year, five colleges recruited him. After discussions with his mother, he decided on Notre Dame in South Bend, Indiana, partly because he viewed the team's graduation rate—almost 99 percent—as a guarantee that he could get a good job one day and help Zora.

When he started at Notre Dame in August 1987, how- 27 ever, Chris was unprepared for the academic rigors of a first-rate university. As a freshman, he partied on weekends and finished the first semester with a 1.9 grade-point-average, which landed him on academic probation.

28   "Mom, I can't do it," he told Zora one night on the phone. "I get these grades again and I'll be kicked out. I'm coming home."

29   Zora was silent for a minute. Finally she said, "And what would you be coming back to?"

30   "You. *You're* there."

31   "Yes, but I won't be here forever," she said.

32   For days Chris mulled over his mother's words. She was right. He knew this was the chance of a lifetime, and in the end he buckled down to his studies and got off probation.

33   Meanwhile, Chris's progress on the playing field was even more impressive. In his sophomore year he became the starting defensive tackle and was named to the 1988 All-America squad.

34   Back home, word got around that the former "fat boy" was an emerging football star. On visits home, the now six-foot-one, 260-pound athlete enjoyed strolling through the old neighborhoods, his mother proudly leaning on his arm. Indeed, Zora became something of a neighborhood hero, signing autographs for fans when Chris was away at school.

35   Chris went on to make All-America for three consecutive years. During his senior year he won the Rotary Lombardi award as the nation's top collegiate lineman. That season ended with a one-point loss to the University of Colorado in the Orange Bowl on January 1, 1991. Still, Chris was named Notre Dame's Most Valuable Player for the game, stacking up ten tackles and one sack.

36   Gloomy over his team's defeat, Chris telephoned his mother, who'd watched on TV. "Hey, I saw all those tackles," she said brightly. "You played some game!" Zora's enthusiasm was contagious, and the two talked and laughed.

37   The next morning Chris caught a flight for Chicago. He had expected Zora to meet him at the airport, but she wasn't there. Racing to his mother's apartment, he found the door locked. He pounded. No answer. Frantic, he went around the back, pulled the screen off a bathroom window and saw Zora lying on the hallway floor, dead of a heart attack. As Chris knelt beside her, his distress gradually gave way to a

feeling of serenity at his core. "Bye, Mom," he whispered, kissing her. "I love you."

At Zora's wake, mourners sang "You Are My Sunshine." 38 Later, at the grave site, Chris placed roses on her coffin. Mom, he thought, I hope you'll be proud of what I'll do with the rest of my life.

* * * *

Chris Zorich played six and a half years for the Chicago 39 Bears and a half-season with the Washington Redskins. Later, he attended law school at the University of Notre Dame. His most important work, however, is honoring Zora's memory. The Zora Zorich Scholarship enables promising students of limited means to attend Notre Dame. Zorich's Care to Share Family Food Program distributes groceries to impoverished families. The Chris Zorich and Friends program takes needy boys and girls to ice shows and other events. And his School Is Cool initiative has him motivating kids by sharing his story.

"I couldn't have accomplished anything without her," 40 Chris says. "She showed me the way; now I just want to show others the way."

DISCUSSION QUESTIONS

1. What are some of the effective descriptions that give you a clear picture of Chris Zorich's appearance? Find the exact words.
2. What reasons does Zorich give for feeling "different" as a child?
3. What did Zora do to make life a little easier for her son at home? What did she do to help him cope with his stuttering problems at school?
4. Describe the incident that made Zorich determined to get himself and his mother out of their bleak environment. How did he know that he would never join a gang?
5. What happened at Chicago Vocational High School that changed Zorich's life?
6. How did Zora convince her son to stay in college?
7. How did Zorich honor the memory of his mother?

WRITING OPTIONS

Collaborate with Peers

1. With two or three classmates, brainstorm and discuss some of the effects teasing at school can have on young children. Also consider why some children enjoy teasing or bullying others. Based on your notes, write a short essay on the causes or effects of teasing.

2. Chris Zorich felt like giving up on college because he found the work too rigorous. However, he persevered and succeeded. With two or three classmates, collaborate on what perseverance means. Then write individual summaries of the best examples of perseverance drawn from several walks of life: education, business, entertainment, sports, medicine, and so forth.

Connecting with the Author's Ideas

3. Susan Straight says that the bond between Chris Zorich and his mother was very tight because it was formed in the "shared adversity" of their circumstances. Write about two people you know whose bond became strong because they shared trouble and pain.

Other Options

4. Write a short essay about a time in your life when someone influenced you to do something you never thought you could do. Include details about your life before, during, and after this accomplishment.

5. The relationship between Zorich and his mother was a particularly close one. Describe a parent-child relationship that you feel is as meaningful as the one described in "Winning for Zora."

6. Chris Zorich now motivates children to strive to be the best they can be. If you could establish your own charity to help or motivate others, what kind of charity would you like it to be? Write an essay about whom this charity would help, how you could get others to contribute money, and the type of special events you would plan that could include volunteers.

No Turning Back:
The Singer Named "Jewel"

Suzanne Chazin

Years before becoming famous for her poetic songs, the singer now known simply as "Jewel" refused to play it safe. She and her parents struggled financially, but they never lost confidence in themselves or each other.

Words You May Need to Know

willowy (para. 1)	gracefully slender
mutely (2)	silently
straits (4)	predicament, distress
skeptical (6)	doubtful, unbelieving
Spartan (10)	severely simple, without luxuries
honed (12)	developed, sharpened
yodeling (15)	singing with alternations between an ordinary voice and an artificially high voice
relentlessly (15)	with determination, strictly
devastating (16)	overwhelming, destructive
seedy (17)	run-down, shabby
patrons (17)	customers
shot glasses (18)	glasses that hold a small quantity, usually an ounce, of liquor
grizzled (18)	graying
prestigious (21)	honored
formal (21)	academic
shimmering (24)	shining, vibrating in faint light
acoustic (24)	performed without electric guitar
derision (25)	ridicule, mockery

cynical (25)	distrustful, unbelieving
undeterred (25)	not discouraged
garish (26)	loud, crudely colorful
exuberance (27)	joyfulness, vitality
catcalls (27)	cries of disapproval
admonitions (27)	advice
undiminished (28)	unreduced
scoffed (28)	mocked, sneered
carping (29)	complaining, faultfinding
charisma (29)	a special power for attracting enthusiastic popular support
riveting (29)	attention-grabbing
ignited (29)	set fire to, started
following (31)	group of admirers
virtually (32)	almost completely

1   Jewel Kilcher was just eighteen, fresh out of high school and completely unsure of what to do with her life. She had moved from Michigan to San Diego to be with her mother and was working a series of disappointing, low-paying jobs—waiting tables and punching cash registers. There was little time or money for exploring careers. In fact, she was barely scraping by.

2   Things only worsened when a burning began in the willowy teenager's back and traveled all the way down her groin. Her long blond hair was damp with fever on the day she mutely followed her mother into a hospital emergency room. It was the eighth medical facility mother and daughter had visited that hazy spring afternoon in 1993. Three hospitals and four clinics had already refused to treat the girl's raging kidney infection because she was broke and lacked medical insurance.

Finally they found a doctor who would attend to her, 3 but it was a physical and spiritual low point. In the weeks that followed, Jewel poured out her anxieties to her mother, Nedra Carroll. What should she do? She loved the arts—literature, drawing, dance, music. But how could she possibly pursue any of these demanding careers when just surviving was claiming so much of her energy?

Nedra, in tough financial straits herself, came up with a 4 novel solution: they'd give up their shared apartment and move into vans near the beach. Without the pressure to meet their rent, Jewel could focus on her life goal and make it happen.

After searching her soul, Jewel decided that singing and 5 songwriting meant the most to her. But Nedra probed further, asking why. Jewel thought about her reasons. Money? She'd always had so little; she'd even grown accustomed to living on what she could carry in a knapsack. Fame? She'd always felt like an outsider, so that didn't matter. The one thing that she really cared about was her songs—inspiring people with her words and voice. "I want to sing to remind people to live their dreams," she told her mother.

Still, she couldn't help feeling a flicker of fear. Friends 6 were skeptical of her plans, and their doubts were contagious. What if she failed at the one thing she wanted to do? Perhaps she should look for a safer way to use her talent—singing on tour boats, for instance, or teaching grade school music, like her father in Alaska.

"Maybe I should have a fallback plan," she suggested to 7 her mother.

Nedra shook her head. "If you have a fallback plan, 8 you will fall back. You are young. Be brave. Have faith in yourself."

So the decision was made: the two would live like fron- 9 tier women on the beach with the sound of the Pacific surf rolling in their ears. And Jewel would put her talents and ambitions to the test.

It was not the first time either had lived such a Spartan 10 life. Nedra and Jewel's father, Atz Kilcher, a social worker, were raised on the Alaskan frontier. Though the Kilchers moved often when Jewel and her two brothers were small, she spent a good part of her most formative years on her Swiss grandparents' 640-acre homestead, 225 miles southwest of Anchorage.

Frontier Child

11 The homestead was a place of rugged beauty, surrounded by soaring tree-covered canyons and snow-capped mountains. But it was also isolated and harsh, with only a coal stove for warmth and an outhouse for plumbing.

12 There, learning to do tough, physically demanding work, Jewel honed a spirit of determination. Even before the move, she had shown a single-mindedness that impressed her family. In third grade, for instance, she was diagnosed with dyslexia, a disability that affected her reading and coordination. Later that year, she was rejected from an after-school gymnastics program she desperately wanted to join because she couldn't do somersaults and cartwheels.

13 "That doesn't mean you can't do gymnastics," her mother told her. "It just means you'll have to work harder."

14 So Jewel began practicing three hours a night until she could do the maneuvers as well as the natural athletes in her grade. She was accepted into the program.

15 Jewel showed the same determination singing. Watching her folksinging parents perform, Jewel delighted in her father's yodeling and wanted to learn how to do it herself. But her parents, feeling it would strain her six-year-old vocal cords, were reluctant to teach her. So she practiced relentlessly on her own until she could do it with ease.

16 But the young girl with the golden voice couldn't will away the most devastating event of her childhood. When Jewel was eight, her parents divorced. Nedra remained in Anchorage, and Atz moved to his parents' homestead. The children spent time with both parents but lived mainly with their father. They took over the barn at the homestead and lived simply off the land—bleeding birch trees to make

syrup, canning vegetables, smoking and drying salmon they caught themselves. Atz even taught the children to weave baskets from willow roots.

He and Jewel became a singing duo. But unlike her parents' singing engagements, some of these were in seedy taverns and veterans' halls, often reeking of smoke and spilled beer. The patrons included tattooed bikers, drifters, and women past their prime still trying to squeeze into skintight jeans. At a biker bar in Anchorage, Jewel watched a man collapse in a parking lot from a drug overdose. "What I saw in those places turned me off drugs, drinking, and smoking for life," she says. She also saw what happens to people who lose their passion for life and end up merely existing. And she vowed it would never happen to her. 17

Singing to the clink of shot glasses and the chatter of crowds taught Jewel something she might never have learned any other way. One night, shortly before one of their performances, she and her father got into an argument. Already upset, Jewel broke into tears when her father reminded her to leave her personal life behind when she went onstage. What did it matter, she thought, since the audience consisted of just a few drunken, grizzled veterans? 18

Then a man in the crowd scolded her. "Stop looking so depressed," he called out. The words had a humbling effect. Jewel suddenly understood that her job was to please the audience, not herself. She stopped crying and finished the set flawlessly. And she determined never to take an audience for granted again. 19

By age thirteen, restless and wanting to spend more time with her mother, Jewel packed up and moved in with her mother in Anchorage. But she was no longer the child her mother had tucked into bed each night five years earlier. "I was bitter about the divorce, angry and mistrustful when I first moved in with my mom," explains Jewel. She developed friendships with members of street gangs. She dated older guys. She even shoplifted a few times. 20

21   But Jewel's life took yet another new turn when a teacher from the Interlochen Arts Academy in Michigan heard her sing at a summer music festival. Impressed by her voice, he encouraged her to apply to the prestigious arts school. Jewel did, and won a voice scholarship. Interlochen gave Jewel formal training in dance, writing, and theater and broadened her artistic horizons.

On the Beach

22 Growing up without running water turned out to be good preparation for living in a van beside the Pacific. Used to quick scrubdowns in Alaska's subzero temperatures, Jewel was expert at washing her hair efficiently in public restrooms at Kmart and Denny's. She was comfortable with thrift-shop clothes and could get by on little more than carrots and peanut butter while looking for work.

23   Eventually, she found a regular spot performing at a Pacific Beach coffeehouse called The Inner Change. While there, she wrote a song entitled, "Who Will Save Your Soul?" about those who lead lives of physical comfort but spiritual emptiness.

24   By the middle of 1993, Jewel was attracting overflowing crowds to the coffeehouse and drawing the attention of record-industry talent scouts. Then in December 1993 her shimmering voice and folk-style acoustic songs landed her a recording contract with Atlantic Records.

25   Jewel might have hoped that the worst of her struggles were behind her. But yet another round was just beginning. When her first album, *Pieces of You,* was released in February 1995, it sold fewer than 500 copies a week. Her sweetly innocent voice and uplifting songs were met with derision by the often-cynical entertainment industry. Unde-terred, Jewel traveled the country alone, usually with only a road manager to keep her company. Back in San Diego, her mother helped to manage her career. Jewel played mostly small clubs, sometimes forty concerts in thirty days, never staying more than a couple of nights in any one city.

Worse still were some of her bookings. She would occa- 26
sionally open for heavy-metal bands with screaming electric
guitars and fans wearing garish clothes and makeup.

Once Jewel was booked to play a black high school in 27
Detroit. She peeked through the curtain before the show,
delighted to see a full auditorium of excited students. But
the noisy exuberance turned to boos and catcalls when the
curtain went up. They had expected a rap singer called
Jewell, and a young woman with an acoustic guitar didn't
turn them on. Many of the students walked out. Still, recall-
ing her father's admonitions years earlier, Jewel realized it
was her job to give a good show. So she sang with undimin-
ished passion for those who stayed.

Radio stations refused to play her. Music critics scoffed 28
at her lack of hipness. She was derided for everything from
her crooked teeth to her constant encouragement that fans
follow their dreams. But Jewel stayed on the road, playing
coffeehouses, signing CDs in suburban stores and thanking
everyone who came to her performances.

Despite the carping of critics, more and more people 29
took note of her talent and charisma, and word spread
about her riveting live performances. As her fan base grew
by word of mouth, the critics counted for less. By appealing
directly to those who mattered to her—those for whom she
wrote her music—Jewel ignited her career.

The decisive breakthrough came in mid-1996, when 30
Pieces of You went gold more than a year after its release,
selling 500,000 copies. With radio stations responding at
last to her fans, the single "Who Will Save Your Soul?"
climbed the charts until it was a top-ten hit.

By the time her second CD, *Spirit,* was released in late 31
1998, Jewel had an international following. *Spirit* went on to
sell three million copies, and her admirers still couldn't get
enough. Jewel would soon appear in her first movie, a Civil
War drama called *Ride With the Devil.* The film extended her
reach as a star.

All of this is a stunning journey for a young woman 32
who was virtually homeless just a few years earlier. But Jewel

Kilcher understands how it happened. In fact, she relives the conversation with her mother that made all the difference.

33   "If she'd encouraged me to have a fallback plan, I'd have made one. I was scared. But being safe didn't mean being happy." Nedra understood this, and so, eventually, did Jewel. Happiness came instead from following her passion— and realizing there could be no turning back.

DISCUSSION QUESTIONS

1. When Jewel was a teenager, what medical condition drained her energy, and why did most medical facilities refuse to treat her?
2. To help her daughter focus on songwriting and singing, what changes did Nedra make in their living arrangements?
3. Why did Jewel's mother caution her daughter against having a "fallback plan"?
4. Where was Jewel raised, and what were some hardships of this environment that helped make her determined to succeed on her own?
5. What made Jewel refuse to try drugs, alcohol, or tobacco?
6. What was a turning point for Jewel regarding her attitude toward performing and her responsibility to her audience?
7. When she first signed a recording contract, her struggles were not over. Why was she criticized by music critics?
8. Jewel's fan base gradually increased, largely because of Jewel's commitment to her fans. What are some examples of this exceptional commitment?
9. Although Jewel was often frightened about her future, what did her mother understand that Jewel eventually learned for herself?

WRITING OPTIONS

Collaborate with Peers

1. Jewel suffered through hard times and rejection before she found success in the music industry. With two or three of your class-mates, brainstorm and discuss three other stars of the music world who faced personal, financial, or career difficulties before

they became famous. Then write individual paragraphs on one of those stars.

Connecting with the Author's Ideas

2. Suzanne Chazin writes that Jewel had "always felt like an outsider" in her childhood and teens. Write about one incident when you felt like an outsider.

Other Options

3. Jewel's mother urged her not to have a "fallback plan." Write a paragraph or short essay about the benefits or drawbacks of having a fallback plan.
4. At one time in her life, Jewel lived on what she could carry in her knapsack. Do you think you could simplify your life to this extent? Write a short essay on how you could lead a much simpler life than you have now.
5. What individual has had the most positive impact on your life thus far? Write a short essay about this person. Be sure to use specific details so the reader can understand the extent to which this person helped you.

Chapter Six
Triumphs in Education

"Only the educated are free."

Epictetus

"A teacher affects eternity; he can never tell where his influence stops."

Henry Brooks Adams

Driven Teen Goes from Hell to Harvard

Linda Matchan

Liz Murray, daughter of cocaine addicts, dropped out of school in the ninth grade, lived on the streets of New York City, and survived by picking food from trash cans. But she never gave up on learning and was eventually accepted at Harvard University, freshman class of 2000. She was determined to succeed and noted, "I'd either make it good for myself . . . or submit to everything that was happening and live a life of excuses."

Words You May Need to Know

snare (para. 1)	catch
execute (1)	carry out
statuesque (2)	like a statue in grace or beauty
poised (2)	dignified, self-assured
pop icon (2)	popular figure
reversed (2)	turned around
fortunes (2)	fate, destiny
prestigious (3)	honored
honchos (3)	bosses
under their wing (3)	under their support
decrepit (5)	broken down
stoic (6)	calm, composed
panhandling (11)	begging
progressive (13)	creative and experimental
conventional (13)	standard, customary
profound (14)	deep
unfathomable (14)	mysterious

genteel (15)	polite
personable (15)	attractive
single-minded (15)	dedicated, firm in purpose
agenda (15)	plan
ecstatic (16)	intensely emotional
awe (17)	overwhelming feeling of admiration and reverence
feverishly (18)	restlessly, excitedly
hectic (18)	confused, rapidly moving
venues (19)	scenes of any event or action
disdain (19)	scorn
apathy (19)	lack of interest
irony (21)	unexpected outcome
consumed (21)	absorbed
gratifying (21)	satisfying
relinquish (22)	give up

1   Liz Murray is standing on the stage of the auditorium of Public School 95 in the Bronx, telling 400 fifth- and sixth-graders about her life. Several of the children are holding pieces of paper, ready to snare her autograph. One girl has a strategic plan (which she will later successfully execute) to pull out a strand of Murray's hair.

2   The nineteen-year-old in faded jeans, worn sneakers, and flannel shirt—though statuesque and poised—isn't the typical adolescent pop icon, a basketball star or a rock singer or an actress. The truth is far more spectacular. The daughter of two cocaine addicts, Murray dropped out of school in the ninth grade, lived on the streets of New York from the age of sixteen until eighteen, slept on subway trains and park benches, and finally, through sheer force of will, reversed her fortunes.

This fall, Murray is headed to Harvard, accepted as a 3
freshman the year the university reported a record number
of applications. As word has gotten out about Murray's
accomplishments (she won a prestigious *New York Times*
College Scholarship last year, which led to a segment about
her in December on ABC's *20/20*), Hollywood honchos have
taken her under their wing.

Now, the girl who picked food out of trash cans and did 4
her homework in stairwells is checking her voice mail on her
cell phone and asking a reporter if she can "expense" the
taxi she's flagging down. "It's completely wild," Murray says
of the arc—from homeless to Harvard to Hollywood—that
her life has made. "For a long time I was just stuck in one
place, saying, 'You were there, and now you are here?'"

———

But ask Barbara Franceschini and Helene Lorinsky— 5
teachers in the audience who taught her in elementary
school—and they'll say nothing would surprise them about
the girl they used to call Elizabeth. They taught her at Public
School 261 in the Bronx, a windowless school so decrepit it
was declared a health hazard and closed the year Murray
graduated.

Her teachers describe her as a tough and stoic child 6
who was placed in the intellectually gifted class, talented at
math, and so driven to work hard she chose to play Brutus
in the class production of *Julius Ceasar*. There were hints,
big hints, that something was wrong at home. Murray's
mother once showed up at school in a nightgown, with feces
on her shoes. During one period, Elizabeth wore the same
pair of pants to school every day for months.

But her teachers didn't have the whole story. They 7
knew her mother had been in and out of hospitals, but not
that she was an alcoholic, or that her parents did cocaine in
the kitchen, without trying to hide their habit. Nor did they
know that the apartment where she lived with her parents
and sister was filthy, with two cats and a dog that no one

walked or cared for. (Murray would have to step over piles of feces covered with maggots to get to her bedroom.) On good days, Elizabeth's mother read her Dr. Seuss stories and listened to old records; her father—he is "extremely intelligent"—would quote from 1940s novels but "then go into the kitchen and shoot up drugs."

8   Neither parent was a provider. At the age of "eight or nine," Murray recalls, she worked bagging groceries at a twenty-four-hour supermarket. "I was the only one putting food in the fridge," she tells the hushed schoolchildren in the PS 95 auditorium. She also pumped gas for tips at self-service gas stations. Money was so tight her mother once sold her sister's winter coat to get some cash.

9   After her parents separated when she was thirteen, her father ran out of money and lost the apartment. Murray went into a city youth facility for a few months but couldn't bear to stay there. She went to live with her mother and god-father. "They were old drinking buddies," Murray explains. But that didn't last long, since her mother was diagnosed with AIDS and tuberculosis; she died in December 1996.

10   In the ninth grade, Murray dropped out of school. To pass the time and lift her spirits, she often went to libraries to read *Hamlet* and Shakespeare's sonnets. She quotes by memory a favorite poem by Edgar Allan Poe, called "Alone."

> From childhood's hour I have not been
> As others were; I have not seen
> As others saw; I could not bring
> My passions from a common spring.
> From the same source I have not taken
> My sorrow; I could not awaken
> My heart to joy at the same tone;
> And all I loved, I loved alone.

11   At age sixteen, Murray hit the streets. Sometimes she'd sleep at friends' houses, "until I'd hear their parents talking in low voices and I knew I was wearing out my welcome," she says in an interview. Other times, she slept on park

benches or subways, panhandling for spare change to get on the trains.

The decision to return to school came at the lowest point 12 of her life—the day she saw her mother's coffin at the cemetery, a donated pine box with her name misspelled in Magic Marker. "Everything really hit me," she tells the children. "Everything I knew about had messed up. And I understood it was important to push myself, that I'd either make it good for myself . . . or submit to everything and live a life of excuses."

One teacher she contacted recommended the Humani- 13 ties Preparatory Academy, a small progressive school in Manhattan known for working with students who are lost in the conventional school system. Despite the fact that her transcript was "one big blank," says Perry Weiner, the school's co-director, her intelligence impressed officials, and she was accepted.

Terrified to fail and determined to distinguish herself, 14 Murray studied wherever she could find a place to sit and managed to complete four years of high school in two, graduating with grades "in the high 90s," Weiner says. Even he was not aware that she was homeless. "I knew she stayed at friends' houses a lot. . . . New York is a very profound and unusual city. The lives of students are quite unfathomable here. I know kids who slept on rooftops. I didn't question it closely. I knew her mother had died of AIDS, but she didn't say much about her life."

Weiner describes her as "genteel" but also sad, yet "very 15 personable and funny, and fun-loving in her own way. She is also a very single-minded person, very intellectual, with a real love of learning. She knew she needed to go to a very, very good college. That was her agenda."

Her opportunity came when she was selected as one of 16 ten top students at the academy to take a field trip to Boston. "That's when she found out about Harvard," says Weiner. "That's when she had her first ecstatic vision."

Standing in Harvard Yard, she had a look of pure awe 17 on her face, Weiner recalls. He says he knew what she was thinking. "I just walked over to her and said, 'It's very improbable, but still possible.' In fact, it happened."

────────

18   Until she starts school in the fall, she is keeping feverishly busy. She has an apartment in the Bronx that she shares with a friend. She works as a clerk for the *New York Times*. She keeps a hectic schedule of appointments, including going to the dentist for the first time since she was nine. She sees her father frequently—"He lives in the Bronx and has AIDS, but he's doing very well."

19   She sees her sister occasionally; she lives in the Bronx, too, but they don't get along well, Murray says. She has a boyfriend and a lot of friends from her homeless days, whom she is helping out with money, "and in every way I can." And she makes frequent appearances at schools and other venues where she talks about subjects close to her heart: the danger of using drugs, the importance of embracing every day, her disdain for people who have an "apathy for living."

20   Then there is the manuscript she is working on, a draft of a book about her life. The celebrity she now calls "Candice" (Bergen) gave her the name of her own literary agent, who has asked to see it. Another agent she met plans to talk to Jodie Foster about Murray's life as a potential movie project.

21   The irony of the shifts in her life is not lost on her, but she is no longer consumed with how strange it is. "For a long time I kept saying that this makes no sense. But I think my life has taught me it makes perfect sense. Everything I've experienced has taught me that things in life can change in an instant. But this is that lesson on a positive level, and it seems so gratifying and exciting at the same time."

22   On the other hand, she says, she would relinquish all the literary agents and talk shows in the world for just one thing, something so simple most people take it for granted. "Sometimes I go to my friends' houses and hear them call for their mom. Or I am with my sister and father and see an empty place where my mother should be. If I could trade what I have now for that, I absolutely would."

DISCUSSION QUESTIONS

1. Liz Murray's family background was full of hardships. What are some of the hardships she had to overcome?
2. How did Murray's elementary school teacher describe her desire to learn?
3. What were some of the clues her teachers noticed that indicated something was wrong at Murray's home? What were the teachers unaware of regarding Murray's living conditions?
4. Why do you think one of Murray's favorite poems is Edgar Allan Poe's "Alone"?
5. Describe the unique characteristics of the Humanities Preparatory Academy in Manhattan.
6. What does Murray think her life has taught her so far? What does she feel most people take for granted?

WRITING OPTIONS

Collaborate with Peers

1. Brainstorm with two or three classmates about the definition of "determined to succeed." Based on your notes, write your own paragraph or short essay defining what this phrase means.
2. Interview a classmate about the most determined person he or she knows. Summarize your interview in a paragraph or short essay.

Connecting to the Author's Ideas

3. Liz Murray says she looks down on people who have an "apathy for living." In an essay or short paragraph, explain what this phrase means to you, give examples of how people with this attitude behave, and explain why people must rid themselves of this attitude.

Other Options

4. Describe a turning point in your life when you were determined to accomplish a goal. To what extent did you succeed?
5. Describe a past or present obstacle that you feel you must overcome in order to make progress in school or at work. Be sure to describe the obstacle in detail, and then explain what you will do (or have done) to make progress.

Field of Dreams: From Farm Work to Medical Work

Alfredo Quiñones-Hinojosa

Quiñones-Hinojosa delivered this commencement address to the Harvard Medical School in 1999, when he graduated with an M.D. Through determination, persistence, and the support of family, Quiñones-Hinojosa learned that he could be "the architect of his own destiny."

Words You May Need to Know

perseverance (para. 1)	steady persistence in something undertaken
commencement (1)	graduation
mentors (1)	wise advisors, trusted teachers and counselors
simultaneously (2)	at the same time
shoulder (2)	take responsibility for
novel (3)	new
incredible (3)	unbelievable
stark (5)	complete
terra firma (9)	solid ground
rejuvenated (9)	renewed
academia (11)	an academic environment
contemplation (11)	thoughtful observation
discipline (11)	control
thrive (12)	grow and develop
ignited (12)	started
primed (14)	made ready
embody (16)	represent
inculcated (16)	instilled, implanted
neurosurgery (19)	surgery related to the brain and nerve tissue

My father used to tell me when I was a little kid that 1
"aunque no tengas buena punteria, si le tiras al cielo, a lo
mejor le pegas a una estrella" (Even if you do not have good
aim, if you shoot at the sky, you may hit a star). Well, I am
not known for my baseball abilities, so Pedro Martinez does
not have to worry about his job. I am better known for my
perseverance. I am thankful and honored to have the opportunity to give this commencement speech. Please, let me
echo what was told to me by many of my friends and classmates graduating today from Harvard Dental and Medical
School. It was the support of our loved ones and mentors,
our determination, discipline, and dreams that have taken
us here today.

"Con trabajo, determinación, y apoyo, puedes llegar a 2
ser el arquitecto de tu propio destino" (With hard work, determination, and support, you can become the architect of
your own destiny), my family constantly told me. Growing
up in Mexicali, Mexico, I developed self-confidence and a
sense of independence at an early age. In order to help my
parents financially, as the oldest child, I was simultaneously
attending elementary school and pumping gas in my parents' small gas station at the age of five. Helping to shoulder
the financial burdens we carried developed my determination and inner strength while I was quite young—qualities
for which I continue to be thankful today.

The idea that our dreams are within our reach is not 3
novel. I am no different from any of my classmates graduating today. We are all here with incredible and interesting
stories. The only difference, perhaps, is that I am in front of
you willing to share my own.

My story in the United States began one night in January 4
1987. As an eager, ambitious young Mexican, I crossed the
border illegally, landed in the fields of California, and became
a migrant farm worker. I packed the little I had, and with $65
in my pocket, decided to explore "El Norte." I migrated to the
United States to fulfill a dream: the dream that many people,
like myself, have of escaping poverty and one day returning
"triumphant" to our countries.

5   The reality was a stark contrast. I spent long days in the fields picking fruits and vegetables, sleeping under leaky camper shells, my hands bloodied from pulling weeds, eating anything I could. My only comfort was that I had a good tan and I was in top shape.

6   One day in the fields, while I was talking with a co-worker, I told him that I wanted to learn English and go to school. He laughed and said, "This is your fate; you will spend the rest of your life working in the fields." Those words were painful to hear. I realized that without English language skills, without an education, and without support, this predicted fate of being a migrant farm worker for the rest of my life seemed very likely.

7   I wish I could tell you what inspired me to leave the fields of the San Joaquin Valley that day. What possessed me to move without a job, the ability to speak English, and knowledge of what was going to happen next? I do not know, but I did it. I think that my dream, although it was fogged by uncertainty, was more powerful than the fear of the unknown. It was one of those decisions that changed my life entirely since, miraculously, four years later, I ended up at the University of California at Berkeley.

8   This experience has always reminded me of what Henrik Ibsen once said: "Rob a man of his life-illusion, and you rob him also of his happiness."

The Importance of Mentoring

9 After the fields, I began to work in a rail car repair company in Stockton, California. I first cleaned railroad cars. Then I was a welder, a painter, and a high-pressure valve specialist, and within sixteen months, a supervisor. On April 14, 1989, an event took place that made me reevaluate my direction and my life. I fell into a tank carrying liquified petroleum gas—I almost died! I woke up in the hospital and saw a person dressed all in white; I felt assured to know that a doctor was taking care of me. I had a feeling of being on *terra firma*. This

brush with death gave me the strength to continue pursuing my dreams with a rejuvenated force.

I constantly daydreamed. I have learned that if our minds can conceive a dream and our hearts can feel it, it will be much easier to achieve that dream. At night, I attended community college. I started out taking English as a Second Language courses. Less than three years of hard work later, I was a member of the track and field team and captain of the debate team. As a member of the track team, I found that a race does not end once you reach the finish line; rather, every time you reach the end, a new race begins. During my speech class, a mentor who believed in me made me the captain of the debate team. I began to appreciate that the ability to work as part of a team is vital to succeed.

Everything went well in community college; my life in academia was beginning to take off. My mentors helped me to get to my next stop, the University of California–Berkeley. I met more important role models and mentors. I learned from them that "knowledge is better learned by action than by contemplation." I also learned that it takes much more than intelligence to succeed; it also takes discipline, dedication, determination, and a dream. Without knowing it, I was being prepared for medical school. When one of my mentors told me that I should apply to Harvard, I thought that he was a very nice man but clearly *living la vida loca* (or a little insane in the brain).

After my acceptance to Harvard Medical School, I hesitated to attend. I was not sure it was the institution where a poor student who grew up in small rural community in Mexico, like I did, would thrive. My mentors at Berkeley insisted that I travel to Boston and visit Harvard. During that visit, I met two distinguished professors, Drs. Edward A. Kravitz and David D. Potter. From them and other important mentors at Harvard, I have learned to see academic medicine as an opportunity to understand and treat human diseases better, but more, as an opportunity to provide leadership and support to future physicians-scientists in order to serve our communities the best possible way. These outstanding professors embody the words of Plutarch: "The mind is not a vessel to be filled but a fire to be ignited."

13 Like many others here today, I realized long ago the great extent to which I have depended on the help received from my mentors in pursuing my dreams of being a physician-scientist. Henry Brooke Adams once said that "A teacher affects eternity; he can never tell where his influence stops." I, like many of us, hope that I can begin to have the same impact as a mentor to future medical students and graduate students—to change their lives for the better.

Our Dreams Have No Barriers, No Borders, and No Limits

14 It is no secret that minority communities have the highest dropout and lowest educational achievement rates in the country. The "pipeline" to higher education and especially in professional programs is not fully "primed" for minority students. Although members of minority groups make up about 18 percent of the U.S. population, in 1994, they accounted for only 3.7 percent of the M.D. faculty at the nation's medical schools. Recent investigations found that Black and Hispanic physicians are much more likely to serve minority communities and to include minorities and poor people among their patients. Minority physicians are twice as likely to work in locations designated as health workforce shortage areas by the federal government. Minority patients are more than four times as likely as Whites to receive their regular care from a minority physician. I have been very fortunate in my involvement in education to meet outstanding minority role models—the quality of the role models is high, but the numbers are low.

15 Drs. Willam Bowen and Derek Bok, in their book, *The Shape of the River*, point out that a "healthy society in the 21st century will be one in which the most challenging, rewarding career possibilities are perceived to be, and truly are, open to all races and ethnic groups." The effort to recruit underrepresented minority students in selective institutions has come under "heavy fire." Changes in admissions policies in places such as California and Texas have

occurred recently. The astounding effects that a "race-neutral admissions policy" has had in decreasing the number of Blacks, Hispanics, and Native Americans being admitted to institutions in these states indicate that the time is "ripe" for re-evaluating how race-sensitive admissions policies have been applied and what their consequences have been during the past thirty years.

Recently, while having dinner with some of my friends, 16 we spoke about Harvard's contributions and commitment to making our institution a leader in science, in community service, and in recruitment of underrepresented students. We felt privileged and honored to be part of this family that has demonstrated dedication, discipline, love and passion for everything it has done. Many of us have constantly commented that we hope one day as future physicians we can all embody the value that this institution and its dedicated faculty has inculcated in us—the value of being a role model, a mentor, an outstanding physician, a colleague, and a friend.

Like many other illegal immigrants, I arrived able only 17 to contemplate what my dreams might be. Now, due to the support I have from my family; my wife, Anna; and our dear daughter, Gabriella; the support of my friends and mentors; and the backing of vital organizations such as our institution, I feel that I can contribute greatly to our community as a physician-scientist.

Today, we graduate from this fine institution, happy, 18 ready to take on the world, perhaps also slightly nervous about starting residency. Let us not forget that thanks to our loved ones and our mentors, and the determination we all carry, we have been able to fulfill our dreams.

I now can welcome and accept my fate of "working in 19 the fields" for the rest of my life—but in the "field of academic neurosurgery."

DISCUSSION QUESTIONS

1. As a child, how did Alfredo Quiñones-Hinojosa help his parents financially?

2. When Quiñones-Hinojosa once told a co-worker that he wanted to learn English and attend school, what was the co-worker's response? Did this response discourage Quiñones-Hinojosa? Explain.

3. What was the experience that made Quiñones-Hinojosa even more determined to make his dream become reality?

4. What ability does Quiñones-Hinojosa feel is "vital to succeed"?

5. Several teachers became mentors to Quiñones-Hinojosa while he attended community college, the University of California, and Harvard. What advice did these mentors offer him?

6. What does Quiñones-Hinojosa mean when he states that academic medicine is an opportunity "to serve"?

WRITING OPTIONS

Connecting to the Author's Ideas

1. Quiñones-Hinojosa says that all of his classmates have "incredible and interesting stories" about their background. Write a paragraph or short essay telling one incredible or interesting story about your own background.

Other Options

2. A co-worker in the fields laughed at Quiñones-Hinojosa's wish to attend school. In a short essay, describe a goal of yours that others might feel is unrealistic. How do you plan to show them that they are wrong to doubt you?

3. Describe how someone is, or was, a mentor for you. How did you get to know this person, and how has he or she helped you?

4. Investigate a volunteer agency in your community that seeks mentors, such as the Big Brother, Big Sister organization. In a short essay, summarize the goals of this organization and explain how hard it is to recruit mentors. If possible, interview one of the volunteers about his or her reasons for participating in the program.

5. Imagine that you are asked to deliver a speech for your own graduation ceremony. (It can be a high school or college speech.) Write that speech. Include an acknowledgment of the people who helped you achieve your educational goals, description of your future goals, and advice to students who come after you.

The Education of Berenice Belizaire

Joe Klein

Faced with taunts from classmates and a new language to learn, a shy Haitian immigrant used her thirst for knowledge to turn challenges into opportunities and graduate at the top of her class.

Words You May Need to Know

cramped (para. 1)	too small
taunts (1)	insults
elite (3)	best, highest class
alma mater (3)	old school
Ruth Bader Ginsberg (3)	a Supreme Court Justice
valedictorian (4)	the student, usually the one with the highest academic ranking, who delivers the farewell speech at the graduation ceremony
modest (4)	humble
burdens (5)	heavy loads
corroded (5)	deteriorating
cited (5)	referred to, mentioned
liberal (5)	generous, open
policies (5)	rules, codes
sop it up (5)	absorb it
preconceived (5)	formed in advance
reinvigorated (6)	refilled with life and energy
retail (6)	sales to consumers
raft (6)	large number
entry-level (6)	low-level, simple

spurn (6)	reject
enlightened (6)	intelligent, open-minded
vast (6)	great in size
hothouse (6)	heated greenhouse where plants are grown
cultivation (6)	growing, development
classic (7)	standard
median (7)	average
fraternal (7)	brotherly
extended families (7)	families consisting not only of a mother, father, and their children, but also of aunts, uncles, cousins, grandparents, and so forth
nuclear families (7)	families consisting of a mother, father, and their children
perverse (8)	contrary
propriety (8)	standards of behavior
menial (8)	lowly, degrading
discipline (8)	control
inebriated (8)	made drunk
phenomenon (8)	occurrence
ironic (8)	unexpected
at bay (8)	away, cornered

1   When Berenice Belizaire arrived in New York from Haiti with her mother and sister in 1987, she was not very happy. She spoke no English. The family had to live in a cramped Brooklyn apartment, a far cry from the comfortable house they'd had in Haiti. Her mother, a nurse, worked long hours. School was torture. Berenice had always been a good student, but now she was learning a new language while enduring constant taunts from the Americans (both black

and white). They cursed her in the cafeteria and threw food at her. Someone hit her sister in the head with a book. "Why can't we go home?" Berenice asked her mother.

Home was too dangerous. The schools weren't always 2 open anymore, and education—her mother insisted—was the most important thing. Her mother had always pushed her—memorize everything, she ordered. "I have a pretty good memory," Berenice admitted last week. Indeed, the other kids at school began to notice that Berenice always, somehow, knew the answers. "They started coming to me for help," she says. "They never called me a nerd."

Within two years, Berenice was speaking English, 3 though not well enough to get into one of New York's elite public high schools. She had to settle for the neighborhood school, James Madison—which is one of the magical American places, the alma mater of Ruth Bader Ginsburg, among others, a school with a history of unlikely success stories. "I didn't realize what we had in Berenice at first," says math teacher Judith Khan. "She was good at math, but she was quiet. And the things she didn't know! She applied for a summer program in Buffalo and asked me how to get there on the subway. But she always seemed to ask the right questions. She understood the big ideas. She could think on her feet. She could explain difficult problems so the other kids could understand them. Eventually, I realized that she wasn't just pushing for grades, she was hungry for *knowledge*. And you know, it never occurred to me that she was also doing it in English and history, all these other subjects that had to be much tougher for her than math."

She moved from third in her class to first during her 4 senior year. She was selected as valedictorian, an honor she almost refused (still shy, she wouldn't allow her picture in the school's yearbook). She gave the speech, after some prodding—a modest address about the importance of hard work and how it's never too late to try hard—an immigrant's valedictory. Last week I caught up with Berenice at the Massachusetts Institute of Technology where she was jump-starting her college career. I asked her what she wanted to be doing in ten years: "I want to build a famous computer, like IBM," she said. "I want my name to be part of it."

5   Berenice Belizaire's story is remarkable, but not unusual. The New York City schools are bulging with overachieving immigrants. The burdens they place on a creaky, corroded system are often cited as an argument against liberal immigration policies, but teachers like Judith Khan don't seem to mind. "They're why I love teaching in Brooklyn," she says. "They have a drive in them we no longer seem to have. You see these kids, who aren't prepared academically and can barely speak the language, struggling so hard. They just sop it up. They're like little sponges. You see Berenice, who had none of the usual, preconceived racial barriers in her mind—you see her becoming friendly with the Russian kids, and learning chess from Po Ching [from Taiwan]. It is *so* exciting."

6   Indeed it is possible that immigrant energy reinvigorated not just some schools (and more than a few teachers)—but the city itself in the 1980s. "Without them, New York would have been a smaller place, a poorer place, a lot less vital and exciting," says Professor Emanuel Tobier of New York University. They restored the retail life of the city, starting a raft of small businesses—and doing the sorts of entry-level, bedpan-emptying jobs that nonimmigrants spurn. They added far more to the local economy than they removed; more important, they reminded enlightened New Yorkers that the city had always worked best as a vast, noisy, dreamy hothouse for the cultivation of new Americans.

7   The Haitians have followed the classic pattern. They have a significantly higher work-force participation rate than the average in New York. They have a lower rate of poverty. They have a higher rate of new-business formation and a lower rate of welfare dependency. Their median household income, at $28,853, is about $1000 less than the citywide median (but about $1000 higher than Chinese immigrants, often seen as a "model" minority). They've also developed a traditional network of fraternal societies, newspapers, and neighborhoods with solid—extended, rather

than nuclear—families. "A big issue now is whether women who graduate from school should be allowed to live by themselves before they marry," says Lola Poisson, who counsels Haitian immigrants. "There's a lot of tension over that."

Such perverse propriety cannot last long. Immigrants 8 become Americans very quickly. Some lose hope after years of menial labor; others lose discipline, inebriated by freedom. "There's an interesting phenomenon," says Philip Kasinitz of Williams College. "When immigrant kids criticize each other for getting lazy or loose, they say, 'You're becoming American.'" (Belizaire said she and the Russians would tease each other that way at Madison.) It's ironic, Kasinitz adds, that "those who work hardest to keep American culture at bay have the best chance of becoming American success stories." If so, we may be fixed on the wrong issue. The question shouldn't be whether immigrants are ruining America, but whether America is ruining the immigrants.

DISCUSSION QUESTIONS

1. Although Berenice Belizaire was taunted when she started attending her new school in America, students soon recognized a special quality in her. What was it?

2. What were the special qualities of Belizaire that her math teacher noticed?

3. What honor did Belizaire receive during her senior year of high school, and what did she state that she wanted to be doing in ten years?

4. Joe Klein states that "Berenice Belizaire's story is remarkable but not unusual." He explains that the New York City schools are filled with "overachieving immigrants." What, according to Belizaire's math teacher, makes her a pleasure to teach?

5. One educator states that New York City would have been "a lot less vital and exciting" without the contributions of hard-working immigrants in the 1980s. What are the reasons he gives to support this statement?

6. What are some of the accomplishments of Haitian immigrants that may surprise people who stereotype immigrants?

WRITING OPTIONS
Collaborate with Peers

1. Interview a classmate who has moved to America in the past few years. Why has he or she moved here? What are some difficult adjustments he or she has had to make? What was surprising about American customs? What are his or her goals? Based on your notes, write a detailed paragraph or short essay summarizing this individual's challenges as an immigrant.

2. Interview a family member who immigrated to the United States. Take notes based on the same questions listed for Writing Option 1, and write a detailed paragraph or short essay based on the information you gather.

Other Options

3. If you are an immigrant, write a detailed paragraph or short essay about yourself using the same questions as Writing Option 1.

4. If you have spent an extended period of time (several months or years) in a country where customs were much different from those in your native country, what were some basic cultural differences between the two countries? You can discuss language, clothing, food, housing, and so forth. How did you learn to cope with, or adjust to, these differences? Answer these questions in a short essay.

A Garden of Honor

Maria Fleming

At Roosevelt High School in East Los Angeles, Latino students plant a tribute to Japanese Americans who attended the school over fifty years ago but never graduated because they were interned in prison camps during World War II.

Words You May Need to Know

sprawling (para. 1)	spread out
abundant (1)	plenty of, a great quantity of
murals (1)	paintings painted on walls
depicting (1)	showing, representing
Aztec (1)	of a native civilization of Mexico
swell (1)	increase of voices
mariachi (1)	a type of Mexican music
Cinco de Mayo (1)	May 5
chilies (2)	peppers
incongruous (2)	out of place
marker (2)	mark, indicator
sushi (2)	a Japanese way of preparing fish
taquerias (2)	taco restaurants
skirting (2)	on the border of
fitting (2)	appropriate
emblem (2)	sign, symbol
heritage (2)	tradition
interned (2)	confined
sleuthing (3)	investigating, tracing
alumni (3)	former students

eerily (4)	weirdly, strangely
initiated (5)	started
atrocious (5)	shockingly wicked, brutal
reparation (5)	compensation
dovetailed (6)	coincided
momentum (6)	force or speed of movement
belated (7)	delayed
crushing (7)	shattering
juxtaposed (7)	placed side by side
garnered (10)	gathered, collected
mobilized (12)	brought together for action
implement (12)	put into effect
oasis (13)	place of pleasant relief
pulses (13)	throbs
encompasses (13)	encloses
flora (13)	plants
meander (13)	wind
fruit (14)	results
plaque (14)	a tablet, usually put on a wall
enhance (14)	improve the quality, make more effective
haiku (14)	a Japanese form of poetry
sizable (15)	large
identified with (15)	associate oneself in feeling with another person or persons
rectify (16)	set right
resonance (17)	impact
lingering (17)	remaining

The sprawling three-block campus of Roosevelt High in 1 East Los Angeles offers abundant evidence of the school community's Mexican American roots. Bold murals depicting Aztec images are scattered through the buildings. Chicano heroes and pop idols peer out from posters tacked on doors. Spanish and English mingle in the swell of voices that rises in hallways between class periods. Mariachi music drifts up from the street through the classroom windows, three days early for the Cinco de Mayo celebration scheduled for the weekend.

Hidden away in a quiet corner of the campus—a few 2 yards beyond the fiery chilies ripening in the school's pepper patch—stands a seemingly incongruous cultural marker: a traditional Japanese garden. At first glance, the garden appears as out of context as a sushi dish at one of the taquerias skirting the campus. But as principal Henry Ronquillo likes to point out, it is a fitting emblem of the school's cultural heritage. A group of students built the garden in 1996 as a memorial to Japanese Americans who attended Roosevelt more than fifty years ago but never got the chance to graduate because they were interned in prison camps during World War II.

Students stumbled upon this disturbing fact while 3 studying Roosevelt's history for a school project. Some sleuthing through old yearbooks and interviews with alumni also revealed that the school once boasted a lovely Japanese garden. Flipping through the 1941–42 Roosevelt yearbook offers glimpses of the original garden, with its magnificent cherry trees and graceful Japanese pines. "It was a beautiful spot," remembers Jun Yamamoto, a member of the class of 1941 and former internee. "It was a typical Japanese garden with a waterfall, a pond, and a bridge. It was a place to sit and relax in the shade, to rest your mind for a little while."

But just one year later, both the garden and the faces 4 of the 400 Japanese American students then attending Roosevelt are eerily absent from the yearbook's pages. Shortly after the students and their families were interned, the garden was destroyed. "No one knows exactly how or when, but it happened, and it broke a lot of people's hearts," Ronquillo says.

5   When the younger generation of Roosevelt students made this discovery, they were shocked and angry. "Nobody should have gone through what the Japanese Americans did," says Gloria Antunez, a 1997 graduate and former member of Youth Task Force L.A., a Roosevelt community service organization that initiated the garden project in the spring of 1995. "Many of them were citizens. They belonged in this country. Then to be imprisoned like that . . . it was atrocious." Students decided to replant the garden as reparation for this past injustice.

6   Plans to rebuild the garden dovetailed with the 50th reunion celebration of the classes of 1942–45, a coincidence that added momentum to the project. In May 1995, the school's alumni association held a special ceremony to honor Japanese American classmates who had been interned and to award diplomas they were denied five decades earlier. A hundred Japanese American alumni attended the celebration, some traveling to Roosevelt from as far away as Japan.

7   Henry Ronquillo, who presented the diplomas at the ceremony, remembers the reunion as a deeply emotional event. The belated graduates shared memories of life in Manzanar, the relocation camp they were sent to during the war. Other alumni recalled the crushing task of saying goodbye to their classmates boarding buses bound for the camp in central California. While alumni spoke, a slide presentation juxtaposed images of life at the high school with life in Manzanar.

8   "It was such a moving ceremony that everybody in the place was sobbing. Not crying, but sobbing," Ronquillo remembers.

9   Bruse Kaji, a Japanese American member of the class of 1944, was one of the alumni honored that day. "It was really very touching," Kaji recalls of the ceremony. "We thought that everyone had forgotten us. It was nice to know that wasn't the case, that the people we were growing up with remembered us after all."

Following the reunion, Kaji learned of the students' 10
plan to restore the garden and offered the support of L.A.'s
Japanese American National Museum, where he serves as
founding president. Kaji organized a fundraising effort that
garnered the $30,000 needed to rebuild the garden. A large
percentage of that was donated by Roosevelt's Japanese
American Alumni, who were surprised and grateful to learn
that a group of Latino students had taken an interest in the
earlier graduates' experiences and wanted to commemorate
them.

"It floored me. I just couldn't believe it," says Jun 11
Yamamoto, who helped raise the funds. "It was an honor to have
them do it and to participate with them in the restoration."

Students pieced together what the garden looked like 12
from old yearbook photographs and graduates' recollections.
Then, assisted by the Japanese American alumni, project
organizers mobilized community support to implement their
design. Local landscape architects, contractors, and suppli-
ers donated services and materials.

A Symbol Grows

The 600-square-foot garden offers an oasis of quiet on this 13
urban campus that pulses with the activity of 5,200
students. Situated about fifty yards from the original garden's location—a space now occupied by Roosevelt's auto
shop—the new retreat encompasses cherry trees, azaleas, a
Japanese black pine, and a gingko tree. Scattered palmetto
palms add a California flavor to the otherwise traditional
flora. A small bridge spans a dry pond of granite pebbles.
Pathways meander through the space, punctuated by several benches that invite reflection.

Gloria Antunez sits on one of these benches and gazes 14
upon the fruit of her labor. "I like being here because it's so
pretty," she says, adding that the spot is popular with classmates. Students like to eat lunch and snap photos of friends
there, she says. "It's appreciated and respected. No one
harms any of the trees or anything. We're planning to make

a little plaque that tells about the history." Some teachers use the garden to enhance lessons, as well, bringing students there for inspiration in writing haiku, or for a history class on the internment of Japanese Americans during World War II.

15   The garden is a small patch of green in this sizable inner-city campus, but it commands a large symbolic presence, according to Henry Ronquillo. "It's a symbol of how one minority group, a different minority group, identified with an injustice and wanted to do something about it."

16   Ronquillo, himself a graduate of Roosevelt, believes that the creation of the garden teaches a positive lesson about owning up to, and learning from, the past. "Through this project, students are able to see the other side of man's inhumanity to man, where people come together to rectify. I think it's important for kids to know there's always a time for righting a wrong—whether it's two weeks later or fifty years later."

17   It's a message that has particular resonance for Roosevelt's students, Ronquillo says. They know the history of discrimination against Mexican Americans in the U.S. and are well acquainted with the lingering prejudice they face today. "People run into unfair experiences, and they may give up because they get bitter or lose hope," Ronquillo says. "I think it's important for them to see that people care and that people don't forget."

DISCUSSION QUESTIONS

1. Although the Roosevelt High student body is largely Mexican American, students decided to build a traditional Japanese garden on school grounds. Why?

2. Decades earlier, Roosevelt High had a beautiful Japanese garden. What were the benefits of having the original garden on school grounds?

3. In 1942, five hundred Japanese-American students were "eerily absent from the yearbook's pages," and the garden was destroyed. Why did these sad events happen?

4. In 1995, what special event was held by the school's alumni association? How important was this event to participants? Explain.
5. How did the students determine what the new garden should look like?
6. Why do students enjoy being around the garden? How do teachers use the garden?

WRITING OPTIONS

Connecting to the Author's Words

1. The principal of Roosevelt High says, "There's always a time for righting a wrong—whether it's two weeks later or fifty years later." Write a short essay about a wrong (in your family, in your community, in American history) that was eventually righted or that still needs to be righted.

Other Options

2. In your school or in your community, find a tribute to an individual. It could be a plaque on a wall, a street name, a unique statue, or a monument. Investigate the history of this tribute by describing whom the tribute is named for, the contributions of this individual, and what the tribute means to the community. Summarize your findings in a short essay.
3. Students at Roosevelt High decided that constructing a Japanese garden would be a worthwhile tribute to a special group of former students. Write a paragraph or short essay about a tribute project you would like to see started (or one you could start yourself) at your school. Explain the reasons such a tribute should be made at your school and the form it should take.

A New Game Plan

Lisa Bennett

High school football coach Bill Miller says he "was a jerk" during the years he was an All-American football player and college coach. He insulted opponents, treated women badly, and drank heavily. Now he's a different man, "teaching players to be accountable on and off the field."

Words You May Need to Know

strides (para. 1)	walks with long steps
adorned (2)	decorated
convert (2)	a person who has been persuaded to change his or her beliefs
taunting (3)	insulting, provoking
belittling (3)	treating as if they had little value
accountable (4)	responsible
mandatory (5)	required
pre-empt (5)	prevent
CEOs (6)	chief executive officers, usually a title given to people who head large businesses
ushered (6)	led
anticipated (7)	prevented
monitoring (8)	observing, checking
sexist (8)	biased against one gender
progressive (12)	improving

1   At Brattleboro Union High School, in the southeastern corner of Vermont, football coach Bill Miller sips a Pepsi from an oversized plastic cup as he strides about his office, rarely pausing to sit during a two-hour conversation. Miller is a former All-American football player and Gettysburg College coach. Young people are drawn to him like fans to a

rock star. They stop in his office to talk about a game, a relationship, a drug problem, or anything that concerns them.

When they're not stopping in, as on this cold November 2 morning, Miller stands outside his office and watches them walk by on the way to class: "Did you get a part in the play this semester?" he asks a student at his locker. "Wow, new hairstyle—looks great!" he calls to a girl as she turns the corner, her head newly adorned in braids. "What are you going to do about college?" he asks another. His voice is loud, his posture confident, his dress impeccable. Miller is a man with a mission—a convert, as it were, to the idea that school sports should be about something more than just winning.

"In the old days, I was a jerk," he says, referring to his 3 years as a player and college coach. Miller recalls taunting opponents on the field, belittling women off the field and drinking heavily between games. This, he explains, was what he thought it meant to be a "cool" athlete. But time made Miller see things differently. By his mid-thirties, he recognized not only that his behavior was insulting and beside the point of academic competition, but that it got in the way of his being a good player and coach.

He took the coaching job at Brattleboro eight years ago, 4 armed with a new philosophy: "There's more to football than just playing. Players have to be accountable for their mistakes, on and off the field. And they have to know that everything doesn't revolve around them."

At the beginning of every season, Miller calls a manda- 5 tory meeting for players and their parents, in which he announces his rules of the game. He asks parents to be present, he says, because he wants their support. He also wants to pre-empt complaints if one of their sons or daughters is suspended from a game because of a violation of the rules. In some cases, he also wants parents present because, whatever they teach their children at home, when it comes to football he wants them to know, "It's my way or the highway."

Among Miller's rules: Any player who puts down a 6 teammate, taunts an opponent, argues with an official, or scores a touchdown and does anything but hand the ball to an official *will be pulled from the game.* Further, any player who gets into a fight will be pulled from that game, plus the next two. Even parents who engage in disruptive taunting as spectators at a game will be asked to leave. "We've even had CEOs in this town ushered out of a game for their behavior—and after a warning!" says Brattleboro soccer coach and health teacher Steve Holmes.

7   But not everything in football can be anticipated by a rule, as Miller discovered six years ago when his juniors and seniors taped some sophomore players' legs together and taped another to the locker room bench. In the spirit of the movie "Scared Straight," he took the offending students on a field trip to the county courthouse, introduced them to the district attorney, and required them to observe a full day of court proceedings. Miller recalls their reaction to sentence after sentence that the judge handed down: "It was a shell-shocker. They kept saying, 'You can go to *jail* for that?'"

8   To be sure, Miller takes a broad view of coaching, monitoring his players' behavior off the field as well as on it. If they drive too fast out of the parking lot, he makes them run laps after practice. If they are caught drunk, he requires them to sit out the next two games. If he hears his male players making sexist put-downs—especially to their girlfriends—he confronts both players and girlfriends.

9   "Athletes get away with that because everybody thinks that's the way they're supposed to be," he says. "But I ask the girl, 'Why do you allow him to talk that way to you? Don't you want him to respect you? Walk away. Tell him you won't put up with it anymore until he cleans up his act.'"

10   Recently, Miller required a number of his worst offenders to view a one-woman play and discussion about a teenage victim of dating violence. "You want to talk about eyes opening?" he says. "They got the message because, deep-down, they know it's wrong."

11   Jason Houle, an eighteen-year-old senior who has been on the team for three years, believes that Miller's message is something most athletes want to hear. "It makes me feel respected," he says, "to think that somebody cares about

what others think about us. I don't want to be thought of as a bad person."

For all his progressive efforts, Miller is the first to admit that old habits die hard. "I'm spoiled," he says. "I lose my temper sometimes and yell and swear and get caught up in the moment. And when I first came here, I was called into the office for my language more than the kids. But," he adds, "I've gotten better." 12

DISCUSSION QUESTIONS

1. When did Bill Miller realize that his behavior was destructive?
2. Each year at the beginning of the football season, Miller calls a mandatory meeting for parents and players. Why?
3. What will cause Miller to pull a player out of a game? What can cause a parent to be asked to leave a game?
4. What did Miller do after some of his older players played a practical joke on some sophomores? What were the seniors surprised about, and how was it a good lesson for them?
5. Miller monitors his players' behavior off the field. What are some examples of unacceptable behavior, and what are the penalties Miller imposes?
6. Miller took some of his worst offenders to a play. What was the play about?

WRITING OPTIONS

Collaborate with Peers

1. Working with two or three classmates, make a list of three characteristics of a good football coach. Use that list to write an individual paragraph or short essay on what makes a good coach.

Connecting to the Author's Words

2. Lisa Bennett refers to "the idea that school sports should be about something more than just winning." Write a short essay about what can happen to high school or college athletes, coaches, and programs when winning becomes everything. Give specific examples.

Other Options

3. Do you think a coach should hold players accountable for their actions off the field? Defend your position in a short essay that provides at least three reasons.

4. In a paragraph or short essay, contrast two professional athletes by describing how one is a positive role model, whereas the other is a poor role model for today's youth.

5. Do you think too much emphasis is placed on athletics at the high school level? If so, write a paragraph or short essay describing several examples of the overemphasis on sports competition when you were in high school.

6. If you played on a sports team in high school and now compete on a college team, what are some of the similarities and some of the differences you have observed? Discuss them in a short essay.

Chapter Seven

Race and Tolerance

"I have a dream my four little children will one day live in a nation where they will not be judged by the color of their skin but by the content of their character."

Martin Luther King Jr.
(From his 1963 landmark speech, "I Have a Dream," delivered in Washington, D.C., at the height of the Civil Rights Movement.)

"After all, there is but one race—humanity."

George Moore

"No loss by flood or lightning, no destruction of cities and temples by the hostile forces of nature, has deprived man of so many noble lives and impulse as those which his intolerance has destroyed."

Helen Keller

Rosa Parks: Black Heart

Kareem Abdul-Jabbar and Alan Steinberg

After a long day's work at her job as a seamstress, Rosa Parks just wanted to get home to rest. Little did she know on that fateful day in 1955 that her refusal to give up her bus seat would "transport her straight into history."

Words You May Need to Know

seamstress (para. 1)	a woman whose occupation is sewing
secessionist (2)	a person who believed the Southern states should withdraw from the Union in 1860–1861, right before the Civil War
inaugurated (2)	installed into office with formal ceremonies
irony (3)	language in which the stated meaning is different from reality
rebuke (3)	a scolding or insulting action
Emancipation (3)	the time when slavery was abolished in America
bespectacled (4)	wearing eyeglasses
NAACP (4)	National Association for the Advancement of Colored People
activist (4)	a very aggressive defender of a cause
strife (7)	conflict
instituted (7)	established
boycott (7)	a group movement to refuse to buy from or do business with a person or organization as a means of pressure or promoting a cause
amendment (7)	a change or addition to a law
Jim Crow law (7)	a law meant to discriminate against or segregate Negroes

stipulating (7)	requiring
mandating (7)	ordering
domestic (7)	household
baited (7)	tormented
epithets (7)	words or phrases used to show hatred or contempt for a person

Just after 5:00 P.M. on December 1, 1955, forty-two 1
year-old Rosa Parks concluded her day as a seamstress in
the men's alteration shop of the Fair Department Store in
Montgomery, Alabama. Rosa was weary—her neck and
shoulders ached; her feet were sore. She just wanted to get
back to her little home at 634 Cleveland Court and relax
before having dinner with her husband. She could not have
known that instead of getting to her home on the west side
of town, her Cleveland Avenue bus was transporting her
straight into history.

After leaving work, Rosa strolled to Lee's Cut Rate Store 2
to buy pain pills for her neck. Then she returned to wait for
the bus, as always, at historic Court Square. The square was
a reminder of the Old South racism on which Montgomery
was founded. Slaves had once been auctioned there; in
1861, at the Exchange Hotel bordering on the Square,
secessionist leader William Lowndes Yancey inaugurated
Jefferson Davis as president of the Confederate States,
claiming, "The man and the hour have met"; it was at the
Square, too, where Yancey declared Montgomery the first
capital of the New South and the cradle of the Confederacy.

Rosa rarely thought about that. To her, Court Square 3
was now just part of the bus-stop landscape. And she barely
noticed anymore the familiar Christmas banner proclaiming
PEACE ON EARTH, GOOD WILL TOWARD MEN, though the
irony of that message was a constant rebuke to African
Americans in Montgomery, where white racism and segregation were still the rule ninety-two years after the Emanci-
pation. Still, the only thing on Rosa Park's mind that gloomy
Thursday was finding a seat.

4   Rosa was a slight, bespectacled, soft-spoken woman, well known and respected in the black community. As a longtime secretary in the local NAACP chapter and a dedicated volunteer with the association's youth council, she knew the political scene, but was certainly no activist. (The biracial NAACP was established in 1909 to achieve equal citizenship for all by peacefully opposing discrimination. It was formed in response to the increasing number of race riots, not just in the South but in places like Abraham Lincoln's hometown of Springfield, Illinois, where, in 1908, forty-six blacks were killed and over two thousand fled the city.) In fact, Rosa was so shy and reserved as to be almost invisible; she barely raised her voice, much less confrontational issues.

5   Rosa let the first bus pass because it was too crowded and she wanted to be as comfortable as possible. The second bus looked more inviting. After paying the ten-cent fare, she headed for the one vacant seat left, in the fifth row. This was the first row of the middle section known as "no man's land," customarily open to blacks if no whites were standing. Rosa took this seat on the aisle and thought nothing of it.

6   Residents knew by heart the segregation law cited in chapter 6, section 11 of the city code, and there were printed reminders in every bus, reserving the four front rows for WHITES ONLY. The official policy assigned blacks to the rear, based on the number of blacks and whites on the bus at any given time. As more whites boarded, the imaginary color line was supposed to shift farther back, with blacks nearest the line expected to give up their seats. But drivers made it understood that whites must *never* stand. Blacks also understood that if a white person sat beside a black person, the black had to stand because city regulations prohibited public integration. (In 1955, Montgomery's bus law was already outdated compared to those in other Southern cities. For example, Baton Rouge, Louisiana, passed an ordinance in 1953 abolishing whites-only sections and establishing first-come, first-served seating—though blacks still had to sit in

the rear.) The Montgomery bus system was so corrupt, blacks complained often that it was the city's worst arena of racial abuse.

That was nothing new. From the turn of the century, 7 the city's transportation system had been the focus of intense racial strife. In 1900, segregation was instituted on all streetcars. But a surprisingly effective black boycott resulted in an amendment to the Jim Crow law, stipulating that no black person had to give up a seat in the white section unless another was available in the black section. The problem was that bigoted white drivers ignored the amendment. In 1906, the white city fathers went the other way, mandating separate buses for blacks and whites. By 1955, city buses were the chief mode of transportation for thousands of African Americans traveling to their mostly domestic jobs in the white sections of town. Yet white drivers still baited blacks with racial epithets. Another intimidation tactic was forcing blacks to pay at the front and then reboard at the rear. (It was not uncommon for sadistic drivers to drive away before blacks could reboard.) By the mid-fifties, these drivers had been granted a sort of "special deputy" status by police, empowering them to enforce the segregation law and even arrest violators themselves.

Rosa Parks knew the drill. When she sat in the fifth row 8 that night, she also knew her rights. At the next two stops, whites got on and started filling the reserved seats. At the Empire Theater stop, more whites crowded on, leaving one white man standing. That prompted veteran driver James F. Blake to yell back at the four blacks in the fifth row, "All right, you niggers. I want those seats." No one moved. Maybe it was because the demand was so unreasonable. Why should four black people, including three women, have to stand in the unreserved section just so one white person could sit?

Blake was irate. He warned, "Y'all better make it light 9 on yourselves and let me have those seats." When the man next to Rosa stood up, she just shifted her legs to let him pass. The two women opposite her got up, too. But Rosa slid over to the window seat, unwilling to budge. (White reporters would later insist that her reaction that night was due more to fatigue than courage, but nothing could be further from the truth. She had decided firmly that she would not only not move *then,* but that she would never again move in that situation.)

10   It isn't hard to understand why she "suddenly" decided to resist. It really wasn't so sudden. Never mind her devoted work for the NAACP, Rosa was aware, as a citizen, that in the last twelve months alone three African-American females had been arrested for the same offense. One incident made the newspapers in March; it even happened on the same bus line. Of four black passengers asked to surrender their seats in no-man's land, two refused—an elderly woman and fifteen-year-old Claudette Colvin. "I done paid my dime," Colvin had said. "I ain't got no reason to move." The elderly woman got off the bus before police arrived. Colvin refused to move, so police dragged her, fighting and crying, to the squad car, where she was rudely handcuffed. That brought protests from the black community: Was it really necessary to manhandle and handcuff a fifteen-year-old girl, especially since she had acted within her rights?

11   Colvin was charged with violating the city segregation law, disorderly conduct, and assault. With the NAACP defending her, she was convicted but fined only for assault, the most absurd of the three trumped-up charges. It was a shrewd ruling; it sent a tough message to blacks while avoiding NAACP appeal of a clearly unconstitutional law. Afterward, E. D. Nixon, former Pullman porter and president of the local NAACP chapter, met with the indignant young Colvin to determine if she might make a strong plaintiff in a test case. But she had recently become pregnant, which spelled trouble; Nixon knew that Montgomery's churchgoing blacks would not rally behind an immature, unwed, teenage mother who was also prone to using profanity. She would have problems, too, with the biased white press. So he advised black community leaders: "She is not the kind we can win a case with."

Rosa Parks was intimately involved with the case; she 12
was still disgusted by the outcome. She felt the same about
another incident. In October, a white woman on the High-
land Avenue bus had asked the driver to force eighteen-
year-old Mary Louise Smith to give up her seat for her.
When Smith refused, she was arrested, convicted, and fined
nine dollars under the segregation law. She might have been
ideal for a test case, except that her father was a known
alcoholic. Nixon ruled her out as another bad risk.

Rosa was also distressed over another bus outrage. 13
After a heated exchange on a city bus between a white driver
and an infirm black passenger, the driver had dropped him
off, returned shortly, found him at the same stop, and beat
the disabled man with a metal coin changer. The NAACP
brought suit; predictably, the ailing black man was convicted instead of his brutal, racist attacker. Well aware of
this in her own present dilemma, Rosa knew there might be
more in store for *her* right now than just an arrest.

Something more personal was troubling her, too: James 14
Blake was the same driver who had humiliated her once before. In 1943, after she had paid at the front of his crowded
bus, he asked her to get off and reboard at the rear. When
she refused, Blake evicted her. She never forgot the indignity; it was on her mind when Blake snarled the word
"nigger" a moment earlier, and hovered over her now, threat-
ening, "Look, woman. I told you I wanted the seat. Are you
gonna stand up?"

So Rosa said, "No, I'm not."   15

"Well, if you don't stand up, Blake threatened, "I'm 16
gonna have to call the police to come and arrest you."

This was usually all it took. But Rosa did not flinch. The 17
words came rolling off her tongue: "Well, then, you may do
that." In this simple act of defiance, obscure, nonconfronta-
tional Rosa Parks became one of our greatest African-
American heroines. Here was a quiet, courteous, law-
abiding woman, seeking only a comfortable ride home; yet in
another of those accidents of fate that draw forth character,

she decided to challenge not only the law and history, but racism itself.

18   Even then, her voice was so soft that Blake could barely hear her. He chewed it over and stomped off the bus for the corner phone. While she waited calmly, others piled off. Rosa thought about her childhood, when she had to walk to a ramshackle, one-room, all-black school in rural Montgomery while white kids rode buses to their brand-new school a few blocks away. She never forgot those buses; they symbolized a separate world for whites that was always closed to blacks. And here she was, so many years later, still fighting for a seat on a Montgomery bus.

19   When the police finally arrived, Rosa was still by the window, cradling her Lee's Cut Rate bag and her purse. One policeman asked if she had understood the driver's request. She coolly said yes.

20   He could not understand her stubbornness. "Then why didn't you get up?"

21   "I didn't think I should have to. Why do you push us around?"

22   That caught him by surprise. He just shrugged. "I don't know. But the law is the law, and you are under arrest."

* * * *

[Rosa Parks's action and the resulting Montgomery bus boycott made national news. Nearly a year after Rosa refused to surrender her seat, the Supreme Court ruled that Alabama's bus segregation laws were unconstitutional.]

DISCUSSION QUESTIONS

1. Rosa Parks never intended to make history on December 1, 1955. What was her job, and why did she stop at Lee's Cut Rate Store before waiting for the bus?

2. Mrs. Parks waited for the bus at historic Court Square. How was the square a reminder of racism in the old South?

3. What did Mrs. Parks do at her local chapter of the NAACP?

4. Why was the NAACP established?
5. Describe what was meant by the term "no man's land" regarding bus seats and the "shifting" of an imaginary "color line."
6. How was Montgomery's bus system outdated and even more strict than the bus systems in other Southern cities?
7. How did bigoted white bus drivers harass and intimidate black passengers?
8. What made the veteran bus driver's remark so unreasonable?
9. The authors note that Mrs. Parks's decision not to change seats was not a sudden decision. What other bus incidents helped her remain determined to fight for her beliefs?

WRITING OPTIONS

Collaborate with Peers

1. With a group of three or four classmates, brainstorm ways there could be more positive interaction between different cultures and ethnic groups at your school. Make a list of your ideas, and then use that list to write your own essay about how to bring groups closer at your school.
2. Many colleges and universities sponsor activities to celebrate and increase awareness of the multicultural nature of their student populations. With two or three of your classmates, investigate what your school has planned to celebrate diversity on your campus. Then use that information to write individual essays about how your campus promotes cultural awareness.

Connecting with the Author's Ideas

3. Kareem Abdul-Jabbar and Alan Steinberg describe Rosa Parks as "so shy and reserved" that she is "almost invisible." Write an essay about someone you know who appears shy and quiet yet who stood up for himself or herself.

Other Options

4. Write a letter to Mrs. Parks complimenting her or thanking her for her courageous stand. Include reasons why you consider her a role model for current and future generations of concerned citizens fighting to preserve basic human rights and dignity.

5. Summarize an incident when you felt you were unfairly treated because of one of these factors: your race, religion, nationality, age, gender, or beliefs. Did you take any action? Why or why not?

6. Interview someone who differs from you in race, nationality, or religion. In your interview, try to find three similarities and three differences between you and this person. For instance, you may both like the same music but celebrate different holidays. Use the information you gather from the interview to write an essay comparing and contrasting the two of you.

Heal Thyself

Christina Cheakalos and Linda Kramer

Dr. Ben Carson conquered poverty, racism, and rage to become a top pediatric neurosurgeon and a folk hero. Once a "poor, inner-city kid with a hair-trigger temper," he is now well known for his surgical skills and his generosity.

Words You May Need to Know

elegant (para. 1)	fine
rapt (2)	deeply absorbed
Siamese twins (2)	twins who are born joined together
wizardry (2)	magic
pediatric neurosurgery (2)	surgery of children's brain and nerve tissue
earmarked (3)	set aside
showcase (3)	display, exhibit
put on a pedestal (3)	glorify, praise
bigamist (5)	someone who married one husband or wife while another legal partner was still living
destitute (5)	lacking any money
tenement apartment (5)	an apartment in a poor, crowded part of a city
aromas (6)	odors
formulations (6)	mixtures
diminish (7)	reduce, lessen
berated (7)	scolded
Seventh Day Adventist (7)	a member of a Christian group that makes Saturday its chief day of rest and religious activity.

1   The Baltimore sixth grade students who crowded into Johns Hopkins Medical Institutions' auditorium one day last April had already been told the rags-to-riches story of the sharply dressed man with the elegant hands. So when he began to speak, they fell silent, their eyes upon him. "There is a tendency in people to try to make you believe only a few people are smart," he said. "As a brain surgeon, I know better than that."

2   Dr. Ben Carson, 47, also knows how to keep his audience rapt with tales about separating Siamese twins and other surgical wizardry. But these days, Carson—whose third motivational memoir, *The Big Picture,* was published in February—is also preaching the values the enabled him to make the transition from poor, inner-city kid with a hair-trigger temper to chief of pediatric neurosurgery at Johns Hopkins.

3   Carson puts his money where his microphone is. Through the five-year-old Carson Scholars Fund, which he and his wife, Candy, founded, they have earmarked $500,000 of their own money to create college scholarships. So far, about 160 students in Maryland, Delaware, and Washington, D.C., have been awarded $1000 grants. Scholars must have a 3.75 grade point average and leadership skills and, Carson says, "We also want people who care about other people." He started the fund after noticing that schools routinely showcase athletes but rarely put "our academic superstars on a pedestal. No wonder they're looked at as nerds."

4   Carson's own nerdiness was hard won. "I was the worst student you could imagine," he tells the Hopkins audience. "My favorite subject was recess. Fortunately for me, I had a mother who believed I was smart."

5   Sonya Copeland, now 71, was only thirteen when she moved from Chattanooga to Detroit to marry twenty-eight-year-old Robert Carson, who worked on a Cadillac plant assembly line. They split after she learned he was a bigamist. Destitute, she took her two boys (Curtis, now 49, is a mechanical engineer in South Bend, Indiana) to live in her sister's tenement apartment in Boston. "After my husband left,

it was worse than the depths of hell," says Sonya, who worked as a maid but now lives with Carson and his family in an eight-bedroom hilltop estate outside Baltimore. "I knew my boys needed me. I'd do any sacrifice to get them educated."

When Ben was eight, she bought him a chemistry set. 6 "It was like magic," he recalls, "to take all these chemicals and create incredible aromas and colors and formulations." Reality was harsher. In 1961, Sonya moved her family back to Detroit, where, by fifth grade, Carson was failing all his subjects. Determined to help, Sonya ordered her sons to read and write reports on two books each week, which she, with only a third-grade education, pretended to review. Within two years, Carson ranked at the head of his class at mostly white Wilson Junior High School.

That didn't diminish his rage against the racist treat- 7 ment he encountered. One memorable day in eighth grade, his teacher berated his white classmates for allowing him, the black boy, to win the outstanding student award. At fourteen, Carson's fury erupted: he tried to stab a fellow ninth-grader who had changed the station on a transistor radio. "He had a large metal belt buckle, and the knife blade struck it and broke," Carson recalls. Terrified by his own temper, he ran home, where he locked himself in the bathroom and prayed for hours. A Seventh Day Adventist like his mother, he says he never lost his temper again.

Carson went on to win a scholarship to Yale, where he 8 met music student Candy Ruskin; the two were married in 1975. They moved to Ann Arbor, Michigan, where Candy earned a master's degree in business and Carson attended medical school at the University of Michigan. He was accepted into the neurosurgery program at Johns Hopkins, where in 1984, at age 33, he became the youngest chief of pediatric surgery in the U.S. Since then, he has made a name for himself by separating Siamese twins joined at the head and by performing hemispherectomies—removing one side of the brain to treat those with severe multiple seizures.

At home, Carson relaxes by shooting pool and playing 9 music with his three boys—Murray, 15, Benjamin, 14, and

Rhoeyce, 12. Though the family is wealthy, Carson reminds his sons that privilege comes with a duty to help the less fortunate.

10   At a recent scholarship event, fourteen-year-old Megan Nivens, a grant recipient, approached Carson shyly. "You don't realize how many doors you've opened for me," she said. "Now I know I'm going to college. I feel so fortunate." Ben Carson knows the feeling.

DISCUSSION QUESTIONS

1. What are the eligibility requirements for receiving a scholarship from the fund founded by Dr. Ben Carson and his wife, and how many students have been awarded grants?
2. Why did Carson establish the Scholar's Fund?
3. Describe some of the hardships that faced Sonya Copeland.
4. What did Carson's mother buy for him when he was eight years old, and what did she "order" her sons to do when Carson was failing all his subjects in school?
5. What is an example of the racist attitudes Carson encountered in school, and what was the turning point that forced him to deal with his rage?
6. How old was Carson when he became the youngest chief of pediatric surgery in the United States, and what operation brought him fame in the surgery world?

WRITING OPTIONS

Collaborate with Peers

1. The Carson Scholars Fund recognizes superior academic achievement. With two or three of your classmates, investigate scholarships that have unusual requirements for eligibility. Consult with your campus financial aid counselors for potential sources or ideas.

   Once you complete your investigation, each group member can write a paragraph about a specific scholarship fund by naming it, describing its history (when it began, who founded it), who is eligible to receive money from it, the amount of each scholarship, and how many scholarships are awarded each year.

Connecting with the Author's Words

2. Dr. Carson feels that schools place too much emphasis on showcasing athletes but seldom place "our academic superstars on a pedestal." In a brief essay, describe how your school rewards or recognizes scholastic achievement, and then explain whether these types of recognition are sufficient.

Other Options

3. Carson notes that he was not always in control of his bad temper. Write about a time when your own temper caused you to overreact, and describe the effects this irrational behavior had on you and others. Conclude with stating what you learned from the experience.
4. Carson's mother was determined to help her son succeed in school, and her methods apparently went well. If someone has affected your life positively by helping you to change your attitude about yourself or others, summarize the ways this individual has positively influenced you.

The Ones Who Turn Up Along the Way

Rabbi Jennifer Krause

Rabbi Krause, who lives in New York City, talks about people she knows "who do not fall into the simple categories of family member, co-worker, or friend." Still, she says, "they make real claims on my heart and mind." It was published two months after the tragedies of September 11, 2001.

Words You May Need to Know

rabbi (see author's name)	the spiritual leader of a Jewish congregation
super (para. 1)	a shortened form of superintendent
devout (3)	devoted
Ph.D. (3)	an abbreviation of Doctor of Philosophy, an advanced academic degree
Allah (3)	in Islam (the faith of Muslims), the Supreme Being
Judaism (4)	the Jewish religion
Islam (4)	the Muslim religion
Quran (4)	the sacred text of Islam
socioeconomic spheres (5)	social and economic environments
site-specific (5)	related to a specific place
episodic (5)	casual, related to some other purpose, like shopping or repairing
Book of Exodus (6)	a part of the Old Testament, relating the departure of the Jews from Egypt

Pharaoh (6)	an ancient title for the king of Egypt
multitude (6)	crowd
anonymous (6)	without any names
the golden calf (6)	a golden object of worship
fanned out (6)	spread out
bound (6)	linked
atheist (7)	someone who does not believe God or gods exists

Not long ago my building super, Walter, stopped by my 1
apartment. He rang the bell saying, "Super," in a way to
which I had grown accustomed, dragging out the "u" and
adding a slight roll to the "r." I imagined that he was coming
to fix something or maybe to bring me a package. But when
I opened the door, he was holding the spare set of keys that
he held to my place.

Walter told me he had come to return the keys because 2
he would no longer be working in my building. His family
had gotten too big for the basement apartment that came
with the job, he explained. Walter had been there for eleven
years, ever since coming to the United States from Colombia.
He had been available at all hours for the occasional mainte-
nance crisis, but, more importantly, he always gave me the
sense that he looked out for me—which is a great comfort
when you're living alone in Manhattan. It was hard to imagine the building without him.

Just before Walter came by, I had been unpacking gro- 3
ceries and reflecting on a conversation I had with Ali, the
manager of my neighborhood grocery store. Ali is a devout
Muslim from Bangladesh. He has a wife and three children
and a Ph.D. in geography. On visits to his country, he often
gives lectures on Islam. He hopes to publish a book encouraging Bangladeshi people to see Jews as friends. It's a project he has been working on for some time, and to which he
feels often more committed since September 11. "This is

what Allah tells me I must do," he says. "I must love all people. I cannot hate people and love Allah."

4   I have been shopping in the grocery store for years now, and Ali and I have always waved and said hello. But several months ago, the hellos turned into conversation. When I told him I am a rabbi, we began discussing the connections between Judaism and Islam, the purpose of religion, the sorrow and anger we feel when people use religion as a justification for violence. Every time we talk, I feel as if I have learned Torah—the wisdom of my own faith tradition—from a man who quotes the Quran.

5   I share these stories because they are all part of the puzzle of community. I am well aware that Walter and Ali do not fall into the simple categories of family member, co-worker, or friend. We are from different backgrounds, different countries, and we occupy different socioeconomic spheres. We don't go to each other's home for dinner or make plans to meet for coffee, and we probably won't. Our connections are site-specific and episodic, yet they make real claims on my heart and mind.

6   In the Book of Exodus, even as God continued to harden Pharaoh's heart, the Israelites began their journey out of Egypt. More than 600,000 packed up and headed out on foot, but they were not alone. An *erev rav*—a mixed multitude—went with them. The ancient rabbis' reviews are mixed when it comes to characterizing this anonymous crew. Some see them as a group of hangers-on ultimately responsible for the building of the golden calf. Others suggest that they were Egyptians who simply shared the basic longing to be free. Either way, I imagine that by the time the travelers made it to shore and fanned out into the desert, called to different purposes and directions, they were bound to one another forever.

7   About a year ago, a man came to replace the intercom system in my apartment. While he worked, he told me that he had been born in Ukraine, immigrated to Israel with his family and fought in the country's 1948 independence war. He explained that he was an atheist and knew he could

never believe in God. Nevertheless, as he was leaving he asked in Hebrew, "What blessing may I give you?" Before I could answer, he prayed that I would find my *bashert* (soulmate), kindly even suggesting one of his sons.

When he had gone, I noticed that he had forgotten a 8 bunch of different-colored wires. I saved them. I kept them in a tin with the quarters I save for doing laundry. They remind me that we are traveling not only with the people we have chosen but with the ones who turn up along the way. The repairman, Walter and Ali are all part of my *erev rav*, and I am a part of theirs.

It's been months now since Walter and his family moved 9 across the river to New Jersey. Soon Ali will take another trip to Bangladesh. I don't know what's next for me, but I know I won't be going alone.

DISCUSSION QUESTIONS

1. How did Walter help make Rabbi Jennifer Krause feel more secure as a single woman living in New York City?
2. Who is Ali, and what do you find unusual about him?
3. Despite their different religions, what makes both Jennifer and Ali feel "sorrow and anger"?
4. What does "*erev rav*" mean, and how does it relate to the people Jennifer came to know in multicultural New York?
5. What significance do the different wires left behind by a repairman have for Jennifer?

WRITING OPTIONS

Collaborate with Peers

1. With two or three classmates, try to identify times when people of different colors, backgrounds, and social classes unite. Are they times of danger to the community, or of sorrow, pride, anger, or joy? Identify as many as you can. Then write individual paragraphs about one such time. Be specific about what drew the community together, what emotions people felt, and how they dealt with those emotions.

Connecting with the Author's Ideas

2. Rabbi Krause says that her super, Walter, "always gave me the sense that he looked out for me—which is a great comfort when you're living alone in Manhattan." If several individuals in your neighborhood or street (aside from family members or friends) provide you with a sense of security or well-being, describe who these people are, how each plays a positive role in your daily life, and how your life would be different if you had never met them.

Other Options

3. Rabbi Krause writes of people of differing backgrounds and religions who have helped her. If you have been pleasantly surprised by how helpful and friendly some "different" people have been to you, describe these experiences. Include any incorrect assumptions of these individuals you may have made before they changed your attitudes for the better.

4. Think about two or three people who are not family members or close friends but who brighten your day. They should be people you see regularly, but briefly. Select one of them and write him or her a thank-you letter, explaining what this person contributes to your day and why you are grateful. Such a person could be the friendly nurse at the doctor's office, the cheerful toll taker on the turnpike, or the warm security guard on campus.

Lessons from a Friend

Frank Deford

Arthur Ashe was the first African American Davis Cup competitor and the first black man to win both the U.S. Open and Wimbledon tennis championships. Prior to his death in 1993, Ashe had become a tireless and well-known political activist fighting for racial justice and educational reform. Frank Deford pays tribute to his friend who was "honored more for his nobility than for his celebrity."

Words That You May Need to Know

frayed (para. 1)	unraveled
monumentalized (2)	remembered in a monument in his honor
confounded (3)	amazed, confused
Thurgood Marshall (3)	a former Justice of the Supreme Court
Dizzy Gillespie (3)	a legendary jazz musician
Rudolf Nureyev (3)	a ballet dancer
Audrey Hepburn (3)	an actress
surpassing (3)	going beyond
lionized (3)	treated as a celebrity
eulogizing (4)	praising highly, especially at a person's death
grotesquely (5)	strangely, unnaturally
intriguing (5)	interesting, unusual
divined (5)	perceived by intuition or insight
Warhol (5)	Andy Warhol was an artist who said that in our times, everyone would get to be famous—for ten minutes.
profligate (5)	extravagant

adversity (6)	trouble, disaster
subsequently (6)	later
violated (6)	disrespected, mistreated
"outed" (6)	A person is "outed" when his or her secret is exposed.
palpable (6)	evident, plainly seen
encroachment (6)	trespassing on the rights of another, usually by gradual means
peril (6)	risk, danger
keystone (7)	critical, essential
infiltrated (7)	filtered into
legions (8)	large groups
transcendent (8)	superior, supreme
mortified (8)	humiliated
exalted (9)	praised
effete (9)	lacking energy, worn out
elitist (9)	a person who is proud of belonging to a select or favored group or who believes in rule by that group
dogma (9)	beliefs, principles
cite (9)	refer to as an example
blindsided (10)	startled, surprised
civil (10)	courteous, respectful
estate (10)	condition
engaging (11)	attracting
adulation (12)	admiration, flattery
effluence (12)	outflow
advocate (12)	a person who pleads for a cause
skeptical (13)	doubtful

A personal note to begin with: I remember my grand- 1
father, who grew up in Richmond, telling me about the day
when he was a little boy, and they let all the children out of
school so they could help pull Robert E. Lee's new statue to
its assigned place on Monument Avenue, there to rest
amidst the other statues of all the beloved Virginia heroes.
And my grandfather would then show me a little piece of
frayed rope, which he'd saved all these decades, cut with
his penknife from the tow rope after the general's statue was
safely set. Virginians have always taken their champions
very seriously.

I thought back on that last Wednesday, in Richmond, 2
a century later, when Arthur Ashe, the Virginian, was
monumentalized. I tried to imagine how I could have ever
explained that to my grandfather—how the hero that
came next to Richmond after Robert E. Lee, general in
chief, Confederate States of America—that next Virginian
was merely a tennis player, who was also, of all things,
black.

As much as that would have confounded my grand- 3
father, it is also still difficult for me to understand quite
how deeply Arthur Ashe's death touched so many people.
Bill Rhoden, who is black, a sports columnist for *The New
York Times,* even observed that the outpouring overshad-
owed that which had been bestowed upon Thurgood
Marshall—not to mention surpassing the affection granted
to those other distinguished world citizens who have left
us, one after another, in these first sad weeks in 1993:
Dizzy Gillespie, Rudolf Nureyev, Audrey Hepburn. Has any
athlete—not to mention *former* athlete—ever been lionized
so at his death? It wasn't as if Arthur was the best player
ever; why, he wasn't even the best of his time. Rather, he
was just a very good tennis player who had come to be
recognized as an altogether exceptional human being. I
think that, by the time he died, Arthur Ashe had become
everybody's favorite athlete—not just All-American, more
just all ours.

4   Obviously, there was some rare chord that Arthur plucked on people's heartstrings. Probably, too, that twang reveals more about our society right now than it does about the man himself. Andrew Young, eulogizing Arthur at the service in Richmond, may have drawn closest, saying that Ashe had come to represent "the role of innocence in our time." And, innocence, like love, sometimes is found in funny places—even in professional athletics.

5   It was the tennis player who came to triumph in society even as he was grotesquely defeated by fate, the tennis player who was the one who exhibited the dignity and decency that we simply no longer expect from people of consequence. Jesse Jackson characterized it in an intriguing way, saying that Arthur managed to "build a code of conduct for the gifted." Somehow, the public correctly divined that essential goodness of Ashe, so that he really was honored more for his nobility than for his celebrity—which is truly amazing in these Warholian times. That's what a lot of last week was about: us saying, we will pause now for just a moment to honor honor. It felt good, so we were even more profligate in our giving.

6   Nothing, of course, distinguished Ashe so much as the way he handled adversity. It was enough to suffer a heart attack while still in his thirties—while still, for that matter, ranked in the top ten of tennis players. But then, to contract AIDS from a blood transfusion given after heart-bypass surgery . . . well, that was just impossibly unfair. The intensity of anger that the public feels about how he was subsequently violated by the media, when he was forced to reveal his condition or be "outed" by USA Today, remains palpable. Anybody in the press who dismisses the public's disgust at the encroachment upon a private man's privacy does so at his or her future peril.

7   But above all, race was forever crucial in understanding the way in which the world dealt with Arthur Ashe. He was, I came to think, in matters of race, The Universal Soldier, some kind of keystone figure we need if ever brotherhood

is to triumph. He was black, but he perfectly infiltrated white society as much as he needed to, and even beyond that he was just terribly interested in everybody everywhere in the world.

Those legions who paid tribute last week kept talking 8 about how Ashe was a "transcendent figure" above tennis, but, I'm sorry, the much greater, dearer point was quite the opposite: he was the sort of person who was always down in the ditches, connecting things, tying people together. Arthur would have been mortified to have been reduced to being labeled transcendent.

Anyway, even if we throw around high-falutin' words 9 like "transcend," most everybody sensed otherwise; by the end, all the world wanted to associate itself closely with Arthur. The International Olympic Committee made him the first athlete member of the Olympic Order never to have had anything to do with the Olympics. The bell was sounded ten times for him at the Bowe-Dokes championship fight, the first time that any but a fallen fighter had ever been so honored. African-Americans exalted him as one of theirs, even though there were occasions in the past when Arthur was painted as effete for failing to scream out and painted as an elitist for failing to go along with politically correct racial dogma. And whites, of course, wanted to cozy up to Ashe and cite him as a black ideal—why can't they all be like him?—missing the point that there are precious few whites that live up to that standard, either.

As a matter of fact, nothing blindsided some whites as 10 much as Ashe's recent comment that, difficult as it was having AIDS, that wasn't nearly as trying as being black. "No question," he snapped. Arthur Ashe said that? Certainly not Arthur. Not the man who was always so civil and understanding. But the thought wasn't anything new with him. I can remember him years ago instructing me that "equal" though things may seem, he could never achieve that estate because so much of his time—of any black person's time— must be spent simply thinking about race. "You can get up in the morning and just walk outside and start your day. I can't do that. I always have to think: well, here goes a black guy walking outside. So you see, you'll always have an advantage over me."

11   But the fact that Arthur Ashe could say things about race, however passionately, without bitterness, is what made them so meaningful. Obviously, Arthur Ashe meant more to black people, but, notwithstanding, he was capable of engaging white people; he was capable of causing changes in them and their world. In the end, the outpouring of emotion we gave to him spoke selfishly to our hope—that if we could not save his life, what he stood for might help save us.

12   Although this adulation Arthur received this past week would have embarrassed him terribly, he must have sensed the effluence of affection that would flow with his death. In a way, you see, the revelation of last April* that was wrenched from him produced the first draft of his obituaries while he was still alive to read them. His pre-death also, he recognized, made him a more valuable advocate of the causes he cared about, so he could make us cosign for his borrowed time. He wanted to steal a few more months, too, and he thought he would, but he was accepting of what would come of him, whenever it did.

13   The last time I saw him was only a couple of weeks before he died, but it preceded any sense of urgency. Still, he was in the hospital, so he wanted to put me at ease. "You know," he said, "everything in my life is just wonderful now—except for the hospital stuff." When I looked a little skeptical—as if to say out loud: excuse me, you are reducing AIDS to "hospital stuff"?—he added, "Really, everything is almost perfect." I left almost believing him. Arthur Ashe had a very good attitude, and it was catching. He was a more infectious person even than what incidentally killed him.

*In April, Arthur Ashe had revealed that he had AIDS.

DISCUSSION QUESTIONS

1. What does author Frank Deford say would have been difficult to explain to his grandfather?
2. The author states that "by the time he died, Arthur Ashe had become everybody's favorite athlete." What do you think Jesse Jackson meant when he said that Arthur Ashe was able to "build a code of conduct for the gifted"?
3. What does the author state was "impossibly unfair" about Arthur Ashe's life?
4. Why was the public angry about the way the media planned to report the athlete's illness?
5. What did Arthur Ashe feel was even more difficult than having AIDS?

WRITING OPTIONS

Collaborating with Peers

1. With two or three of your classmates, discuss whom you would choose as the most influential athlete of your time. Your goal is not to come up with one name, but to consider several names, and to discuss the reasons for your choices. Consider whether each candidate has been a positive or negative influence on sports or in society. After this discussion, write an individual essay on your choice for the most influential athlete of your time. Be sure to give the reasons for your choice.

Connecting with the Author's Ideas

2. This article is a tribute in honor of a man who triumphed over difficult circumstances. In a short essay, select one of the compliments author Frank Deford makes about Ashe, and describe how the compliment also applies to someone you know and admire.

Other Options

3. This article mentions that the media violated Arthur Ashe's right to privacy concerning his disease. Write a short essay about how

you feel the media violates the privacy of either ordinary citizens or celebrities.

4. Some professional athletes or celebrities are poor role models for today's youth, but others are positive role models away from the spotlight. Write an essay describing how a well-known sports or media personality is a positive or negative role model for young people today.

Chapter Eight

Physical Challenges, Boundless Possibilities

"I know things are possible. I've always known that."
Stanley Buckley, recent college graduate and first wheelchair-bound
person to graduate from Northeast High School (Florida)

"All serious daring starts from within."

Eudora Welty

On Their Own

Susan Schindehette and Cindy Dampier

Dr. Mridula Prasad is a skilled neurosurgeon, but her own childhood convinced her that quiet compassion and the spirit of giving can help disabled individuals gain a sense of freedom and dignity. Her MS (multiple sclerosis) patients, she says, are her real heroes.

Words You May Need to Know

modest (para. 1)	inexpensive, not showy
teeters (1)	wobbles
haltingly (1)	hesitantly, unsteadily
neurologist (2)	a doctor who specializes in diseases to the nerves and nervous system
multiple sclerosis (2)	a nerve disease that begins slowly, usually in young adulthood, and continues through life. Its characteristics include speech and vision difficulties, and muscular weakness. There are cycles when the symptoms worsen or become weaker.
languishing (2)	fading away, weakening
characteristic (2)	typical
simplicity (2)	openness, sincerity
pied-a-terre (3)	a small place meant for temporary use
ravaged (3)	damaged, ruined
debilitated (3)	weak
disability payments (3)	payments sent to people whose physical handicap prevents them from leading a normal life or holding a job

benefactress (3)	a woman who gives money to help others
compassion (4)	deep sympathy and desire to help
nurtured (4)	nourished, encouraged
self-esteem (5)	self-respect
epilepsy (5)	a disease of the nervous system that usually includes seizures
empathy (5)	sympathetic understanding of another person
calling (6)	a strong impulse to follow a special career
escrow (7)	financial trust
compromising (8)	unfavorably affecting
zoning variance (8)	official permission to use the townhouse for the patients
spurred (9)	encouraged
realize (9)	make real
communal (9)	group

In a modest living-room in Merrillville, Indiana, a middle- 1
aged woman, her face red with effort, struggles to move
forward. She teeters, regains her balance, then haltingly
places one foot in front of the other. Having achieved a few
short steps, she reaches out to embrace her doctor. "I did it!"
Phyllis Walsh cries into the shoulder of Dr. Mridula Prasad.
"I *walked*!"

As a neurologist who specializes in the treatment of 2
patients with multiple sclerosis, Prasad is used to giving
emotional support along with physical care. But for three
patients who might otherwise have spent their lives lan-
guishing in nursing homes, she has provided something
even greater: the simple dignity of a place to call home. "If
we needed it, we would want other people to come and help,"
says Prasad, 49, with characteristic simplicity. "I want
people to realize that we are all a big family."

3   In a two-story townhouse Prasad bought as a pied-a-terre located near Methodist Hospital where she works, Walsh and her two housemates, all ravaged by a disease that leaves them physically debilitated but intellectually intact, are living independent lives. Though they receive regular visits from nurses' aides and volunteers, they pool their disability payments to pay for groceries and take care of each other as best they can. "The freedom is the best part," says, Walsh, 51, a former schoolteacher. "We can do what we want." And the fact that their benefactress is Prasad—who contributes roughly $2,500 a month for the mortgage and their care—hardly surprises them. "It's nothing more than I'd expect of her," says housemate Sharon Smith, 48. "She's got a lot of God in her."

4   Prasad's quiet compassion was nurtured during childhood in India, when a mysterious illness that took the life of her two-year-old sister also killed her brother at age eleven. "My parents took him to all the hospitals in the country, but nobody knew what was wrong with him," says Prasad. "I grew up thinking that I would find a cure."

5   At Osmania Medical College in her hometown of Secunderabad, she met a young psychiatry student, Bhawani Prasad, now 49. "It was a big surprise to me that someone that intelligent would talk to me," she says. "I had no self-esteem at all." Still, the two married, and in 1976, after they graduated, she followed him to the U.S., where both eventually set up practices in Indiana. But, says Prasad, it was the 1984 diagnosis of the second of their three daughters, Ambika, then ten months old, with a form of epilepsy that inspired her true empathy for patients. "I was one of them now," she says. "The parent of a sick child."

6   Prasad slowly nursed her daughter back to health and over time began to realize a special calling. "Some people cried on your shoulder for an hour because they had a headache," she says. "Others, who couldn't move at all, were smiling and doing everything they could. I became attached to my MS patients because they were the heroes."

One of those was Sharon Smith, a divorced escrow 7 agent from Gary, Indiana, diagnosed with MS in her early forties. After suffering depression and bedsores in 1997, she begged not to be returned to her nursing home. "At that point, it became very simple to me," says Prasad. In July 1997, she moved Smith to her townhouse, fifteen miles from the home where Prasad lives with her family. Smith was joined by Walsh, Daisy Smith, 49, a former computer-programming student, and Sharon's disabled sixteen-year-old son, Vincent. "Now that I have him with me," says Smith. "I can sleep through the night."

Once they had settled in, however, Prasad's retreat 8 came under unexpected fire. Neighbors and the town council accused Prasad of compromising the residential nature of the neighborhood by operating an illegal nursing home. When the town fined Prasad, she refused to pay. And in August, after a judge ruled in her favor, the town granted Prasad a zoning variance. "I haven't heard any more complaints," says Councilman Rick Bella. "I think it's going to work out just fine."

Spurred by the victory, Prasad now hopes to realize an 9 even bigger dream. Last year she founded the nonprofit group People Helping People to encourage the establishment of other communal homes for the disabled. "I want to plant the seed in many hearts," she says, "so that this can go on after I am gone."

DISCUSSION QUESTIONS

1. According to Dr. Prasad, what is the source of "simple dignity" for her MS patients?
2. What do Phyllis Walsh and her housemates use their disability payments for, and what financial contribution does Dr. Prasad make for them?
3. What happened to Dr. Prasad's brother and sister that motivated her to find a cure some day?

4. What did some neighbors and the town council accuse Dr. Prasad of doing? How was the issue resolved?

5. What has Dr. Prasad established to help disabled people in the future?

WRITING OPTIONS

Collaborate with Peers

1. The goal of many physically challenged individuals is to become as independent as possible. Working with a partner or small group, summarize the reasons why a group home is preferable to a nursing home for the disabled. Use the ideas you gather to write an essay.

Connecting with the Author's Ideas

2. Dr. Prasad takes care of many of her patients' physical and emotional needs. To explain her motives, she says, "If we needed it, we would want other people to come and help." Write about a time when you needed physical, financial, or emotional help and about the person(s) who helped you.

Other Options

3. If you are thinking about a career in the healthcare field or in counseling, investigate what types of group living arrangements are available for the physically challenged citizens in your community. In a short essay, describe the types of homes, their various services, and the monthly or yearly costs for the residents. Also include how much independence the residents experience.

4. Dr. Prasad is described as a generous, quiet, and compassionate individual. In a short essay, describe a similar individual that you know or have known in your community or in your family.

5. Have you ever had an illness or injury that temporarily prevented you from performing a physical activity you took for granted? For instance, you may have twisted an ankle or broken a bone. Write an essay about what it felt like to be limited in your physical activity and how you coped. What was the toughest part of the experience?

On Having Adventures

Nancy Mairs

Nancy Mairs, stricken with multiple sclerosis years ago, has learned to redefine what "adventure" means, but she knows how to appreciate her life on <u>her</u> terms.

Words You May Need to Know

multiple sclerosis (para. 1)	a nerve disease that begins slowly, usually in young adulthood, and continues through life. Its characteristics include speech and vision difficulties, and muscular weakness. There are cycles when the symptoms worsen or become weaker.
minutiae (2)	small details
delight in (2)	find pleasure in
Peter Matthiessen, John McPhee, Annie Dillard, David Bain, Ed Abbey, Robert Pirsig, George Dyson, Isak Dinesen (3)	writers whose subjects are nature and adventure
trekked (3)	traveled, with difficulty
trudged (3)	walked, in a tired way
hostility (3)	unfriendliness, opposition, or hatred
forgo (4)	give up
bettas (5)	brightly colored fish that originated in Southeast Asia

Nearly ten years ago, I was told that I had a brain 1
tumor, and this experience changed my attitude about

adventure forever. I thought that I was going to die and that all my adventures were over. I did not have a brain tumor, it turned out, but rather multiple sclerosis, which meant that, although they were not over, the nature of my adventures would have to change.

2   Each morning that I wake up, that I get out of bed, is a fresh event, something that I might not have had. Each gesture that I make carries the weight of uncertainty, demands significant attentions: buttoning my shirt, changing a light bulb, walking down stairs. I might not be able to do it this time. Inevitably, the minutiae of my life have had to assume dramatic proportions. If I could not delight in them, they would likely drown me in rage or self-pity.

3   I admire the grand adventures of others. I read about them with zest. With Peter Matthiessen I have trekked across the Himalayas to the Crystal Mountain. One blistering July I moved with John McPhee to Eagle, Alaska, above the Arctic Circle. I have trudged with Annie Dillard up, down, into, and across Tinker Creek in all seasons. David Bain has accompanied me along 110 miles of Philippine coast, and Ed Abbey has paddled me down the Colorado River. I've ridden on the back of Robert Pirsig's motorcycle, climbed ninety-five feet to George Dyson's tree house, and grown coffee in Kenya with Isak Dinesen. I relish the adventures of these rugged and courageous figures, who can strike out on difficult trips—two miles, 250 miles, 3,000 miles—ready to endure cold, fatigue, human and natural hostility—indeed not just to endure but to celebrate.

4   But as for me, I can no longer walk very far from the armchair in which I read. I'll never make it to Tibet. Maybe not even to Albuquerque. Some days I don't even make it to the backyard. And yet I'm unwilling to forgo the adventurous life: the difficulty of it, even the pain, the suspense and fear, and the sudden brief lift of spirit that graces a hard journey. If I am to have it too, then I must change the terms by which it is lived. And so I do.

5   I refine *adventure*, making it smaller and smaller. And now, whether I am feeding fish flakes to my bettas or crawling across the dining room helping my cat Burton look for his

blind snake, lying wide-eyed in the dark battling yet another bout of depression, cooking a chicken, gathering flowers from the garden at the farm, meeting a friend for lunch, I am always having the adventures that are mine to have.

DISCUSSION QUESTIONS

1. What does Nancy Mairs feel is a "fresh event" each morning?
2. How does she find an escape through reading?
3. What do you think Mairs means when she says she redefines the word "adventure"?
4. Mairs says that the small details of her life bring her happiness. What are some of her small moments of happiness and adventure?

WRITING OPTIONS

Collaborate with Peers

1. Interview a partner about some great adventure he or she has always dreamed of. In an essay, compare and contrast that dream with your own dream of adventure.

Connecting with the Author's Ideas

2. Mairs says that adventures contain difficulty, pain, suspense, and fear, but they also contain "the sudden brief lift of spirit" that is part of "a hard journey." Write about a time when you had an experience that included all these elements: difficulty, pain, suspense, fear, and a sudden, short lift of the spirit.

Other Options

3. Nancy Mairs's life changed suddenly years ago, but she learned to adapt. In a short essay, describe how your life, or the life of someone you know well, changed suddenly one day. Consider if there was anything you (or the person you know) once took for granted but do not any longer.
4. Mairs mentions that she has adventures through reading books. In a short essay, describe how a certain book, author, or movie enables you to escape from daily pressures.

It Took True Grit and Ten Years, but He Won

Jill Rosen

Stanley Buckley has cerebral palsy, but that didn't stop him from pursuing a college degree. Others doubted he could do it, but he never doubted himself. With his condition, he knows he has limits, but as he says, "Within reason, I know things are possible."

Words You May Need to Know

grit (see title)	spirit, firmness
painstakingly (para. 12)	carefully
sap (12)	weaken or destroy
sustain (12)	keep up
commencement (13)	graduation ceremony
registrar (13)	a college official who maintains students' records and issues grade reports

1   He's got the suit, the tie, and the shiny black shoes. His mom's getting her hair done. And days ago, they fetched the cap and gown. So now, all that's left for Stanley Buckley is anticipation for the moment they call his name. Stanley Buckley, they will say, the graduate. It's taken Buckley ten years to earn his degree, which he will receive this morning from Florida Atlantic University in Boca Raton.

2   He has taken it so slowly because he has cerebral palsy, a disorder where messages from the brain never make it to the muscles. It's a disease that makes everything hard—moving, talking, breathing. And going to college has been the hardest thing he has ever done.

3   "People have a tendency to say they didn't think I could do things," says Buckley, who will be thirty-two next week. "But I knew I could. I just wanted to prove them wrong."

It wouldn't be the first time. In 1988, Buckley, who is 4 from Fort Lauderdale, Florida, became the first wheelchair-bound person to get through Northeast High School in Oakland Park, Florida. He made it past staring kids, impatient teachers and buildings that, despite all those federal laws, are so much easier for "normal" people to navigate. No one expected him to continue to college. But he knew he had to try. "I get frustrated," Buckley says, "but I knew it would pay off in the end."

Buckley, like everyone with cerebral palsy, was born 5 with it. Although he was eight weeks premature, it took months before his mother, Mary, knew anything was wrong with her youngest child. Stanley, Mary Buckley says, was the most sweet-tempered of babies, but he couldn't crawl and he couldn't sit up. So she took him to a doctor who delivered the bad news—along with a bit of good. "The doctor said he's going to be very intelligent," said Mary Buckley, who, after her divorce, raised and took care of her son without much help. "Somehow he just knew that." That was true—as were all the difficulties the doctor predicted.

Though he wears high-top Reeboks, Stanley can't walk. 6 He can feed himself, but he doesn't have full use of his arms. And he has been in and out of hospitals his whole life. But he is bright and quick, particularly quick to lose patience with those who can't keep up with him. "I hate repeating myself," he said.

He knows all too well that for him, the sky is never the 7 limit—his limits are much, much closer to Earth. But he's adopted a motto for himself: "Within reason, I know things are possible." In his own way, he gets things done. It's just that his way is always the long way.

Stanley Buckley started classes at Broward Community 8 College after he graduated from high school. There he spent a couple of years taking care of the basics like literature and math, and then he enrolled at Florida Atlantic University's criminal justice program.

Nothing about it was simple. The things other students 9 just do and forget about became issues. Getting to campus meant he had to ride with his mother in the family's specially equipped van from their home in Fort Lauderdale. Once on campus, he had to find someone to wheel him from class to class.

10　　　In class, someone with FAU's Office of Students with Disabilities had to take notes for him because, while he can write, he can't match the speed of a lecturing professor. Test taking especially was a production: essay tests were the worst. He had to form answers in his head and tell it all to a transcriber who would put it on paper. And those were the good days when he was feeling well and could make it to class.

11　　　Stomach surgery kept him out for a whole semester. The very next session he was back in the hospital for hip surgery because one day he just could not sit up. But Buckley kept coming back. He would file into his front row seat in criminal justice professor Richard Mangan's class. Mangan could only marvel. "He could have just lain down and played dead," Mangan said. "But he's going to achieve, regardless."

12　　　He will graduate today with a C average. It is a bachelor's degree earned painstakingly slow, with class loads light enough not to sap what little energy he managed to sustain.

13　　　On Thursday, Stanley Buckley's mother wheeled him into FAU's cavernous gym where the commencement will be. The school registrar pointed to the spot that would be reserved for Buckley in the student section. Then he led Buckley to the ramp he will use to get onto the podium to claim his diploma.

14　　　Buckley could not keep a smile from spreading over his thin face. In a corner near the bleachers, he talked about what's next. Unlike his fellow criminal justice majors, he knows he will never be an FBI agent or a lawyer. He has set his sights on something behind the scenes, maybe working with troubled young people.

15　　　Persuading someone to hire him, like everything Buckley has done, won't be easy. But Mangan has faith Buckley can do it. "I know things are possible," Buckley says. "I've always known that."

DISCUSSION QUESTIONS

1. Stanley Buckley took ten years to earn his college degree. Some doubted he could do it, and even in high school, Stanley had to struggle. What are some of the obstacles he had to overcome at Northeast High?
2. What disease has Stanley endured since birth, and what did his mother notice about him when he was a baby?
3. Whom does Stanley lose patience with, and what does he hate to do?
4. After he enrolled at his university, what were some of the challenges he faced getting to campus and keeping up with his classes?
5. What kind of work does Stanley hope to do? Do you think he will be successful? Explain.

WRITING OPTIONS

Connecting with the Author's Ideas

1. Author Jill Rosen says that Stanley "always gets things done. It's just that his way is always the long way." Write about someone you know who has to take the long and harder way to reach his or her goals.

Other Options

2. If your college has an Office of Disability Services (or some similar service), arrange to interview a student who uses its services about his or her typical day. In a short essay, summarize the challenges this student faces each day on campus.
3. Are there any buildings or walkways around your campus that you think may cause problems for physically challenged students? If so, summarize the types of problems these areas pose for wheelchair-bound and other physically challenged students.
4. Have you (or anyone you know) experienced unfair treatment because of some physical impairment? In a short essay, describe this form of prejudice and explain how you (or the person you are writing about) dealt with it.

Blind Commuter

Douglas Martin

Albert Torres's two-hour commute to work could be an ordeal for anyone, let alone for a blind man. His job developing X-rays at a hospital is demanding work, but he thinks his day is nothing out of the ordinary. That attitude is what makes him extraordinary.

Words You May Need to Know

inflammation (para. 1)	swelling
optic nerve (1)	a nerve connected to the eye
retinal (1)	related to the retina, a nervous tissue membrane of the eye
ailing (2)	sick
mind-numbing (2)	making the mind dull and stupid
radical mastectomy (3)	surgical removal of the breast, with the chest muscles, lymph nodes, and other nearby tissues
chemotherapy (3)	treatment of disease with chemicals or drugs
radiation treatments (3)	treatment of disease with energy, rays, or waves
labyrinthine (4)	complicated
invariably (5)	always, constantly
interminably (5)	endlessly, for a long time
provisions (5)	arrangements
rehabilitating (6)	restoring to good health or the ability to work
the visually impaired (6)	those with difficulty seeing

to no avail (6)	with no success
arduous (7)	difficult
data (8)	information
concession to (8)	allowance for
transcends (9)	goes beyond
briskly (9)	quickly

You could feel sorry for Albert Torres, who is blind. The 1
last thing he remembers was seeing his daughter, Lauren,
being born thirteen years ago. Then the world went blank;
he can only imagine what his only child looks like as a
cheerleader and honor student. Total darkness came as a
result of an inflammation of his optic nerve—a condition
that was unrelated to the retinal disease that had obscured
his vision since birth. "I went to sleep and woke up with
nothing," he said.

Bad luck is no stranger to this warm and thoughtful 2
thirty-seven-year-old man. His mother died of cancer when
he was four, and Mr. Torres's ailing father had to give him
up to foster care when the boy was eleven. He later worked
for nineteen years in a workshop assembling mops and
other household goods, mind-numbing stuff.

Earlier this month, Alberto Torres's wife Idalis, who had 3
just been laid off from her job as a receptionist, had a radi-
cal mastectomy and now faces a year of chemotherapy and
radiation treatments. Even Mr. Torres's good luck has a
dark side: Five years ago, his beloved seeing-eye dog,
Gambler, got him out of the path of a truck. Mr. Torres was
unharmed; Gambler died. But know this and know it well:
Mr. Torres does not feel sorry for himself. "These are just
little bumps you have to go over in your life," he said.

At 5 A.M. on a recent morning, we caught up with 4
Mr. Torres at the Nassau Avenue subway stop in Greenpoint,
Brooklyn, where he lives in a third-floor walkup. He had
been up since 3, feeding Greg, his new dog, making coffee,
getting ready. "When you're blind, it takes a little longer to do

things," he said. Mr. Torres was beginning the labyrinthine two-hour trip to his job developing film in the X-ray department of the emergency room of the Bronx Municipal Hospital Center. He would take the G train to Queens Plaza where he would walk up a set of stairs and down another to the Manhattan-bound R train; he would then ride the R to 59th Street where he would walk upstairs to switch to the No. 6.

5   At one point along the journey, he might chat with a stranger. At another, someone would pat Greg, calling him by name. People offered assistance, even seats. At 125th Street, Mr. Torres would transfer to the No. 4 by crossing the platform. At 149th Street, he would descend to the No. 2. He would take that to East 180th Street where he invariably waits interminably for his final train, the Dyre Avenue shuttle to Pelham Parkway. Then he and Greg would walk twenty minutes to the hospital. "They shouldn't make any special provisions for me," Mr. Torres said. "It's a job, and I should be on time."

6   It was a hard job to come by. Before he got the job, Mr. Torres was determined to escape the workshop run by the Lighthouse, an organization dedicated to rehabilitating the visually impaired, and to try to make it on his own. He wanted a job developing X-ray film, something that everyone must do in the dark. The Lighthouse called many hospitals, to no avail, even though they offered to pay his first three months' salary and provide training.

7   The Lighthouse people would have much preferred something closer to his home. But they believed he could handle the arduous trip, as well as the work. "Our philosophy here is that blind people can do just about anything besides drive buses," said Marianne Melley, who tries to place blind people in jobs. And that, as it turned out, was also the thinking about disabled people at the Bronx hospital. "We find what a person can do rather than what he can't do," said Noel McFarlane, the hospital's associate executive director. "The point is that it works," Pamela Brier, executive director, said.

One day a while ago marked the first anniversary of 8 Mr. Torres's hiring. He will likely develop 150 or so X-rays, his usual output, to celebrate. The cards with names and other data will be folded on the upper right hand corner so he can photograph them right-side-up. That is the only concession to his blindness. Mr. Torres works by himself in a small, chemical-scented darkroom. He cannot wear protective gloves because he needs to feel. It is exacting work, and, since this is an emergency room, lives are at stake. His immediate supervisor, Alcides Santambrosio, says he trusts him one hundred percent.

Mr. Torres makes $20,000 a year. He could be pocket- 9 ing more than $12,000 from disability payments. But his motivation transcends money. "If I start feeling like a victim, that makes me bitter," he said. "And why be bitter? That makes you go into a hole and stay there." Just then, a technician rushed in undeveloped X-rays of a teenager who had jumped from a window and was in critical condition. "I'm not doing anything out of the ordinary," insisted Mr. Torres as he briskly completed the task.

DISCUSSION QUESTIONS

1. Douglas Martin, the author, notes that Albert Torres "is no stranger" to bad luck. What are some of the setbacks and problems he has endured?

2. Albert Torres is quoted several times in this article. Which statement do you believe best reflects his positive attitude and sense of purpose?

3. What is the Lighthouse, and what is this organization's philosophy regarding the blind?

4. What is Albert Torres's job, and why can't he wear protective gloves while he is at work?

5. How does Albert Torres think he would act if he started "feeling like a victim"?

6. Albert Torres says he's not doing "anything out of the ordinary." Would you agree or disagree?

WRITING OPTIONS
Collaborate with Peers

1. With a partner or small group, share your ideas on society's stereotyping of blind people. Consider these questions: Do you think society still stereotypes blind people? What, exactly, is the stereotype, and why do you think it exists? After you have discussed these ideas, write individual essays on the reasons (causes) for this misconception or the effects of it.

Connecting with the Author's Ideas

2. The author says that "Mr. Torres's good luck has a dark side" sometimes. For example, Mr. Torres was lucky to have a guide dog that saved his life, but the dog was killed in the effort. Write a short essay about a time when you had good luck that turned out to have its dark side.

Other Options

3. The author, Douglas Martin, describes the difficult and complicated process Mr. Torres goes through each morning as he wakes up, prepares for work, and makes the long commute. In a short essay, describe the process you go through each morning from waking up, to getting ready for work or school, and to getting there.

4. Write a short essay about a remarkable individual you know who has succeeded in life despite a disability.

5. Investigate how dogs are trained to become "seeing-eye" dogs. Summarize how dogs are selected and describe the stages of the training process.

6. Investigate agencies and support groups in your community that try to help disabled individuals find employment and lead productive lives. If you do not know where to start, contact your college's Office of Disability Services or make an appointment with a counselor to get some ideas. In a short essay, summarize the purpose of the agency, and if possible, include details about the agency's success stories.

Looking Forward, Looking Back

Robert DeBlois

This is a first-person account of one man's adjustment to life as a quadriplegic. Television movies, Robert DeBlois notes, focus only on things physically sound people can relate to. Here is an alternately humorous and serious account of the annoyances, compromises, and possibilities in his life.

Words You May Need to Know

amid (para. 1)	among
repertoire (1)	list of songs they are prepared to perform
irony (1)	contradictory meanings
looms (1)	seems
pondering (1)	considering, meditating on
neurosurgeon (2)	a surgeon who deals with the brain and nerve tissue
in effect (2)	for practical purposes
bet the ranch (2)	hold out much hope for
in stride (2)	calmly
prognosis (4)	forecast or prediction
solemn (4)	serious
quadriplegic (4)	a person who suffers paralysis of the arms, legs, and the body below the level of a spinal cord injury
VA (5)	Veterans' Administration
claustrophobia (7)	fear of enclosed or narrow places
whim (7)	desire, odd idea
compromised (8)	damaged
nebulously (9)	vaguely, indistinctly
intrigued (10)	fascinated

the long haul (10)	long time period
ideals (10)	concepts or beliefs
simplicity (10)	freedom from complications
naive (10)	inexperienced, unsophisticated
imply (12)	indicate, suggest
mused (12)	thought, meditated
ambivalence (12)	uncertainty, mixed feelings
discernible (13)	distinguishable
evidenced (13)	shown
salvaged (13)	saved
stagnation (13)	not growing, not developing
stasis (13)	standing still, inactivity
anticipation (13)	hope, expectation
hokey (14)	excessively sentimental
absurd (14)	ridiculous

1   When I was in the spinal-cord injury, intensive-care unit of a Boston VA hospital, some union musicians would come in once a month, set up amid the beds of men who would not be walking again, and go through their repertoire. They always started with "The Way We Were" and seemed not to notice the irony of it. I hope they never came to a realization of its significance and stopped playing it out of fear of offending someone. It was an appropriate song. Time looms large at the beginning of the ordeal, and looking back at the past is more pleasant than pondering the future.

2   May 19, 1975, was a warm day in New Hampshire. I was twenty-one years old and had just finished my junior year at the University of New Hampshire. I went swimming in a nearby river, where I broke my neck when I dove onto a rock. Although not the most intelligent thing I had ever done, it was certainly the most dramatic. A few days later, when a neurosurgeon solemnly told me that, in effect, he

wouldn't bet the ranch on my walking again and that my arms would not be of much use, either, I took the news right in stride. The doctor was surprised and, I have always suspected, just a little disappointed. I think he was ready for a Hollywood performance in which I would rant and rave and swear through my tears that he was wrong and that, by God, I would walk again and, in fact, would start training for the next Olympics right then and there. "Bring me some barbells, please, Doctor."

Shortly after the doctor gave me the news, I was awakened one morning by my new nurse, Lollie Ball. As a symbol of snuffed-out youth, I had been getting the royal treatment by the staff, and Lollie was determined to put some discipline into my life. If the Pillsbury Doughboy had a middle-aged daughter, she would look like Lollie—a powdery white complexion, plump, and jolly behind her no-nonsense manner. "Time to wake up, Robert. Today we are going to brush our teeth." 3

Lollie was one of my first real annoyances after I got hurt, and in this respect she served an important purpose. Annoyances were something I was going to have to get used to. The doctor knew this when he gave me his prognosis. He was solemn because he understood the significance of my injury. Quadriplegic, to me, was just a word. 4

The most immediate annoyance I encountered was hospitals. One of the first thoughts I had after I came to on a grassy slope next to the river was that I would have to endure a couple of weeks in a hospital. It turned out to be six months, and all but the first was spent in a VA hospital, where I was given special permission to occupy an empty bed. 5

Another annoyance I couldn't anticipate when the doctor told me of my future was the lack of privacy I would have. This didn't mean I wouldn't be alone at times (although these times are infrequent). It did mean, though, that I could never really do anything while I was alone. Privacy is being able to do something with your aloneness. 6

The personal-care attendant entered my life. One spends a lot of energy when he has to spend forty hours a 7 week with someone who is paid to be a companion. Things can get annoying. Like the premed student who didn't know how to make a peanut-butter-and-jelly sandwich. Or the woman who insisted I was discriminating against her when I (my wife, really) wouldn't let her go topless when she worked around the yard, as had been the case with male attendants. Or the woman who had claustrophobia and could not ride elevators, sometimes leaving me to travel through a building at the whim of those who pushed the elevator call buttons.

8   Don't get the feeling it's all fun and games, though. Life became considerably more complex and required more compromise. I began to realize this when I moved to a VA hospital that specialized in spinal-cord injuries. Here the compromised future forced itself upon me in the form of bent-over old men in wheelchairs and men of all ages bedridden with urinary tract infections, made noticeable by blood-red urine in the bags attached to their beds.

9   If someone were to ask me what I feel I missed out on most, it would not be sex, athletic ability, or even the ability to walk. These are things that TV movies concentrate upon because they are easy for physically sound people to understand. What I feel I missed most was the opportunity to experiment with my ideals and ideas as I moved into adulthood, that "real world" which floats nebulously outside the gates of colleges where American adult-children prepare to answer the question, "What now?"

10   The question intrigued me. I was anxious to get to the real world, but in an instant the future was transformed into "the long haul." I found myself unable to test my ideals of simplicity, unable to learn that these ideals may have been naive, unable to learn through trial and error that life is, after all, complicated, that it is the rare person who gets to have his life on his own terms and call his own shots. The fact that I have come to these conclusions through another route is no consolation. The pain is in opportunity lost, experience missed.

11   When I graduated from college, I began teaching, which is what I had planned to do before I got hurt. Before the

accident though, teaching was just one of many possibilities. Afterward, it was one of the few realistic choices. And then marriage to the woman who was my girlfriend at the university, whose sense of loyalty is equal to our golden retriever's. Still, the romance was difficult, as was the decision to get married.

None of this is to imply that I regret what has happened 12 since the accident. But I cannot keep from wondering. As I understand it, Franklin Roosevelt once mused over whether he became president in spite of his paralysis or because of it. He was referring, I think, not to the public's sympathetic view of him but, rather, to his own ambivalence about his motives to take on challenges and, in effect, to prove himself.

For persons who wish to assign qualities of heroism to 13 those of us who have to live with readily discernible disabilities, I would suggest caution. That "normal" people are fascinated by different handicaps is evidenced by the way the media latched onto the disabled a few years ago. For a while there, being crippled almost became chic. The poorer films depicted characters who heroically salvaged happiness from pathetic despair. The better movies, such as "Coming Home," and "The Other Side of the Mountain," showed that courage does not really enter into the picture. The lack of alternatives takes the heroism out of it. Growth may be painful, but stagnation is more so. Being disabled, like being normal, is a process, not a stasis for which one easy approach or formula can be developed. This is an optimistic idea, not a pessimistic one. It means an anticipation and enthusiasm for the future can still be present. Time will not be denied, but it need not only be faced and endured.

This may be a little hokey, but then, being crippled is 14 also a little hokey, a little absurd, a little tragic, a little funny, a little fascinating, plenty weird, and plenty frustrating. Eleven years later, this is the way things are. Not exactly the way things were, but at least, looking forward is now about as easy as looking back.

DISCUSSION QUESTIONS

1. How did Robert DeBlois (the author) become paralyzed?
2. DeBlois says he took the news of his paralysis "in stride." How does his sense of humor emerge in this essay when he describes his doctor's "disappointment"?
3. What are some of the "annoyances" he encounters? Which annoyance seems to have bothered him the most?
4. When DeBlois talks about his regrets, what opportunity does he feel he missed out on the most?
5. "While growth is painful," he says, what is even more painful for him?

WRITING OPTIONS

Collaborate with Peers

1. Working with a partner or group, make a list of famous people whose lives changed suddenly because of an accident or illness. Discuss how these people coped: Did they continue to grow, exhibit courage, become advocates for the ill or disabled? Using the ideas you gather, write individual essays on two or three famous people who handled their physical misfortune with goodness and strength.

Connecting with the Author's Ideas

2. Read Robert DeBlois's description of his former nurse, Lollie Ball. Have you ever known such a "no-nonsense" person? If so, write a short essay describing how you met the person, how he or she acts, and how you respond to this type of person.

Other Options

3. Robert DeBlois clearly has a sense of humor that has helped him cope with adversity. In a paragraph or short essay, describe how a sense of humor helped you to cope with life's pressures or your relationships with others.
4. In a short essay, describe how a movie or television show unrealistically depicts the life of a disabled individual, and then describe how another movie or television show realistically depicts the life of a disabled person.

Chapter Nine
Victims into Victors

"You gain strength, courage, and confidence by every experience in which you really stop to look fear in the face . . . you must do the thing you think you cannot do."

Eleanor Roosevelt

The Siege of Khe Sanh

Rocky Darger, Captain, Helicopter Pilot, U.S. Marines

In 1968, the U.S. Marines combat base in Khe Sanh, South Vietnam was encircled by twenty thousand or more North Vietnamese troops. There was no place to hide. For seventy-seven days, the marines crouched in underground bunkers they built themselves, surrounded by the rumble of artillery, the relentless enemy shelling, and the U.S. bombing and shelling of North Vietnamese camps. Rocky Darger, a helicopter pilot, flew relief missions into Khe Sanh. In this article, which is a transcription of a taped interview, he describes those missions.

Words You May Need to Know

transcription (see above)	written record
LZs (para. 1)	landing zones
external (1)	outside
hover (1)	hanging suspended in the air
mortar rounds (2)	cannon fire
M-16s (3)	rifles
grunt (4)	foot soldier
taking rounds (5)	being hit by enemy fire
fuselage (5)	central structure
apt (5)	appropriate
hooch (6)	group
medevacs (7)	soldiers needing to be medically evacuated (rescued)
harrowing (7)	distressing
dire (7)	fearful
socked in (7)	surrounded by fog

forced recon team (8)	a reconnaissance (secret surveillance) team on an emergency search for military information in the field
NVA (8)	North Vietnamese Army
suppressing (8)	crushing or subduing
inevitability (8)	unavoidable outcome
thereafter (8)	afterwards
camaraderie (9)	close friendship, comradeship
duplicated (9)	copied
foxhole (9)	a small pit used for cover in a battle area

The zones that we went into consistently—Hill 861, 881 1
North, 881 South—those were the three primary zones we seemed to work the most. The weather was an absolute nightmare. We would single-handedly go in there because all the LZs were so small, you couldn't get in with more than one aircraft. But after a while, it seemed to be kind of a safer bet to go in with a lot of helicopters. Usually the number seemed to be eight, and then we would coordinate our timing to be in the LZ maybe thirty seconds apart, so you get all eight helicopters in there and out of there maybe in four or five minutes at the very most. We'd carry external loads when we were just doing resupply that would be hanging underneath the helicopter, and we would actually go in, do a quick hover, release the load in the zone, and then get out of there.

Occasionally, though, you'd be going in, and you'd be 2
dropping off troops, or you might be picking troops up, and then you would have to land. And when you did, the co-pilot's responsibility when you touched down to the ground was to push the stopwatch on the panel, and at twenty seconds, he'd start lifting the power, and we'd have to be out of there because within thirty seconds there'd be mortar rounds in the zone.

3   One day I remember sitting in the zone and looking down at a couple of Marines. They were in a trench right below me as we were sitting in the LZ, and they were sticking the M-16s up over the edge of the trench and shooting over the top of their heads. They didn't want to get their heads over the trench in view because all eyes were on us when these helicopters were in those LZs.

4   The one grunt on the ground I would have really liked to have met was the radioman that directed us to the LZ on Hill 861. Sometimes when we'd be coming there, knowing we were going to start taking fire and stuff right away, he would be standing on top of the command bunker to get a better view to help us get into the LZ. He didn't use normal radio chatter. It was more a real down-to-earth way of talking, and he was very comforting and very helpful. He actually got in trouble with some of the officers in his company because of the way he was talking to the pilots. We frankly got word out there and said, "Leave the guy alone. He's tremendous." I don't know his name. I'd sure love to find out.

5   When you're taking rounds, you can hear the clicking when they're hitting the fuselage of the plane, or you can see the instruments jump out in your lap because .30 caliber rounds come through the front of the helicopter. But you wouldn't hear anything other than when it finally hit the plane. You didn't know the mortar was there till it hit you. You might fly into 881 four days in a row and take no fire at all and the next day just get the living hell shot out of you. So you never knew. It was a big surprise, the biggest surprise. I remember someone describing being a helicopter crewman as hours and hours of boredom punctuated by moments of stark terror, and I think that's a pretty apt description because you might fly for three or four weeks and nothing would happen, and then in a period of one day, you'd be changing helicopters because the other ones were too shot up. And that's the way it went. Khe Sanh was like that.

6   Early on it was pretty intense. It was a major changing point in my life, going up there. You have to keep doing what

your job is, and you just get along. I don't know how else to describe it. There was a period in the hooch that I was in. We had ten pilots in there, and we lost four or five pilots in three days, not counting the crewmen that were on board, and you, you just go on.

The weather at Khe Sanh seemed to be a constant over- 7 cast. Sometimes, to resupply the hills leading to Khe Sanh, we would actually slide over the side of the mountain and just start sliding up through the fog, trying to get up to the top of the mountain to the outposts to resupply them and then, in turn, pick up medevacs and slide back down the side of the mountain till we had visual flight again. That could get a little harrowing. The difficulty in dealing with grunts is that they may be in dire need of ammunition or food or water, and because they were all socked in, they couldn't understand why we couldn't come in and just hover down through the clouds and land in their zone. Once you can't see outside, you don't know if you're flying backwards, forwards, sideways, or what. It was very frustrating sometimes when we wouldn't fly into their LZ that was completely zero-zero weather. That is to say, no visibility forward. You couldn't see anything. It was solid overcast. Solid fog.

I remember sitting in an LZ while we were trying to load 8 on a forced recon team of about five or six Marines; three of them were trying to carry two dead fellow Marines and all their equipment. We were trying to get them on board the helicopter. And they were under fire from a large number of NVA. We sat in the zone for over a minute and a half. I knew we weren't going to get out of there because we were taking all of this fire and we had no suppressing fire, and I accepted the fact that we were going to die there. I looked at Captain Weigand, and the only thing I could think to say was, "This is it," and he just nodded his head because we weren't going to leave until all those Marines were on board. At the same time, fifty to one hundred yards away, you could see these flashing lights all in the tree line shooting at us and lots of flashing lights. And it amazed me that anyone carrying a rifle could have just killed us because we were sitting there in this little glass cockpit and crewmen are in the back with little pieces of thin aluminum between them and death. We got everyone out of there, and no one was injured. I still don't understand it, to this day. I had accepted the inevitability that I was going to get killed. And once I did that, my sanity—I just didn't worry about it any more, and that was real early on. And thereafter, I had a different attitude about what I was doing. I have a different attitude about death today because of that.

9   The camaraderie that you have with people in that type of situation can't ever be duplicated. Things you do for the grunt on the ground, it's hard to imagine. You're willing to sacrifice your life, and if you're the decision maker, the aircraft commander, you may sacrifice the lives of four other people on the aircraft for one person. The one thing more than anything else I got of the entire experience was it seemed like everyone wouldn't trade places with the other guy. The grunts would always look at the helicopter crewmen and say, "God, I wouldn't do that for anything. At least I can hide in my hole." I think, on the other hand, when we were able to fly out of an LZ and fly back to the security of a larger base, we wouldn't have crawled into that foxhole for anything.

DISCUSSION QUESTIONS

1. According to Darger, how fast could eight relief helicopters get in and out of an LZ (landing zone) in Khe Sanh, a U.S. Marines combat zone in South Vietnam?
2. When a helicopter had to land to drop or pick up troops, what was the co-pilot's responsibility? What was the maximum amount of time the helicopter was supposed to stay on the ground? Why?
3. Why did Darger especially look forward to communicating with one of the foot soldiers, even though he did not know that "grunt's" name?
4. What is the "biggest surprise" for a helicopter pilot?
5. The job of a helicopter crewman is described as "hours and hours of boredom punctuated by moments of stark terror." Why does Darger think this description is an accurate one?

6. Why is overcast weather so frustrating for helicopter pilots, and what wouldn't the "grunts" understand?
7. What were the circumstances that made Darger believe he had no chance of surviving? Did this realization help or hurt his attitude?
8. What was "the one thing more than anything else" Darger learned from his experience as a helicopter pilot during the Vietnam War?

WRITING OPTIONS

Collaborate with Peers

1. With a group, discuss any war movies you have seen. Consider which movies seemed most realistic and what kinds of scenes and characters are often in war movies. After this discussion, write individual essays on how Rocky's Darger's personal account of war compares to the way war is depicted in many movies.

Connecting with the Author's Ideas

2. Darger describes the job of a helicopter crewman as one that involves mostly boredom with occasional "moments of stark terror." Write an essay describing three jobs that you feel fit this description. You can base your essay on dangerous jobs you have heard about, one you may have held, or ones that you research. If any of your friends or family members have held dangerous jobs, you may want to interview them for potential ideas.

Other Options

3. One of the jobs Rocky Darger says he would have liked was that of a radioman. In your own words, summarize that job of a radioman and his importance to pilots like Darger.
4. Darger states that the "camaraderie" he had with others who were in life or death situations "can't be duplicated." If you have experienced similar ties to others, describe the circumstances that led to this close bond, and then summarize some of the benefits you received from this relationship.

The Victim's Voice

Richard Jerome

Julie Alban is no stranger to violence. In 1988, after she tried to break up with her boyfriend, he shot her in the back. Paralyzed and confined to a wheelchair, Julie "channeled her pain, anger, and frustration" into earning her law degree. Determined to be "the best prosecutor ever," she now helps victims become victors not only in the courtroom but also in reclaiming their lives.

Words You May Need to Know

haltingly (para. 1)	hesitantly, in a stumbling manner
turbulent (1)	disturbed
jarred (3)	shocked
dilemma (3)	problem, difficult situation
launch (5)	started
crusade (5)	movement to promote a cause
advocate (5)	lawyer
avenger (5)	someone who seeks punishment for a wrong done to someone else
gilded (6)	bright, attractive
elite (6)	upper class
orthopedic (6)	related to the spine and bones
literally (6)	actually, really
oppressively (8)	like a burden
pressing (8)	urging
obsession (8)	domination of one's thoughts by one idea or desire
assumed (8)	supposed
hacienda (9)	ranch
whimpered (13)	cried with a low, broken sound

seeping (13)	oozing
compounding (14)	increasing
arraigned (16)	brought before the court to answer a charge
anguish (18)	suffering
immobile (18)	motionless
despondent (19)	depressed
Valium (19)	a tranquilizer
spasms (21)	sudden muscular contractions
gurney (22)	a four-wheeled structure for transporting hospital patients from place to place
adversaries (24)	opponents
recant (24)	withdraw a statement
confront (25)	face

A frightened woman speaks haltingly to Julie Alban, a thirty-one-year-old deputy prosecutor. Julie nods sympathetically as Lisa describes the night her boyfriend punched her in the eye. It was one blow too many in their turbulent relationship: For the first time, Lisa called the police. Now she must decide whether to speak out against the father of her baby—a man she says she still loves—or go home and forgive him once again.

Julie's advice is firm. "You don't want to stay with your boyfriend unless he gets counseling," she says, leaning forward in her wheelchair. "I'm very familiar with domestic violence. I'm in this chair because my ex-boyfriend tried to kill me."

Jarred out of her own dilemma, Lisa asks, "Oh my God, what happened?"

"I was breaking up with him," Julie answers, "and he shot me in the back."

That bullet shattered Julie's spine, paralyzing her below the waist. But she did not let it shatter her spirit. Instead, she used her anger, pain, and frustration as fuel to launch a legal career and a personal crusade against domestic violence. Since joining the Long Beach district attorney's office in 1993, she has prosecuted thousands of domestic violence cases, handling as many as twenty-five a day—mostly on behalf of women battered by their husbands and boyfriends. (Only fifteen of these cases have gone to trial. Most defendants plead no contest, then undergo counseling.) Amazingly, although Julie is a tough advocate, she is not a wild-eyed avenger.

6   Julie once enjoyed a gilded life among the California elite as the daughter of a wealthy orthopedic surgeon and a former teacher. In the fall of 1987, during her senior year at a university, Julie began dating a childhood playmate named Brad. Brad was then twenty-three, a one-time national junior tennis champion who was literally the boy next door.

7   At first, Julie felt she had found a soul mate. "Brad was so sensitive," she says. "He would cut roses from his parents' garden and bring them to my mother. He adored my father and even asked if he could call him Dad."

8   But Brad's feelings intensified too quickly for Julie. He began clinging to her oppressively and pressing her for marriage. However, neither she nor her family recognized Brad's behavior as a real obsession. Everyone assumed his feelings would pass.

9   Just before midnight on June 7, 1988, in the family room of the Albans' hacienda-style home, Julie broke off the affair. "I'll always love you. I'll always be your friend," she told him, "and you'll always be welcomed by my family." Brad's apartment was forty-five minutes away, so Julie invited him to sleep in the guest room.

10   At seven o'clock the next morning, she heard her bedroom door open. "I pretended to be asleep. Then I heard this tremendously loud blast, and I was thrown to the floor."

11   A moment later, Brad pointed the gun at his own chest and fired. Julie watched in horror and shock, not really aware that she had been wounded. She screamed for her parents, asleep at the other end of the house. When they

didn't respond, she dragged herself to the next room, where she called 911.

Finally waking to Julie's screams, her father raced 12 down the hall and gave CPR to the bleeding young man until paramedics arrived. Only then did he realize that Julie, still lying on the floor, was also in danger.

"Dad, I can't move my legs," Julie whimpered. When her 13 father rolled her over, her spinal fluid was seeping out.

Compounding his distress, Julie's father realized his 14 daughter had been shot with his own pistol. He belonged to the county sheriff's reserve, and he had invited Brad to the firing range the day before, afterwards leaving the gun in his unlocked car.

Julie and Brad were rushed to the hospital, where they 15 lay in the emergency room separated by a thin curtain. Julie overheard doctors saying Brad would survive. She told her mother through angry sobs, "He's going to walk out of here, and I'm never going to walk again."

Discharged from the hospital two weeks later, Brad was 16 arraigned for attempted murder. His wealthy parents, members of the same Long Beach elite, posted the five-hundred-thousand dollar bail, and he went home without serving any jail time.

Julie, meanwhile, began physical therapy. "I'd been an 17 active young woman, ready to take on the world," she says. "And here I was, having to learn what to do if I fell in the shower."

After a month, Julie, too, went home. One day, as she 18 lay anguished and immobile, she heard a familiar, repetitive "whup" through her bedroom window. It was the sound of Brad swatting tennis balls on his private court next door.

At his trial in December 1988, Brad claimed that he had 19 been despondent over gambling debts and had shot Julie accidentally, after overdosing on Valium. Unmoved, the jury convicted him. (Ultimately he served half of a fourteen-year prison term before his release on parole. He has since married.)

Julie last saw Brad in prison eight years ago, behind a 20 glass partition. "I wanted to hear him say 'I'm sorry,'" she says. Instead, Brad told the woman he had paralyzed for life, "The worst part of this is, I know your father hates me."

21   With Brad behind bars, Julie got on with her life—a very different life than before. She could no longer participate in the usual social activities of her circle of girlfriends—friendships that had been based mostly, as she recalls, on playing tennis and shopping for cocktail dresses. Instead, Julie learned to operate a specially equipped car, although spasms of pain prevented her from driving it. And in 1990, she entered law school, a lifelong dream.

22   Despite chronic pain—eventually eased by surgery to remove bullet and bone fragments from her spinal canal—Julie fulfilled her ambition. She even took one final exam while recuperating on a gurney, graduating on time in 1993.

23   After passing the bar exam, Julie applied for a job with the district attorney's office. "I told my future boss that I would be the most determined prosecutor he ever hired," she says, "because I had a personal commitment to victims he wasn't going to find in other people."

24   About that, even her legal adversaries agree. "The biggest problem the prosecution has in these cases is that most victims recant," says Bill Hoffman, a public defender who has battled Julie in domestic violence. "But Julie Alban helps these women find a voice."

25   Lisa appears to be one of them. After speaking with Julie, she agreed to confront her boyfriend in court. He pleaded no contest to misdemeanor domestic violence and was ordered to undergo counseling and perform community service.

26   "He can't just smack me whenever he doesn't like what I say," Lisa declares, with new firmness and self-respect. "I can't let what happened to Julie happen to me."

DISCUSSION QUESTIONS

1. Unfortunately, neither Julie Alban nor her parents realized something about Brad's behavior. What did they fail to notice?
2. Whose gun did Brad use, and how did he gain possession of it?
3. What excuse did Brad give for hurting Julie?

4. What did Julie want to hear Brad say, and what did she hear instead?
5. According to Bill Hoffman, a public defender who has argued in court with Julie, what is the main problem prosecutors have in domestic violence cases?
6. What caused Lisa to be more determined not to tolerate abuse, and what happened to her former boyfriend?

WRITING OPTIONS

Collaborate with Peers

1. With a partner or group, discuss why some people confuse obsessive behavior with true love. Consider how popular movies and music often confuse obsession with love. Then write individual essays about (1) the difference between obsessive behavior and loving behavior, or (2) how popular movies and music often confuse love and obsession.

Connecting with the Author's Ideas

2. The author states that "neither she [Julie] nor her family recognized Brad's behavior as a real obsession." If this tragedy had happened recently, do you think you would have considered Brad's behavior obsessive? Justify your view based on what you have experienced or read about obsessive behavior in relationships.

Other Options

3. The article notes that Julie had been shot with her father's pistol. If you or your family keeps a gun in the house, describe the safety measures you take to prevent accidents and tragedies.
4. What do you find most admirable about Julie's outlook? Once you identify that trait, write a paragraph or short essay about someone you know who exhibits the same trait.
5. Investigate an organization that can help individuals who feel threatened by a possessive person. You can start by interviewing some counselors on your campus, legal aid organizations, or law enforcement agencies. In a short essay, describe the types of services available for individuals who find themselves in potentially dangerous relationships or circumstances.

A Day in the Life of a Welfare Mom

Randi Londer Gould

Gloria Trenkle was secure knowing that she had found the right man to match her faith in God and desire for children. But after just a year of marriage, "the good times began to sour," as her husband turned his anger and violence against her. Gloria overcame financial and personal setbacks, enduring the punishing bureaucracy and indignity of the welfare system. She eventually became a straight-A student who knew, "There is no failure except in no longer trying."

Words You May Need to Know

whirlwind (para. 1)	rapid-moving, like a tornado
courtship (1)	the period when one partner romances the other before marriage
endearing (2)	lovable
renovations (2)	repairs and remodeling
dilapidated (2)	decayed, ruined
unencumbered (2)	not weighed down
sour (4)	go bad
Dr. Jekyll and Mr. Hyde (5)	In Robert Louis Stevenson's famous story, Dr. Jekyll was a doctor whose scientific research turned him into the evil Mr. Hyde at night.
fled (6)	ran away
succumbed (7)	gave in to
reluctantly (7)	unwillingly
huddled (7)	crowded closely together

eviction (8)	being forcibly expelled from a building
chaotic (9)	in total confusion or disorder
stifling (9)	suffocating
ushered (10)	led
caseworker (10)	a social worker assigned to study a family or individual's history and to try to improve conditions
scoured (11)	ranged over, in search of something
scrounged (11)	searched thoroughly and actively, especially by moving around, turning over, or looking through contents
self-sufficient (11)	able to supply one's own needs without outside help
super (12)	building superintendent
ironically (12)	in an unexpected twist
Pentecostal (13)	any of the Christian groups that emphasize the activity of the Holy Spirit, stress holiness of living, and express their religious feelings without restraint
fueled (14)	motivated
defunct (14)	no longer in effect; not operating
prerequisite (15)	in college, classes required before other classes can be taken
momentum (15)	moving force
comply (16)	meet with, obey

subsidy (16)	financial support
pro bono attorney (17)	a lawyer who works for the public good, that is, who donates some of his or her time to clients who cannot pay
dons (18)	puts on
geriatric (19)	related to the elderly

1   In the spring of 1988, Gloria Trenkle met the man of her dreams. In a whirlwind courtship, Gloria and Jay Neumair, a carpenter, got along perfectly. They shared a desire for family and a deep faith in God. Together they attended church four times a week. "I had always wanted to settle down and have children," Gloria says. "He was the man for me." In a modest wedding ceremony, the couple were married. "It was the most beautiful day of my life," Gloria says.

2   From the start, the couple lived in an endearing but drafty old house in Port Jefferson, New York, with Jay's elderly aunt. Gloria provided constant care for the 95-year-old, whom she grew to love. Jay kept busy with renovations on the dilapidated 130-year-old house. He brought in money by picking up construction work here and there. Unencumbered by rent, the couple socked away money so that Jay could one day start his own carpentry business.

3   They started a family right away. First came a baby boy, Matthew, and then a girl, Gloria Jean. Jay's business idea slowly took shape as they invested their savings in tools and a utility truck they named Old Blue. "We invested a lot of money," Gloria says. "I encouraged him because I knew he would be happier working for himself."

4   But in the summer of 1989, the good times began to sour. Money was tight, and after Jay's aunt died, they had to pay $600 a month in rent. Jay had trouble finding work, so Gloria sold her car for $11,500. "I let him handle our money, and I took care of the kids," she says. "I didn't even question it."

5   Jay's behavior changed. Often withdrawn and depressed, he disappeared for hours at a time and returned

intoxicated. "There were shouting and cruel insults," she recalls. "He was like Dr. Jekyll and Mr. Hyde when he drank. Sometimes he had this crazed look in his eyes." Gloria felt increasingly frustrated and fearful. "I couldn't understand how something so wonderful could go so bad," she says. "I used to play the audiotapes of our wedding ceremony and remember the happy days. I wished so much it had stayed that way."

One terrible night in March 1991, Jay was in a drunken 6 rage. "He yelled at me and threatened to kill me," she recalls. "He lifted me up by my pink jacket and hit my head against the kitchen cabinets." Screaming, Gloria tried calling the police, but Jay ripped the phone cord from the wall. She broke free and fled to a neighbor's house with the children. She spent the night in the emergency room of Stony Brook University Medical Center, where she was treated for cuts and bruises. Her spirit was badly broken.

Gloria filed a case in criminal court, but later succumbed 7 to Jay's pleading and apologies and dropped the charges. As a last-ditch effort to salvage her family, Gloria agreed to try again. "I prayed in my heart that he would get it right," she says. It was a choice she now regrets. Within weeks, Jay's violent temper resurfaced, but this time she stood up to him. Terrified and shaking, Gloria threatened to have him thrown in jail. Reluctantly, he left the house. Downstairs, Matthew and Gloria Jean huddled next to a bed. "I was scared for our lives," Gloria says. "I didn't know how far he would go."

Armed with a restraining order for protection, Gloria set 8 out to reclaim her life. But with so few options, the road would be a rough one. She had no family of her own to rely on. The bank account was empty, and the rent hadn't been paid for six months. A minimum-wage salary wouldn't cover living expenses and child care. "I felt so low," she says. "I had nowhere to go." Facing eviction, Gloria and the kids piled into their 1983 Volkswagen and drove to the Suffolk County social building in nearby Coram. As a last resort, they would have to sign up for public assistance.

An armed guard directed the young family to a crowded 9 room on the second floor. The walls were scuffed, and the plastic seats were torn and battered. A sign overhead set the tone: "NO WEAPONS, THREATS, CURSING, ALCOHOL, DRUGS, OR DISORDERLY CONDUCT." A clerk offered forms to fill out and point to a handwritten sign above: "PLEASE DO NOT ASK WHEN YOUR NAME WILL BE CALLED. WE DO NOT KNOW." The waiting area was chaotic. People shouted their complaints about the system. Mothers yelled at unhappy children. Men sat on duffel bags that bulged with belongings. The stifling air reeked of urine. "It was disgusting," Gloria says. "It felt like all hope had drained from that place. I worried how it would affect my kids."

10   Matthew and Gloria Jean passed the time playing with coloring books they had brought along. After waiting three hours, Gloria was ushered into a room where a case worker reviewed the family's personal documents—Social Security cards, birth certificates, tax returns, financial books from Jay's home-based business, an estimate on the car, and bank statements. She was told to come back the following week with additional records. But first, she had to be finger-printed. "I felt like a criminal," she says.

11   By early summer, after a half-dozen visits to the social services building, the application was approved. Each month the Neumair family would receive $598 for living expenses (rent, gas, garbage, electricity, and heat) and $198 in food stamps. Their life became an exercise in survival. Gloria clipped coupons to lower the cost of necessities. Diapers and baby formula were donated by local churches. And as neighborhood children grew out of their clothes, Matthew and Gloria Jean inherited them. "I was fortunate to have kind and generous neighbors," Gloria says. Every penny was accounted for, but the money was always gone before the end of the month. That's when family dinners were spent at church-sponsored soup kitchens. To raise cash, Gloria scoured the streets for refundable bottles and cans and scrounged the neighborhood for valuable castoffs. Once she found a patch of carpet, which she used to cover the floor in Gloria Jean's bedroom. Another time she picked up some yellow vinyl kitchen chairs. "I kept telling myself it wouldn't

last forever, and that I'd be self-sufficient again," she says. There were many sleepless nights spent searching for answers. "I never imagined I would end up on welfare."

For Gloria and the kids, the dilapidated old house had become an island of calm. Worried that the high rent would crush their tiny budget, Gloria bargained it down to $375. She also promised to handle maintenance and repairs. After borrowing instruction videos and books from the public library, she became the self-taught super. She installed a new shower. She patched holes in the ceiling and rebuilt the front porch stairs. Ironically, the woodworking skills she had learned from Jay came in handy.

Gloria's faith carried her through dark moments. Every Sunday, she traveled twenty-five miles to a Pentecostal church in Deer Park. Church members offered emotional and financial support. "I felt loved," she says. "It was a very difficult time, and I really needed caring hands." One Sunday, as Gloria prayed for guidance, she remembered the good times she'd spent with Jay's elderly aunt years before. The memories inspired an idea for a career. Gloria wanted to become a nurse. "It felt like a calling," she says. "I had to pursue it."

Fueled by blind faith, she applied to the department of nursing at Suffolk Community College. She was overjoyed when the acceptance letter arrived. To cover the high cost of tuition and books, she applied for financial aid from federal and state agencies. Again, her request was approved. "Things were falling into place," she says. Even welfare officials agreed to continue benefits under a now-defunct program for job-skills training and education. "For the first time in a long time, I had hope," says Gloria.

In the fall of 1993, Gloria became a full-time student. Before she could start the two-year nursing program, however, she had to complete a series of science prerequisites. A dedicated student, Gloria maintained a straight-A average. On the eve of the first semester of the nursing curriculum, however, her momentum came to a screeching halt. At a meeting with two welfare caseworkers, Gloria learned that her benefits had been cut. The two-year limit for education had been reached. She had two weeks to find a job. "I was beyond discouraged," Gloria says. "I felt I had worked so hard for nothing."

16   She appealed the system, but the system would not bend. The only words of advice came from one female caseworker who told Gloria to become a barmaid. "I had no idea what was going to happen," she says. "It was scary, but I focused on my goal. I wasn't about to give up then." A resourceful Gloria pressed on, coming up with different arrangements to comply with the agency's requirements. Finally, caseworkers met her halfway. Her subsidy was reduced by half, and Gloria would have to work part-time. Medicaid and food stamps remained untouched.

17   As the single mom struggled to keep her young family together and to stay in school, another chapter of her life was thankfully coming to a close. A pro bono attorney was putting the finishing touches on the divorce proceedings. In 1995 a judge granted sole custody of the children to Gloria and ordered Jay to pay $1200 a month in child support. By then, Jay had been gone for three years, and it was unlikely that the kids would get the financial support. For Gloria, the victory was bittersweet. "I don't like to think about it, but if he had followed through with his responsibilities, I would never have had to go on welfare," she says. "Even so, I was thrilled with the verdict. It meant that finally a certain kind of justice had been done for me. We may not ever see the money, but at least it's on the record that this man is responsible for the children."

18   Today, the rituals of daily life are the glue that holds the family together. Mornings begin with tooth-brushing at 7:00 A.M. By 7:45, Matthew and Gloria Jean catch the school bus in front of the house. Before Gloria heads off to college, she dons a carpenter's cap to finish a repair on the house. After class, Gloria skips lunch in order to get a head start on homework at the school's computer lab. Afternoons are spent working at an auto repair shop, and by 4:15 P.M., the kids return home. And after dinner, the trio of students gather at the kitchen table for study time. Before bed,

Matthew and Gloria Jean love reading stories and cuddling with their mother. Finally, it's lights out as Gloria breathes a sigh of relief that her family is safe and sound.

In just a few short months, Gloria will graduate with a 19 degree in nursing. After seven long and painful years, she will no longer need public assistance. Not surprisingly, she has chosen to specialize in geriatric nursing. "I love the wisdom of older people," she says. "So many people dismiss them, but they really have so much to contribute." She has already started the job hunt for a position at a hospital not far from home. The future looks bright for the children, too. Matthew, in fourth grade, and Gloria Jean, in third, have never missed a day of school. Like their mother, they are tops in their classes. "I want my kids to have opportunities in life," Gloria says. "I want them to go to college and make the right decisions. It bothers me that I've had to expose them to so much sacrifice, but we stuck it out as a team."

As for the welfare system, Gloria, now 39, has mixed 20 emotions. "They made it very difficult at times, and I wrestled with a lot of discouragement. I did everything they asked, but every interaction with the caseworkers felt like punishment," she says. "It was nerve-racking not to be in charge of my family's financial destiny. I never knew if some bill would pass and our lifeline would be cut. I survived because of my faith in God. The real truth is that welfare kept my family off the streets. And from this experience, I've lived a valuable lesson: There is no failure except in no longer trying. And when I'm independent, I will volunteer at a soup kitchen. I'm looking forward to being on the other side of the counter."

DISCUSSION QUESTIONS

1. What did Gloria Trenkle and Jay Neumair have in common that helped make her feel he was the right man to marry?
2. For whom did Gloria provide care, how did Jay earn money, and what was a long-term goal for Jay?

3. When and how did Jay's behavior change? Why did Gloria agree to try to save the marriage? How did she finally stand up to her husband?

4. Describe Gloria's ordeal of applying for public assistance, and explain why it made her "feel like a criminal." How many trips did Gloria make to the social services building before her application was approved?

5. Describe how Gloria and her children's lives became a collective "exercise in survival."

6. To help lower expenses, what skills did Gloria teach herself?

7. Describe how Gloria's faith and fellow church members helped her through the hard times.

8. What was Gloria's career goal, and what type of student was she at Suffolk Community College? What threatened to end her educational plans?

9. In 1995, a judge granted Gloria sole custody of her children. How much money was Jay ordered to pay for child support? Why is there little chance that Gloria will receive child support from Jay?

10. What are some of the daily rituals Gloria and her children follow? Which ones do you think are most important for providing a sense of stability for her children?

11. Why does Gloria want to specialize in geriatric nursing?

12. Although welfare did keep Gloria's family "off the streets," Gloria has mixed feeling about the welfare system. Explain why.

WRITING OPTIONS

Collaborate with Peers

1. Individuals who receive welfare are often stereotyped by those who have never received welfare or visited such an agency. Working with two or three classmates, list what you believe are the most common and harmful stereotypes about welfare recipients. Then, in individual paragraphs or a short essay, explain how Gloria Trenkle's behavior and attitude do not reflect these stereotypes.

Connecting with the Author's Ideas

2. When Gloria was living in poverty and searching the streets for usable throwaway goods, she comforted herself, she says, by "telling myself it wasn't going to last forever." Write about a time when you used the same words to give yourself hope.

Other Options

3. Gloria Trenkle's life changed drastically after only a year of marriage. In a brief essay, describe a time in your life when your goals or plans changed suddenly. Begin by describing what your life was like before this turning point; then describe what your life was like immediately after this turning point, and, finally, describe what your goals are now.

4. When Gloria first visited the Suffolk County Social Services building to sign up for public assistance, she noticed the bleak atmosphere of the area. In a paragraph or brief essay, describe the bleak atmosphere of an office or agency you have recently visited, and then describe a more cheerful office you have visited. Be sure to include specific and concrete details.

I Want to Save the World:
Ana Rodriguez

John Kasich

Ana Rodriguez was a victim of domestic violence for years. She was only sixteen and pregnant when the beatings began, and even her family thought she was the one at fault. After escaping the cycle of violence, she became a respected detective, telling others her own story in order to "save the world, one woman at a time."

Words You May Need to Know

articulate (para. 1)	able to use language easily and fluently
regarded (1)	thought of
exudes (1)	oozes, sends out
petrified (4)	rigid with fear
paranoid (6)	mentally ill, believing one is being persecuted by a person or persons
Valium (9)	a tranquilizer
spouses (9)	husbands or wives
urged (9)	strongly advised, pushed
incarcerated (11)	imprisoned
trauma (11)	shock
subservient (13)	submissive, inferior
vulnerable (14)	capable of being hurt
ferret (19)	hunt, search
proactive (20)	prepared, acting in advance
impact (21)	effect
panorama (22)	wide, changing scene
overwhelming (22)	overpowering

Ana Rodriguez is a tall, attractive, articulate, and highly 1 regarded police officer in Philadelphia. Today she exudes self-confidence, but that was not always true. Two decades ago, Ana lived with a man who beat her severely. For years, she lived in fear, unable to understand why no one would help her, almost convinced that she was herself to blame. Now, thanks to her remarkable strength of character, she has not only turned her own life around but dedicates herself to saving other women from the abuse that she knows all too well.

Ana's parents moved from Puerto Rico to Philadelphia 2 before she was born. At sixteen, she began living with a Hispanic man. "At sixteen you think you know it all," she says now. "Within a year I was pregnant. That was when the beatings began. My son was born when I was seventeen. After that the attacks became worse. He would beat me, bite me, kick me, give me black eyes, rape me, lock me in a room. Once he hung me out a second-floor window and threatened to drop me. He always said it was my fault, that it was because of things I did, and I accepted his excuses. At first I would fight back, but that only made it worse. I learned to take the beatings and keep quiet.

"When I called the police, they would see my black eye, 3 my split lip, but they would say, 'He's your husband; you have to listen to him, learn to get along with him.' Once I told the policeman, 'I was asleep and he woke me up and started beating me—how was I to blame?'

"I was always afraid. Petrified. When my parents found 4 out, they thought the beatings were my fault, too. I left him many times, but I would always go back. He threatened my parents, and in part I went back to protect them. I also went back because I thought I could heal him. Women are raised to heal. I thought I could change him.

"But there was no pleasing him. He was Latin; he was 5 macho. He was raised that way. His father beat his mother. It's about power and control. It's a man's way of saying, 'I'm the king—you must obey me!' Sometimes he would cry after he beat me. Once he gave me some matches and said, 'Burn my hands—I've got to stop this.' He felt great anger, and he had a problem with drugs and alcohol.

6   "The police, the neighbors, my family, everyone said I was at fault. Once I saw a psychiatrist, and she said I must be paranoid, must be exaggerating. She wanted me to take Valium. Sometimes I felt like I was going crazy. What is most painful now is realizing what my son went through. To live with that hurts a child emotionally. The end came when he beat our son. He was beating me, and our son, who was about three, came forward to protect me, and he hit him. I hit the man with something and knocked him down. When I went to see if he was okay, he sucker-punched me. I woke up in the bathtub, wet and bleeding.

7   "I got my son and caught a bus to New York. I remember how people looked at me—I had blood all over me. In New York, I stood in the bus station for four hours, not knowing what to do. I didn't have any money. Finally, I called my parents, and they said I should come back home and stay with them. At home, it was like I was a prisoner in my parents' house for a year. I was afraid to go out by myself. I was afraid of what he might do to me or to my family. Finally, he found another victim, another woman, and I though I might be safe from him. I'd been with him for five years. I think if I'd stayed much longer he would have killed me."

8   Ana went back to high school and got her degree. She took some college courses and became the manager of a department store. Her father encouraged her to take the test to join the police department, which she did in 1987. She graduated from the police academy and was assigned to patrol duties. "At first, I didn't tell people about my past. Then one day I responded to a domestic violence call. It was a young woman with a child, like I had been. She said, 'What do you know about it? You're a cop!' So I told her my story."

9   In 1990 she joined the victims' assistance program, which helped all victims of crime, including domestic violence, and in 1993 she moved to the department's newly formed Domestic Violence Unit, which focused exclusively on family members—not just lovers or spouses—who

abused one another. By then, things had begun to change. Police were less likely to ignore women who said their husbands beat them. New laws had been passed and were starting to be enforced. An officer didn't have to witness the domestic violence in order to make an arrest. Ana's job was to follow up every report of violence against a woman and offer her help. She urged abused women to consider their options, which include leaving the man and bringing charges against him.

"You really can't understand it unless you've been 10 through it," she says. "Why do they stay? Out of fear. Because it's cultural. For financial reasons. Because of the kids. Out of shame. Or because they think they love him. Domestic violence is a cycle. The woman loses self-esteem. He makes promises, and she wants to believe them. Statistically, women leave five to seven times before they leave for good. I left five times. I realized I had to talk about my past to make it heal."

Over the years, investigating hundreds of cases of 11 abuse, Ana has seen it all. "I've lost two women in five years, killed, and I take it personally. The two men, one killed himself; the other is in prison. Another woman, the ex-husband slashed her throat; she survived, and he's incarcerated now. Some women have had a finger cut off. Some are beaten unconscious. I deal with a lot of emotional trauma—I keep up contact with the women.

"They want the abuse to stop but not the abuser to 12 leave, for whatever reason, economic or because they think they love him or can heal him. So they go back. They want to believe he'll stop. But we'll see them again if he's not held accountable. The men go into the honeymoon stage—'I love you, I'll stop it'—but then it starts again.

"More women are prosecuting, bringing charges. We let 13 them know they're not by themselves, that they don't have to live that way. But whenever there's a domestic violence homicide, we lose a lot of them. They say, 'She had a protective order, and it didn't save her. I better go back to him—I don't want to wind up dead.' So many still believe it's their fault.

The husband tells them it's their fault. Some cultures tell women that they should be subservient to men. We're slowly changing that. Men need treatment as well as punishment. It's easier to change the law than to change attitudes."

14   Anna says there are two times in particular when women are at risk of abuse. The first is when they are pregnant. "The man doesn't know what will happen. She's not the same person. He's insecure. He thinks she may not love him anymore. He feels financial insecurity. Anger. And she is more vulnerable. She can't fight back. That's what happened to me. I had to protect my unborn child."

15   The other dangerous time is known to most Americans as Super Sunday. "This year, I did a radio show on the day of the Super Bowl, warning women about abuse. It's the combination of men drinking and gambling and getting angry when they lose their bets. They take it out on the women."

16   Asked if many men were getting counseling and if it helped, Anna says, "Men get treatment but no accountability. The judge sends them to an 'anger management' class, but the quality of the treatment isn't good, and they don't change. They just get a piece of paper signed.

17   "We need to reach the kids. I started a program called Positive Rap. I go to schools, and we do role playing. I ask them what a relationship should be. 'Is it okay to hit your girlfriend?' So many boys say yes. They say, 'I have to keep her in line.' He thinks he's the king of his castle. That's what they learn at home. Unless we change that, we're raising the next generation of abusers—and victims. Sometimes I ask the boys, 'Would it be okay for some guy to beat your sister?' They're not so sure about that. We try to talk to them about love, about what a relationship can be. When we raise kids, we have to teach them to be human beings first."

18   In 1997, Anna joined the Philadelphia District Attorney's Family Violence and Sexual Assault Unit, which prosecutes cases of child abuse, domestic violence, and adult sexual assault. She is a Detective One, investigating cases of abuse and preparing them for court. She likes this assignment because she thinks that, along with education and prevention,

some men need jail to stop their violence against women. Often, she says, men are given six months' probation for a first offense, but after that they often serve the time.

Ana's boss, Assistant District Attorney Charles Ehrlich, 19 says of her, "Ana does a great job. She relates very well with victims of domestic violence, and she can ferret out the truth about what really happened to make sure we have the facts before we go to court. She combines street smarts with a special sensitivity to people." In recent years, Ehrlich says, the number of domestic violence cases his office has prosecuted has more than doubled. The biggest challenge is getting women to testify against their husbands or boyfriends, and that is where Anna has been so effective.

Ana's job includes some community education work, 20 and beyond that she volunteers much of her off-duty time to her crusade against violence. "I do a lot on my own time. It's important for us to be proactive." She speaks at schools, churches, housing projects, hospitals, and community groups. She urges doctors to screen patients for signs of domestic violence. She tells of speaking at a medical school and having a student come up afterward and confess that she was a victim of violence.

When she tells audience about her own experiences, she 21 says, "sometimes I get emotional." She has hundreds of letters from abused women and from people who have heard her speak that testify to the impact she is having. Yet her own father told her he disapproved of her talking about her years as a victim. "I told him it was part of my healing," she says.

Asked if she is ever discouraged by the endless 22 panorama of violence she sees, she says, "Yes, sometimes it's overwhelming. I see so much suffering, and I think, 'How far have we come?' I have bad days." But then, she adds, "I get a call or a letter from some woman I've helped, and I can see hope. I want to save the world, but I realize I have to save it one woman at a time. Sometimes I get emotional when I tell the people about the pain I suffered. It's hard. But the only way we heal is to go back and understand what happened. Sometimes I get tired of telling my story, but then a woman says, 'Thank you; you've helped me,' and it's all worthwhile. I believe God put me here for a reason, and the reason is to help people deal with this problem."

DISCUSSION QUESTIONS

1. How old was Ana when she started living with a man, and when did she become pregnant? When did the beatings become worse?
2. What are some examples of the worst attacks she endured, and what does she say usually made her situation even worse?
3. When Ana told police about her circumstances, what was their response?
4. Who thought that Ana's beatings must be Ana's fault? Do these reactions surprise you?
5. What incident involving Ana's son became a turning point for her? What did she do?
6. After a year of living at her parents' house, Ana thought she might finally be safe after she learned something about her abuser. What did she learn?
7. Ana eventually returned to high school and graduated. Later, what did her father encourage her to do?
8. In 1993, Ana joined the Domestic Violence Unit. Among police, how had attitudes changed about domestic violence?
9. Ana believes there are "two times in particular when women are at risk of abuse." What are they?
10. Describe the program Ana started called "Positive Rap."
11. Ana enjoys being a "Detective One" with the Philadelphia District Attorney's Family Violence and Sexual Assault Unit. Why does she like this assignment, and what are her responsibilities?
12. Despite her bad days, what makes Ana believe she is doing important work and making a difference in the world?

WRITING OPTIONS

Collaborate with Peers

1. With two or three classmates, brainstorm some questions you would like to ask a detective who investigates causes of domestic

violence. Arrange an interview by calling your local police station or sheriff's office. After the interview, write an essay that summarizes the most surprising facts you learned. Arrange your details in emphatic order (least to most important).

Connecting with the Author's Ideas

2. Ana Rodriguez says, "The only way we heal is to go back and understand what happened." In a short essay, support her statement in one long or two or more short examples. The examples can come from your own experience of being hurt (physically or emotionally) or from the experiences of others you know or have read about. Describe not only the pain but also the healing.

Other Options

3. Ana Rodriguez speaks at schools and to community groups whenever possible. If you have attended a community or other public meeting where a speaker offered good advice on how to avoid becoming a victim of violence, summarize what the speaker said and why it was valuable information for you and, perhaps, your family.

4. Based on the article about Ana Rodriguez as well as your own observations or research, write a short essay describing some of the reasons that domestic violence happens so often in our culture. For each reason, you can also provide specific examples of the effects of such violence on family members and on family members' relationships.

New Directions

Maya Angelou

Back in 1903, Annie Johnson found herself at a crossroads in Alabama. Her marriage had ended, and she was left with little money and only a one-room house for herself and two toddlers. Even worse, the town's cotton gin and lumber mill would not hire her. Through sheer perseverance and common sense, she figured out a way to "cut a new path" and make the two factories work to her advantage.

Words You May Need to Know

toddling (para. 1)	walking with short, unsteady steps, like a young child
burdensome (1)	troublesome
conceded (2)	admitted
amicably (2)	in a friendly way
domestic (3)	a household worker
cotton gin (3)	a factory with a machine for separating cotton fibers from seeds
lumber mill (3)	a building in which lumber is sawed into boards by machinery
meticulously (4)	very carefully
sawmill (4)	a lumber mill
brazier (6)	a container that holds live coals, covered by a grill, used for cooking
savors (6)	food that smells and tastes good
lint (6)	cotton fibers
specters (6)	ghosts
balmy (9)	mild and soothing
hives of industry (9)	a place swarming with busy workers

assess (11)	evaluate, judge
looms (11)	rises in front of us
ominous (11)	threatening
resolve (11)	determination
unpalatable (11)	not acceptable

In 1903 Mrs. Annie Johnson of Arkansas found herself 1
with two toddling sons, very little money, and a slight ability
to read and add simple numbers. To this picture add a disas-
trous marriage and the burdensome fact that Mrs. Johnson
was "a Negro."

When she told her husband, Mr. William Johnson, of 2
her dissatisfaction with their marriage, he conceded that he,
too, found it to be less than he expected and had been se-
cretly hoping to leave and study religion. He added that God
was calling him not only to preach but to do so in Enid,
Oklahoma. He did not tell her that he knew a minister in
Enid with whom he could study and who had a friendly, un-
married daughter. They parted amicably, Annie keeping the
one-room house and William taking most of the cash to
carry himself to Oklahoma.

Annie, over six feet tall, big boned, decided that she 3
would not go to work as a domestic and leave her "precious
babes" to anyone else's care. There was no possibility of
being hired at the town's cotton gin or lumber mill, but
maybe there was a way to make the two factories work for
her. In her words, "I looked up the road I was going and
back the way I come, and since I wasn't satisfied, I decided
to step off the road and cut me a new path." She told herself
that she wasn't a fancy cook but that she could "mix groceries well enough to scare hunger away from starving a
man."

She made her plans meticulously and in secret. One 4
early evening, to see if she was ready, she placed stones in
two five-gallon pails and carried them three miles to the cotton gin. She rested a little, and then, discarding some rocks,
she walked in the darkness to the sawmill five miles farther

along the dirt road. On her way back to her little house and her babies, she dumped the remaining rocks along the path.

5   That same night she worked into the early hours boiling chicken and frying ham. She made dough and filled the rolled-out pastry with meat. At last she went to sleep.

6   The next morning she left her house carrying the meat pies, lard, an iron brazier and coals for a fire. Just before lunch she appeared in an empty lot behind the cotton gin. As the noon dinner bell rang, she dropped the savors into boiling fat, and the aroma rose and floated over to the workers who spilled out of the gin, covered with white lint, looking like specters.

7   Most workers had brought their lunches of pinto beans and biscuits or crackers, onions and cans of sardines, but they were tempted by the hot meat pies that Annie ladled out of the fat. She wrapped them in newspapers, which soaked up the grease, and offered them for sale at a nickel each. Although business was slow those first days, Annie was determined. She balanced her appearances between the two hours of activity.

8   So, on Monday if she offered hot fresh pies at the cotton gin and sold the remaining cooled-down pies at the lumber mill for three cents, then on Tuesday she went first to the lumber mill presenting fresh, just-cooked pies as the lumbermen covered in sawdust emerged from the mill.

9   For the next few years, on balmy spring days, blistering summer noons, and cold, wet, and wintry middays, Annie never disappointed her customers, who could count on seeing the tall, brown-skinned woman bent over her brazier, carefully turning the meat pies. When she felt certain that the workers had become dependent on her, she built a stall between the two hives of industry and let the men run to her for their lunchtime provisions.

10   She had indeed stepped from the road which seemed to have been chosen for her and cut herself a brand new path. In years that stall became a store where customers could buy cheese, meat, syrup, cookies, candy, writing tablets, pickles, canned goods, fresh fruit, soft drinks, coal, oil, and leather soles for worn-out shoes.

Each of us has the right and the responsibility to assess 11
the roads which lie ahead, and those over which we have
traveled, and if the future road looms ominous or unpromis-
ing, and the roads back uninviting, then we need to gather
our resolve and, carrying only the necessary baggage, step
off that road into another direction. If the new choice is also
unpalatable, without embarrassment, we must be ready to
change that as well.

DISCUSSION QUESTIONS

1. Annie and William Johnson both knew that their marriage was in
   trouble. What did William give as the reason for his wanting to
   leave the marriage, and what did he not tell her?
2. What did Annie keep after the marriage ended, and why did she
   decide not to work as a domestic?
3. Annie decided to "make the two factories" in her town work to
   her advantage. What was her plan, and what did she do to see if
   she was strong enough to put her plan to work?
4. Where and when did she first put her plan to work?
5. What attracted the factory workers to Annie's new business?
6. What did Annie offer "for a nickel each"?
7. What was her plan regarding what to offer at the cotton gin and
   lumber mill on certain days?
8. What did Annie build between the "two hives" of industry, and
   what did it become over the years? What did it offer its customers?
9. What advice does the author give about when we should "gather
   our resolve"?

WRITING OPTIONS

Collaborate with Peers

1. Working alone, freewrite for ten minutes about people (famous or
   not-so-famous) who became successful through hard work, perseverance, and common sense. Then, working with two or three
   people, read your freewriting aloud, and ask the group members
   to point out any part of your freewriting that could be the basis of

an essay called "The Path to Success." Repeat the process for each member of the group.

Connecting to the Author's Ideas

2. Maya Angelou says Annie had "stepped from the road which seemed to have been chosen for her and cut herself a hard, new path." If you or someone you know has taken a different path based on unexpected circumstances, write a short essay that describes the conditions leading up to this turning point, and then describe the changes that resulted from this sudden twist of fate.

Other Options

3. Over the years, Annie's customers were very loyal to her. If you know about a local restaurant or store whose customers are very loyal, write a short essay explaining the reasons for this loyalty. Interview the owner and two or three customers about the reason for the business's success over the years. Summarize these reasons in a paragraph or short essay.

Chapter Ten
Children As Role Models

"Parents learn a lot from their children about coping with life."
Muriel Spark

"No one has yet fully realized the wealth of sympathy, kindness, and generosity hidden in the soul of a child. The effort of every true education should be to unlock that treasure."
Emma Goldman

When Kevin Won

Janice M. Gibson

Kevin, a "slow" learner, loved basketball but had never made a basket. He was on a team that had never won a game, but he captured the hearts of fans and teammates one fateful night when everyone became winners.

Words You May Need to Know

    rapport (para. 1)   connection

    contagious (1)   catching, infectious

    thundered (8)   boomed

    infinite (10)   unlimited

1   If you had to choose one word to describe Kevin, it might have been "slow." He didn't learn his ABCs as fast as other kids. He never came first in the schoolyard races. However, Kevin had a special rapport with people. His smile was brighter than the sun in June; his heart bigger than the mountain sky. Kevin's enthusiasm for life was quite contagious, so when he discovered that the pastor at his church, Randy, was putting together a basketball team, his mother could only answer, "Yes, you may join."

2   Basketball became the center of Kevin's life. At practice, he worked so hard you'd have thought he was preparing for the NBA. He liked to stand in a certain spot near the free-throw line and shoot baskets. Patiently, he stood there throwing ball after ball, until finally it would swish through the hoop. "Look at me, Coach!" he'd yell at Randy, jumping up and down, his face just glowing with the thrill of it all.

3   The day before their first game, Coach Randy gave each player a bright red jersey. Kevin's eyes absolutely turned to stars when he saw his—number 12. He scrambled himself into the sleeves and scarcely ever took it off again. One Sunday morning, the sermon was interrupted by Kevin's excited voice. "Look, Coach!" He lifted his gray wool sweater to reveal his beautiful red jersey to God and everyone.

Kevin and his whole team truly loved basketball. But 4 just loving the game doesn't help you win. More balls fell out of the basket than into it, and the boys lost every game that season by very large margins, except one—the night it snowed and the other team couldn't make it to the game.

At the end of the season, the boys played in the church 5 league's tournament. As the last-place team, they drew the unfortunate spot of playing against the first-place team—the tall, undefeated first-place team. The game went pretty much as expected, and near the middle of the fourth quarter, Kevin's team stood nearly thirty points behind.

At that point, one of Kevin's teammates called time-out. 6 As he came to the side, Randy couldn't imagine why the time-out had been called. "Coach," said the boy, "this is our last game, and I know that Kevin has played in every game, but he's never made a basket. I think we should let Kevin make a basket." With the game completely out of reach, the idea seemed reasonable, so plans were made. Every time Kevin's team had the ball, Kevin was to stand in his special spot near the free-throw line and they would give him the ball. Kevin skipped extra high as he went back onto the court.

His first shot bounced around but missed. Number 17 7 from the other team swiped the ball and took it down to the other end, scoring two more points. As soon as Kevin's team had the ball again, they passed it to Kevin, who obediently stood in his place. But he missed again. This pattern continued a few times until Number 17 grew wise. He grabbed one of the rebounds and instead of running down the court, he threw the ball to Kevin, who shot . . . and missed again.

Soon, all the players were circling Kevin, throwing the 8 ball to him and clapping for him. It took the spectators just a little longer to figure out what was happening, but little by little, people started to stand up and clap their hands. The whole gymnasium thundered with the clapping, hollering, chanting, "Kevin! Kevin!" And Kevin just kept shooting.

Coach Randy realized the game must be over. He looked 9 up at the clock, which was frozen with 46 seconds left. The referees stood by the scoring table, cheering and clapping like everyone else. The whole world was stopped, waiting and waiting for Kevin.

10   Finally, after an infinite amount of tries, the ball took one miraculous bounce and went in. Kevin's arms shot high into the air, and he shouted, "I won! I won!" The clock ticked off the last few seconds, and the first-place team remained undefeated. But on that evening, everyone left the game truly feeling like a winner.

DISCUSSION QUESTIONS

1. Although Kevin was slow in schoolwork, what were some of his special qualities?
2. Before the first game, what did the coach give each player, and what did Kevin do to show his enthusiasm during a sermon?
3. What place was Kevin's team in the church league's tournament?
4. In the last game, what did one of Kevin's teammates do that was both unusual and compassionate?
5. What did all the players, fans, and referees start rooting for?
6. The first place team still remained undefeated, but the author, Janice M. Gibson, notes that "on that evening, everyone left the game truly feeling like a winner." Why?

WRITING OPTIONS

Collaborate with Peers

1. Assume that you are the coach of Kevin's team and that you have to prepare this last-place team to play the league's first-place team. Write the speech (or "pep talk") that you would make to them, emphasizing and praising their spirit of determination despite their being outmatched by their opponents all season. Read your draft to one or two students for their comments.

Connecting with the Author's Ideas

2. Gibson says that Kevin "had a special rapport with people," and his "enthusiasm for life was quite contagious." Have you ever

known a child who has a similar personality and outlook? Describe that individual so that your reader will have a clear idea of the child's admirable qualities.

Other Options

3. You have probably observed or experienced poor sportsmanship at some sporting events, but you have probably observed outstanding conduct at some others. Using as many specific details as possible, describe the worst example of poor sportsmanship you have observed, and then describe the best example of good sportsmanship.

4. Write an essay defending or opposing the emphasis on sports at the high school level. As preliminary work, make a list of pros and cons, see which is longer, and then develop your essay based on the longer list.

My New Hero? She's a Courageous Four-and-a-Half-Year-Old

Dan Evans, Jr.

Heroes come in all shapes and sizes. Here's one example of how a frail four-and-a-half-year-old girl's optimism and compassion during a bout of cancer made her a hero and role model to her father.

Words You May Need to Know

infectious (para. 1)	catching
chemotherapy (2)	treatment of disease with chemicals or drugs
radiation (2)	treatment of disease with energy, rays, or waves
stoically (2)	calmly
stroll (4)	leisurely walk
nobility (7)	superior character

1   My hero? On a good day she weighs forty pounds. Hair? Non-existent. Smile? Infectious. Attitude? It never ceases to amaze me.

2   For the past year, my four-and-a-half-year-old daughter, Eloise, has suffered through thirteen rounds of chemotherapy, twenty-eight days of radiation, several surgical procedures, more than a hundred days in the hospital and countless tests to treat cancer. Through all of this, she has fought her battle stoically and courageously.

3   She quickly became one with her treatment, deeply interested in all that was going on around her. A terrific patient, Eloise was always willing and able to help. "Can I flush my line?" was a common request.

4   I remember one night, early in her treatment, when we took a late-night stroll around our wing at Children's Hospital. We bumped into our nurse, who for various reasons was

having a difficult night. As Tina stopped for a moment to say "Hi," Eloise said to her, "I know you're having a tough night, but I love you." After she fell asleep that night, I held her hand and cried for half an hour, realizing just how lucky I was to have such a wonderful kid.

Sure, she's had bad days. We remember the many times 5 we held her hand as she threw up, saying between gasps, "I'm OK! Don't worry about me!" Or the countless shots I had the privilege to administer as she looked me in the eye and told me it was OK and that I was good at giving the shot. Her reward was a Band-Aid she would pick from the countless boxes that filled our shelves. My reward was a big hug. I know I got the better deal.

We witnessed much in the past year. We came to know 6 families whose suffering was far worse than ours, as cancer took their son or daughter away from them. And others still who survived treatment and are now well on their way to recovery. We grew increasingly frustrated with the health-care system, but at the same time realized how fortunate we are to have great health insurance and a facility like Children's Hospital in our backyard. As Dickens said in *A Tale of Two Cities,* "It was the best of times; it was the worst of times."

Heroism is defined as "great courage, nobility." When I 7 was growing up, my heroes were athletes: Mays, Namath, Biletnikoff, Bench, Clemente, and anyone who played football for the University of Washington. I now have a new hero. Her name is Eloise, and she's four-and-a-half-years old.

(Shortly after this article was written, Eloise completed her treatment and, at age five, had a clean bill of health.)

DISCUSSION QUESTIONS

1. What do you find most admirable about Eloise?
2. What is an example of Eloise's concern for others?
3. What are two examples of Eloise's positive personality?

4. Before his daughter became his hero, who were the author's heroes? What do these earlier heroes all have in common?

5. Eloise's father quotes Charles Dickens's famous line, "It was the best of times; it was the worst of times." Explain how Eloise's bout with cancer reflects this statement.

WRITING OPTIONS

Collaborate with Peers

1. With one or two classmates, brainstorm about what it takes to face a serious illness. You are looking for a list of positive traits that can help a person deal with fear, pain, uncertainty, and loss. Come up with at least five traits. Once you have that list, write individual papers about the three traits you think are most important in facing a serious illness.

Connecting with the Author's Ideas

2. Dan Evans, Jr., Eloise's father, says that some define a hero as a person "of great courage, nobility." Define what the word "hero" means to you, and then describe how an individual you know fits this description. Provide as many example as you can from your observations of, or experiences with, this person.

Other Options

3. Eloise is very mature for her age. In a paragraph or short essay, describe what adults could learn from her about facing challenges.

4. Write about a time when you were ill. You do not have to write about a serious illness, but try to remember a time when you felt bad, both physically and emotionally. Describe those feelings and how you coped with them.

The Bullies on the Bus

Kitty Oliver

Young bullies often gain power on school grounds, but the real world is a different story. In this narrative, the author recounts both her fear of and grudging admiration for a bully whose brief "moment of heroism" occurs on a segregated public bus.

Words You May Need to Know

pitiable (para. 2)	miserable
viable (4)	practical, workable
bravado (5)	bluster, a swaggering display of courage
cringed (6)	crouched in fear
crinolines (6)	stiff petticoats
snickering (6)	laughing disrespectfully
nape (9)	the back of the neck
reprimand (9)	scold severely
defiance (9)	resistance
formidable (10)	strong, intimidating
foe (10)	enemy

The No. 7 bus maneuvered out of late-afternoon traffic 1 toward the three teen-aged black girls who waited at the curb. They were a couple of years older than I and had already graduated, but we had a history.

They used to hang out near our high school and make 2 fun of us underclassmen who wore black and white saddle oxfords instead of pumps, and ribbons instead of barrettes in our hair. "Here comes the girl who looks like she's pregnant in the front and the back," they would catcall at me when boys were around. I started arriving for homeroom at the last bell, and I'd enter through a side door just to avoid their threats and mean-spiritedness. In the minority community I grew up in, however, this was considered a pitiable strategy. Life was cruel, we were told, and we had to be tough to survive. The battle lessons began as soon as we entered elementary school.

3   Once, some class bullies spread the word that I had been "chosen" that week for the Friday after-school fight. I took another route home that day. At one point, panting and praying, I glanced back at the playground to see if I was being followed. To my surprise, the bullies and spectators were still milling around, expecting me to come back.

4   The next Monday, I was forgotten, as they whispered a new victim's name. But avoidance was only a temporary solution. The self-appointed teacher in junior high was a tomboy band trumpeter who hung around the bathroom challenging girls to fight their way out. The day my turn came, my first choice—to take up permanent residence in a stall—didn't seem viable.

5   "Go ahead and hit me," I said, finally walking up to her and swallowing hard. Her stomach punch sucked up all of the air in my body as I coughed and tried not to gag. She waited, fist clenched and ready again, but I didn't fight back, out of paralytic fear, not bravado. She seemed surprised by the reaction. After that, she decided our confrontation had made us friends and would brag about how I could "stand there and take it." But I couldn't understand why our people felt we had the right—the obligation even—to assault each other, just because the world outside could treat us even worse.

6   The girls waiting for No. 7 now wore grown-up variations of the popular French roll and curly hairstyles, but I still cringed at the lingering scent of trouble. Their wide gathered skirts rustled with starch and crinolines as they climbed up the stairs in single file to pay their fares. The first two cut their eyes past the empty seats at the front and

headed to the back and sat down in the seat directly behind me, snickering with mischief.

The third girl's token bounced into the metal container. 7 I don't know what caused me to keep watching her. There was something about the way she stood there for a moment longer than the others, surveying seated passengers as the door closed and the bus grunted off. Her mouth set hard as her head swivelled and stopped, facing the long front seat with a side view of the driver.

A white man, middle-aged and muscular in a white T- 8 shirt, sat alone, hugging the seat corner closest to the door. He braced himself with his right hand gripped around the metal pole. In the split second that it took me to realize her intent, she spun around and sat down, a good foot away from the man. Cradling her shopping bag in her lap, she seemed to concentrate on some point beyond the window, behind the seat, and far past the white people facing her across the aisle.

Not a word was said. The man swung his left hand 9 around her back in a reflex action. His fingers clamped the nape of her neck the way you reprimand a disobedient animal, and he shoved her forward—hard. She lurched off the bench, scrambling to stay upright and keep a hold on her bag. Straightening herself quickly, she swish-hipped toward the back of the bus, her face emptied of defiance. The other blacks in the bus avoided looking her way.

No. 7 squealed and slowed to another stop. Instead of 10 sitting down, the girl nodded a signal to her two friends, who jumped up, and they piled out in a rush. "Troublemakers," muttered the old woman sitting next to me. Good, I thought. All those battle lessons didn't help her much when she encountered a formidable foe in the outside world.

But I couldn't deny her the brief moment of real hero- 11 ism I saw. Not the confrontation. It was when she stumbled, and nearly fell, but managed to regain her footing and keep on moving—past her anger and humiliation. Grudgingly, I felt a tinge of admiration.

DISCUSSION QUESTIONS

1. The author, Kitty Oliver, says she first used avoidance strategies to keep herself safe from the bullies at school. But the minority community she lived in felt she should react differently. Why did the community feel this way, and how did it feel she should react?
2. Oliver says that the girl who hit her "seemed surprised." Why?
3. What was difficult for Oliver to understand?
4. When the three girls boarded the No. 7 bus, what did Oliver already know about them, and what was her experience with them?
5. In the era of bus segregation, one of the three girls who got on the bus sat where she was not supposed to sit. Explain.
6. What did the man "hugging the seat corner closest to the door" do to the girl who sat down "a good foot away" from him?
7. How did the girl react? Did she try to maintain her composure?
8. Who avoided looking at the girl?
9. Oliver was glad the girl had encountered a "formidable foe" in the outside world but couldn't deny her "the brief moment of real heroism." What did Oliver admire about this girl?

WRITING OPTIONS

Collaborate with Peers

1. Working in a group, define the word "bully." What makes a person a bully? After you have agreed on a definition, write individual paragraphs or essays supporting that definition with examples of bullying.

Connecting with the Author's Ideas

2. Oliver says that she was raised to believe that she "had to be tough to survive." Write a paragraph or essay about both positive and negative results of living by this belief.

Other Options

3. In a paragraph, summarize the reasons you think bullies lash out at others.

4. If you were ever the target of a bully, describe this person's behavior, your reaction, and the reaction of others who observed this negative behavior.

5. Some individuals allow themselves to be swayed by peer pressure and may even participate in hurtful behavior. Based on your own experiences growing up, write an essay describing how peer pressure can be a negative influence at school, work, or social events.

The Little Girl Who Dared to Wish

Alan D. Shultz

Ever since Amy Hagadorn started the third grade, she had constantly been teased about the effects of her cerebral palsy. Her simple but heartfelt letter to Santa Claus not only stopped the teasing, but it was literally a wish heard round the world.

Words You May Need to Know

smirk (para. 1)	offensive smile
mimicked (1)	imitated
cerebral palsy (3)	a crippling condition caused by brain injury
glimpsed (6)	briefly glanced
proclaimed (8)	announced, declared

1   As Amy Hagadorn rounded the corner across the hall from her classroom, she collided with a tall boy from the fifth grade running in the opposite direction. "Watch it, Squirt," the boy yelled, as he dodged around the little third grader. Then, with a smirk on his face, the boy took hold of his right leg and mimicked the way Amy limped when she walked. Amy closed her eyes for a moment. *Ignore him,* she told herself as she headed for her classroom. But at the end of the day, Amy was still thinking about the tall boy's teasing. Ever since Amy started the third grade, someone teased her every day about her speech or her limping. Sometimes, even in a classroom full of other students, the teasing made her feel all alone.

2   At the dinner table that evening, Amy was quiet. Knowing that things were not going well at school, Patti Hagadorn was happy to have some exciting news to share with her daughter. "There's a Christmas wish contest at the local radio station," she announced. "Write a letter to Santa and you might win a prize. I think someone with blond curly hair

at this table should enter." Amy giggled and out came pencil and paper. "Dear Santa Claus," she began. While Amy worked away at her best printing, the rest of the family tried to figure out what she might ask from Santa. Amy's sister, Jamie, and Amy's mom both thought a three-foot Barbie doll would top Amy's wish list. Amy's dad guessed a picture book. But Amy wouldn't reveal her secret Christmas wish.

At the radio station WJLT in Fort Wayne, Indiana, let- 3 ters poured in for the Christmas Wish contest. The workers had fun reading about all the different presents the boys and girls from across the city wanted for Christmas. When Amy's letter arrived at the radio station, manager Lee Tobin read it carefully.

Dear Santa Claus,

My name is Amy. I am nine years old. I have a problem at school. Can you help me, Santa? Kids laugh at me because of the way I walk and run and talk. I have cerebral palsy. I just want one day where no one laughs at me or makes fun of me.

Love, Amy

Lee's heart ached as he read the letter: He knew cere- 4 bral palsy was a muscle disorder that might confuse Amy's schoolmates. He thought it would be good for the people of Fort Wayne to hear about this special little girl and her unusual wish. Mr. Tobin called up the local newspaper.

The next day, a picture of Amy and her letter to Santa 5 made the front page of the *News Sentinel.* The story spread quickly. Across the country, newspapers and radio and television stations reported the story of the little girl in Fort Wayne, Indiana, who asked for such a simple, yet remarkable Christmas gift—just one day without teasing.

Suddenly, the postman was a regular at the Hagadorn 6 house. Envelopes of all sizes addressed to Amy arrived daily from children and adults all across the nation, filled with holiday greetings and words of encouragement. During that busy Christmas season, over two thousand people from all over the world sent Amy letters of friendship and support. Some of the writers had disabilities; some had been teased as children, but each writer had a special message for Amy. Through the cards and letters from strangers, Amy glimpsed a world full of people who truly cared about each other. She realized that no form or amount of teasing could ever make her feel lonely again.

7   Many people thanked Amy for being brave enough to speak up. Others encouraged her to ignore the teasing and to carry her head high. Lynn, a sixth-grader from Texas, sent this message:

> I'd like to be your friend, and if you want to visit me, we could have fun. No one will make fun of us, because if they do, we will not even hear them.

8   Amy did get her wish of a special day without teasing at South Wayne Elementary School. Additionally, everyone at school got an added bonus. Teachers and students talked together about how teasing can make others feel. That year, the Fort Wayne mayor officially proclaimed December 21 as Amy Jo Hagadorn Day throughout the city. The mayor explained that by daring to make such a simple wish, Amy taught a universal lesson. "Everyone," said the mayor, "wants and deserves to be treated with respect, dignity, and warmth."

DISCUSSION QUESTIONS

1. When did the daily teasing start for Amy, and how did it make her feel?
2. What contest did Patti Hagadorn encourage Amy to enter?
3. What did Amy's mother and sister think she would ask for from Santa? What did Amy's father think would be her wish?
4. In her letter to Santa Claus, what did Amy ask for?
5. What did the manager at the radio station do after he read Amy's letter?

6. How did the story of Amy's letter spread quickly, and how many people from "all over the world" sent Amy encouraging letters?
7. What advice for Amy did some of the letters contain?
8. As a result of her simple Christmas wish, what special events occurred at Amy's school and at Fort Wayne?

WRITING OPTIONS

Collaborate with Peers

1. With two or three of your classmates, recall some specific examples of teasing you experienced or observed in high school. Then discuss some of the harmful effects of this teasing. Summarize these effects in individual paragraphs or short essays.

Connecting with the Author's Ideas

2. Alan D. Shultz writes about a child who asks for "a simple, yet remarkable gift," one that can't be paid for with money or wrapped in a box and tied with a bow. Write about another "simple yet remarkable gift" that you might wish for, and explain why you want it.

Other Options

3. Assume your brother or sister (or son or daughter) is being constantly teased at school and has told you about it. In a short essay, explain what you would do to find out the nature of this teasing, and summarize the advice you would offer, depending on how serious or hurtful the teasing has become.
4. Sometimes friends tease each other good-naturedly. What distinguishes this type of teasing or kidding from hurtful ridicule? In a short essay, first describe the similarities between teasing and ridicule, and then describe the differences. Use as many specific examples as possible so that the distinctions are clear.
5. Assume you are teaching an elementary school class and that you have become aware that some children are being ridiculed by others. Describe the methods you would use to diminish or stop this type of hurtful behavior in your classroom.

Anne Frank's Legacy

Miep Gies

Miep Gies helped hide Anne Frank and her family for more than two years (1942–1944) during World War II. It was she who found and saved Anne's diary after the Franks were captured by the Nazis. This article is an excerpt from a speech Miep Gies delivered in June 1996 at a meeting of the Anti-Defamation League, an organization devoted to human rights, where she received an award.

Words You May Need to Know

too-liberal (para. 3)	too free
yield (4)	give in
stow (10)	put, pack
Auschwitz (17)	the site of a Nazi concentration camp

1   We should explain to our children that caring only about our own business can be wrong. When in Germany, step by step, Jewish life was destroyed, most people, all over the world, looked the other way because they thought it was safer to keep out. However, during the Holocaust, not only did six million Jews die, but ten times that number of non-Jews as well. Not only Jews lost what they had, but others lost billions and billions, too. This teaches that if injustice happens to your neighbor, there is no guarantee that it will not come to your home, that it will stop at your doorstep. Therefore, we should *never* be bystanders, because, as we have seen years ago, that can be very dangerous to ourselves as well.

2   I feel very strongly that we cannot wait for others to make this world a better place. We ourselves should make this happen in our own homes and schools by carefully examining the manner in which we act and by closely examining the ways we speak and express our opinions about other people, particularly in the presence of children. We should never forget the victims of the Holocaust. I myself always think of the family Frank, the family van Daan, and the

dentist Dussel. Van Daan and Dussel are the names Anne gave them; their names were Van Pels and Pfeffer. Also, some helpers got others names from Anne, but not for me. Why did she decide to use my own name? That answer I will never receive, but it touches me very much. She probably felt too close to me to alter my name.

Together with Jan, my husband, we were a total of five 3 helpers. We all had our own tasks. In the morning, I had to enter the hiding place to pick up the shopping list. When I came in, nobody would speak; they would just stand in line and wait for me to begin. This was always an awful moment for me because it showed that those fine people felt so dependent on us, the helpers. They would silently look up to me, except for Anne, who, in a cheerful tone, used to say, "Hello, Miep, what is the news?" Her mother disliked this very strongly, and I knew that the other people in hiding would afterward blame Otto (Anne's father) for what they would call "proof of a too-liberal upbringing!"

What struck me most about Anne was her curiosity. 4 She always asked me about everything that went on outside and not only that. She knew that I had just married, and therefore, she hoped that I would tell her more about being so close to another person. Well, I did not yield to that, and that must have disappointed her. However, usually I shared all my information with her.

Anne felt very strongly about her privacy, which I discov- 5 ered when I once entered the room where she was writing her diary. From her eyes, I saw that she was angry; maybe she thought I was spying on her, which was not true, of course. At that moment, her mother came in and said, when she noticed the tense situation, "Oh, Miep, you should know that our daughter keeps a diary." As if I did not know that; I was the one who always gave her the paper. Anne closed her diary with a bang, lifted up her head, looked at me, and said, "Yes, and I am writing about you, too." Then she left, slamming the door behind her. I hurried back to my office, quite upset.

However, usually Anne was a friendly and very charm- 6 ing girl. I say "girl," but talking to her gave me the surprising feeling of speaking to a much older person. No wonder, since the situation made Anne grow very quickly from child to young adult. I did not pay much attention to this because there were all the other things, like my daily care for eleven people: my husband and I, eight in the attic and also a non-Jewish student, wanted by the Germans, who we were hiding in our home. Otto Frank did not know about this student. He would have forbidden it. "You take too much risk, Miep," he would have said.

7   The children-in-hiding had a hard time. They missed so much. They could not play outdoors and could not meet with friends. They could hardly move. We did all that was possible to help them, but freedom we could not give them. This was one of the most painful things for me.

8   Every year on the fourth of August, I close the curtains of my home and do not answer the doorbell and the telephone. It is the day that my Jewish friends were taken away. I have never overcome that shock. I loved and admired them so much. For two years, eight people had to live together in a very small space. They had little food and were not allowed to go out. They could not speak to their friends and family. On top of that came the fear, every hour of the day. I have no words to describe these people who were still always friendly and grateful. Yes, I do have a word: They were *heroes, true heroes.*

9   People sometimes call me a hero. I don't like it because people should never think that you have to be a very special person to help those that need you. I myself am just a very common person. I simply had no choice because I could foresee many, many sleepless nights and a life filled with regret if I refused to help the Franks. And this was not the kind of life I was looking forward to. I have wept countless times when I have thought of my dear friends, but I am happy that these were not tears of remorse for refusing to help. Remorse can be worse than losing your life.

10   I could *not* save Anne's life, but I could help her live another two years. In those two years she wrote her diary, one in which millions of people find hope and inspiration. I am

also grateful that I could save this wonderful diary. When I found it, lying all over the floor in the hiding place, I decided to stow it away in order to give it back to Anne when she would return. I wanted to see her smile and hear her say, "Oh, Miep, my diary!" But after a terrible time of waiting and hoping, word came that Anne had died. At that moment, I went to Otto Frank, Anne's father, the only one of the family who had survived, and gave him Anne's diary. "This is what Anne has left," I said to him. "These are her words." Can you see how this man looked at me? He had lost his wife and two children, but he *had* Anne's diary. It was a very, very moving moment.

Again, I could not save Anne's life. However, I did save 11 her diary, and by that I could help her most important dream come true. In her diary she tells us that she wants to live on after her death. Now her diary makes her really live on, in a most powerful way. And that helps me in those many hours of deep grief. It also shows us that even if helping may fail to achieve everything, it is better to try than to do nothing.

Those who read the diary are surprised by Anne's wis- 12 dom. Even Otto Frank had no clue about the deep thoughts of Anne. "I must have made a mistake," he once said. "I loved her so much, but at the same time I must have given her the feeling that I looked at her as just a child, and she therefore kept her ideas for herself, being afraid that I would not accept them." Otto also felt that this explained her sometimes angry and unruly behavior. So, what about our own children? Do we really respect them, and do we really listen to them? Under our own roof, they may feel just as lonely as Anne Frank once did.

Otto told me to read the diary, but in the beginning, I 13 refused because I was afraid that it would give me more pain. But when I finally started to read it, all my dear friends came back to life. Again, I heard their voices, their laughs, their arguments. It was really wonderful. Of course I wept a lot while reading, but basically I felt very happy. Anne and all the other people were back with me again. "Thank you,

Anne," I often thought, "you gave me one of the finest things I ever received."

14   I had been asked many times to tell my side of Anne's story, but I always refused because I felt that Anne's diary told everything we should know. But then I met Alyson Gold, an author from Los Angeles. She said something I had not thought of myself. "Anne," she said, "is telling her story from the inside of the hiding place and you, Miep, should tell how it was outside." Still, I wondered whether I should be the one to do that because many others in Holland could also tell about Jews they helped. "That is true," Alyson said, "but how do I know I am told the truth? Your story I can check against Anne's diary." And so I gave in, and Alyson helped me to get everything on paper. It was not an easy decision, but reading the many letters I receive, I feel it was the right one.

15   As I told you, I was born an Austrian girl. For a long time I was deeply ashamed of both my home country and Germany. My biggest joy was on the day that I became a Dutch citizen. Then I felt free to hate *all* Germans and Austrians because of what they did to my friends. I could not see that there was anything wrong with that. However, it was wrong, and, as you will see, I learned that the hard way.

16   After that war, the business of Otto Frank, where I worked in the office, was still in the same building where he had been hiding. After the diary was published, people started to visit the place, including Austrians and Germans! Otto knew about my blind hate for them, and therefore, he would never let me near them. But one day, fate caught me. When I suddenly faced Germans, I jumped at them, calling them everything I could think of. I shouted, "You always say that you did not know what happened to the Jews! You really want me to believe that you were that stupid?" The visitors were clearly afraid of me and backed off to the wall. I also saw that the wives were taking position in front of their husbands, trying to protect them from my violent outburst. I really had my go at them! In a certain way, I even enjoyed it. But then Otto told me that these German people had been

for many years in concentration camps themselves for opposing Hitler. Can you understand how I felt, and can you see me standing there? I really did not know where to look, and what to say, and how to make good for it. At that moment I started to understand the wisdom of Otto Frank, who always said that we should never, never lump people together. "We all make our own decision," Otto said. "Even parents and their children do not act and think the same." Therefore, Otto Frank asked us to stop talking about "the Jews," "the Arabs," "the Asians," "the Germans," "the Blacks," or whomever. Lumping people together is *racism*, Otto said. It led to the Holocaust and still destroys countless lives today, in Cambodia, Ireland, Rwanda, Bosnia, and many other places.

It does happen that people ask me what I would answer 17 to those that deny that the Holocaust ever took place. My response to them is that on August 4, 1944, at nine in the morning, I did meet a healthy and strong fifteen-year-old girl: Anne Frank. A few hours later, I heard her footsteps on the inner stairs, leaving our office building, where she had been two years in hiding, and I also heard the sound of boots belonging to the Austrian policeman who had arrested her. The next thing I saw was her name on a German list of people on a cattle train to Auschwitz.

DISCUSSION QUESTIONS

1. Miep Gies notes that picking up the shopping list from the people in the "hiding place" was an "awful moment" for her. Why?

2. What did Anne Frank always want to find out from Gies?

3. How many people were hiding out in the Gies home, and how did the children-in-hiding have an especially difficult time?

4. What does Gies do every year on August 4? Why?

5. Why doesn't Gies like to be considered a "hero"? Whom does she regard as true heroes?

6. When Gies first found Anne Frank's diary, what did she decide to do, and how did she imagine Anne would react?

7. Whom did Gies finally give the diary to, and why was it a "very moving moment"?

8. According to her diary, what was Anne Frank's most important dream? Reading Anne's dream in the diary helped Gies realize something important about trying to help others. What did Miep Gies realize?

9. Otto Frank admitted that he must have made a mistake as Anne's father. What is his honest admission?

10. Gies states that she initially refused to read Anne's diary. Why was she so reluctant at first, and how did her attitude change once she started reading the diary?

11. Gies says she was once "deeply ashamed" of her own country, Austria, as well as of Germany. How did she behave around Germans who visited her house after the war was over?

12. What did Otto Frank tell Gies that helped her face and eventually overcome her racist attitudes? How relevant is this lesson today?

13. What is Miep Gies's simple response to those "who deny that the Holocaust even took place"?

WRITING OPTIONS

Collaborate with Peers

1. Anne Frank, a teenager, was in hiding from the Nazis for two years. She lived in a small, secret space with her family, another family, and another man. With two or three classmates, imagine the experience, and discuss what would have been the worst aspects of the experience for you if you had been hiding there. For instance, would it have been the constant fear? The lack of freedom to come and go? What else? Make a list of the worst parts of this hidden life, and write a paragraph or short essay about them.

Connecting with the Author's Ideas

2. Miep Gies admits that she once "felt free to hate all Germans and Austrians because of what they did to my friends." If you or someone you know has ever been unfairly judged or stereotyped,

describe the experience as well as the effects this judgment had on your behavior or attitude at the time.

3. Otto Frank advised Miep Gies and others to "stop talking about 'the Jews,' 'the Arabs,' 'the Asians,' 'the Germans,' 'the Blacks,'" and so on, because "lumping people together is racism [which] led to the Holocaust." Based on what you see depicted on some television series today, do you think some programs reflect harmful stereotypes by "lumping" people into certain groups? If so, select three series (dramas or comedies) and describe how each one reinforces negative stereotypes.

Chapter Eleven
Heroic Animals

"Animals are agreeable friends—they ask no questions, they pass no criticisms."

George Eliot

Profiles in Courage: All God's Creatures

Eric Swanson

Cats and dogs may be common household pets, but these following brief selections spotlight some uncommon acts of courage, compassion, and conviction for these furry friends of humans.

Note: In this reading, discussion questions will accompany each brief selection. Writing options related to this reading are located after the final selection.

Brat, the Cat: A Gutsy Feline Saves Her Owner's Life

Words You May Need to Know

gutsy (see title)	brave
feline (see title)	cat
disheartening (para. 1)	discouraging
frowsy (1)	dirty
exhibit (2)	show
degree (2)	amount
humble (2)	respectful
gratitude (2)	thanks
digs (2)	home
undeniable (2)	obvious
application (4)	appeal
rousing (4)	waking
emanating (5)	coming from
thrashing (5)	tossing
throes (5)	violent attack

seizure (5)	a sudden, violent, uncontrollable contraction of a group of muscles
lapsed (6)	fell, slipped
coma (6)	a state of deep unconsciousness
grim (6)	harsh, frightening
monitored (6)	observed, oversaw
verbally (6)	in words
subsided (7)	gradually decreased
circulate (7)	spend
intervention (7)	involvement, interference
crucial (7)	important, vital
succinctly (7)	in a few words
proclamation (8)	official announcement
citing (8)	praising
ingenuity (8)	cleverness
persistence (8)	steady determination
flurry (9)	sudden excitement
nonchalant (9)	calm, unexcited
resume (9)	go on with after an interruption

1   For his fifteen birthday, Jose Ybarra of Wheeling, Illinois, hadn't wanted just any old kitten. The cat he wanted would be the one he "couldn't imagine not taking home." Visits to breeders and pet stores proved disheartening, however, until one July afternoon, when a somewhat frowsy black kitten with a white marking on her chest popped up in a store window. As the kitten curled up in his arms, Jose knew he'd found the companion he'd been looking for.

2   The pet store owner told Jose and his mother, Karen Hummerich, that the kitten had been found in an abandoned car. One would naturally assume that an orphan thus

rescued might be inclined to exhibit a certain degree of humble gratitude upon finding herself in a warm, comfortable home. After settling into her new digs, however, the kitten began making an undeniable—if amusing—nuisance of herself. After playfully bopping Karen on the head one day, she earned the nickname by which she has been known ever since: Brat.

Early on, the cat established a habit of looking after any 3 member of the family who showed signs of illness. When Karen returned from work one March afternoon, she found the cat curled up with Jose, who had come home from school early feeling sick to his stomach. Later that evening, red spots began to appear on Jose's arms and chest, and Karen suspected an attack of the measles. She decided to take her son to the doctor the following morning.

Jose turned Brat out of his room that night so he could 4 sleep in peace. During the early morning hours, Karen Hummerich was awakened by the odd sensation of something wet and scratchy pressing against her eyes: Brat was licking her face in an attempt to wake her. Since feline behavior of this sort can usually be taken as a direct application for food, Karen simply shooed the cat away. Brat, however, persisted and, after rousing her mistress from sleep, ran down the hall to Jose's room and began scratching furiously on the door.

As Karen followed Brat, she began to hear strange, 5 thumping noises emanating from her son's room. "It sounded as if he was rearranging the furniture," she later recalled. Yet nothing could have prepared her for the shock, upon opening the door, of seeing Jose thrashing around unconscious in the throes of a seizure.

Rushed to a hospital in Glenview, the young man 6 lapsed into a coma. Doctors prepared the family for the worst as they related the grim news that Jose's seizure had been brought on by bacterial meningitis, an often fatal infection of the brain and spinal cord. The boy was transferred to Lutheran General Hospital at Park Ridge, where a team of intensive-care specialists monitored his symptoms. Against all odds, Jose awoke from his coma on the fifth day after his seizure and began responding verbally to family and other visitors. Within weeks, he made a full recovery.

7   News of Jose's illness spread quickly through the community. As fears of a more widespread infection subsided, the details of his unusual rescue began to circulate. While the efforts of hospital workers undoubtedly saved Jose's life, Brat's intervention played a crucial role. As Dr. Myron Singer, the Hummeriches' family physician, succinctly explained, "Without the cat, Jose would have died."

8   Ultimately, Brat's heroic response came to the attention of both Wheeling Village officials and Illinois State Senator Martin Butler. Two months after the rescue, both governing bodies rewarded Brat with a proclamation citing her "ingenuity and persistence" in the face of a medical emergency. The proclamation, presented in a public ceremony on May 12, 1996, represents the first such honor bestowed on a cat in Illinois history.

9   Brat's attitude to the flurry of public attention surrounding her role in Jose's recovery has been characteristically nonchalant. Whatever opinions she may have formed, she has chosen simply to resume a normal life of pouncing, racing, and lying in wait for the unsuspecting ankle or foot to enter her range of vision.

DISCUSSION QUESTIONS: "Brat the Cat"

1. Where did Jose Ybarra find his kitten, and what convinced him that this animal was the right one to go home with him?
2. How did this kitten get the name of "Brat"?
3. What unusual habit involving Jose and his family did Brat have?
4. What did Brat do to get Karen's attention regarding Jose, and what shocked Karen about her son's behavior?
5. According to Dr. Singer, how vital was Brat's "intervention"?
6. How did Brat make Illinois history?

Tramp and Lady: A Bold Rescue Beats the Odds

Words You May Need to Know

disheveled (para. 1)	untidy
burrs (2)	prickly, irritating seeds
rural (3)	rural
evergreen, elm, and hemlock (3)	three kinds of trees
accordingly (5)	therefore
canine (5)	dog
sprint (8)	run
customary (9)	usual
formality (9)	stiffness

Matt Drummond vividly remembers the late autumn 1
afternoon when a cat—whom he later named Tramp for its
disheveled appearance—arrived at his home in Barclay,
Pennsylvania.

"He was filthy," Drummond says. "His hair was matted, 2
he was covered with burrs and twigs. I couldn't even tell
what color he was till we got him cleaned up. It looked like
he'd been living in the woods for a long time."

Indeed, Matt and his wife, Surya, live in a pleasant, rural 3
area in Barclay, Pennsylvania, where broad fields are occasionally broken by thick patches of evergreen, elm, and
hemlock. Not far from their house runs a wide stream that
eventually feeds into the Delaware River. Frequent trips down
the stream became a regular part of the Drummonds' daily
life when Lady, a golden retriever, joined the Drummond
household about a year after Tramp arrived.

Despite the warmth and familiarity of a pleasant 4
home, Tramp never lost his attraction to the natural world
and would complain bitterly if forced to stay inside all day.
Still, Surya made sure that he came inside at night. The
surrounding woods were full of foxes and other small wild

animals, and she worried that Tramp might be hurt in a fight or caught in one of the metal traps laid by local hunters.

5   Accordingly, when Lady—barely more than a puppy— slipped out of her collar, Surya feared the worst. Although she could make out canine footprints in the mud along the banks of the stream near their home, she couldn't tell if they were Lady's or where they led. When Matt came back from running errands in town, he joined his wife in exploring the woods and fields around the stream. They returned home near dusk, hoping perhaps that Lady had wandered back to the house on her own. Only after night had fallen did they realize that Tramp was gone as well.

6   "After dinner we sat on the back porch with dishes of dog food and cat food laid out," Matt recounted, "hoping maybe they'd be attracted by the smell. Then this *thing* sort of wandered up out of the field at the edge of the property. All we could see was a pair of glowing eyes that wouldn't come any closer."

7   Finally, Matt stepped down off the porch to investigate. Greatly to his surprise and relief, the creature turned out to be Tramp—as matted and dirty as the day he'd first arrived on the Drummonds' doorstep. However, the cat refused to come any closer. As Surya approached, the cat turned and headed back into the field.

8   Years later, it's difficult for either Matt or Surya to recall what made them both creep silently after the cat rather than sprint after him. After passing through the field into a more densely wooded area, both Drummonds became aware of a distinctly canine whimper in the darkness ahead. Surya called out Lady's name and was answered by her pained but unmistakably familiar bark. Breaking into a run, they arrived in short order at the spot where Lady lay with her front leg caught in a fox trap. Surya knelt by Lady's side while Matt worked the trap's metal jaws open.

9   After an overnight stay at the animal clinic, Lady returned home. The trap had broken her front leg, but after a round of antibiotics and several weeks in a cast, she was in the pink once more. Though relations between Tramp and

Lady seem to have resumed their customary formality, neither Matt nor Surya are likely to forget Tramp's compassion that night.

"I've never seen a cat, before or since, behave so tenderly toward another creature," Surya later recalled. "I used to think they were pretty selfish, but now I guess you could say I'm a believer."

DISCUSSION QUESTIONS: "Tramp and Lady"

1. When Matt Drummond first encountered Tramp, what did the animal look like?
2. Why did Surya make sure Tramp stayed inside at night?
3. When Matt and Surya realized that both Lady and Tramp were gone, what did they do to lure the animals home?
4. When the Drummonds spotted a "creature," who did it turn out to be? What did this animal do as Surya approached it?
5. What did the couple do after hearing a familiar bark?
6. What surprised Surya about Tramp's behavior toward Lady?

Frankie and Johnny: Two Species, One Enduring Bond

Words You May Need to Know

scheme (para. 1)	arrangement
inevitable (3)	unavoidable
cataract (3)	a condition in which the eye lens loses its clearness
feline (4)	cat
reprimanded (4)	scolded
skittering (6)	skipping
craning (7)	stretching
literally (7)	actually
pounces (10)	dashes

1   Frankie, a Labrador mix, was already getting on in years when Johnny became a member of the Watson household. Adopted from a Massachusetts shelter, the gray-and-white tabby kitten seemed instinctively to know his place in the social scheme and never challenged Frankie's authority. According to their human companion, Geoff Watson, Frankie appeared at once amused and protective of the new member of the family.

2   "When Johnny got tired, he'd fall asleep between Frankie's front paws," Geoff recalled. "Frankie would just lie there—sometimes staring up at you with these big, sad, doggy eyes, as if to say he'd give anything to be able to get up and go to the bathroom, but he just couldn't bring himself to wake up the baby."

3   In time, however, the inevitable occurred: Frankie grew old. He developed a cataract in one eye. When Frankie was thirteen, his back legs had grown so weak that he could barely stand, and Geoff would often come home and find the poor dog lying helplessly in a puddle of urine. Eventually, Frankie was fitted with a diaper.

4   Oddly enough, though he seemed to be eating less, Frankie wasn't losing any weight. Geoff thought he'd hit on the reason when, upon coming home from work, he'd find Johnny's dry-cat-food bowl sitting empty beside Frankie's bed. Evidently, the dog was stealing food from his feline friend. Geoff reprimanded him, but the food kept disappearing, so he moved Johnny's bowl to the kitchen counter.

5   "For the next few days, I'd come home and find the bowl on the floor," Geoff explained. "The food would be scattered everywhere, and while I was sweeping up, I realized some of it seemed to lead in a kind of trail right toward Frankie's bed."

6   Finally, on the weekend, Geoff thought he'd watch and wait and catch Frankie knocking the food off the counter. Instead, Geoff fell asleep on the living-room couch and didn't even hear the bowl clatter to the floor. "I woke up to hear this strange sort of skittering sound," he recalled. "I couldn't imagine what it was."

Craning his neck to peer into the kitchen, Geoff imme- 7
diately noted the overturned bowl. What he wasn't prepared
for, however, was the sight of Johnny standing by the bowl,
literally batting kernels of dry cat food toward Frankie's bed.
Whenever a kernel rolled close enough, Frankie leaned over
and gobbled it up.

"All this time I thought Frankie was stealing food," Geoff 8
concluded, "and it was actually Johnny feeding him. I could
have wept. I *should* have wept. But Johnny looked so serious, I had to laugh."

Two months later, after his veterinarian discovered a 9
tumor in the dog's chest, Frankie was gently put to sleep.
For a long time afterward, Johnny padded through the
apartment, crying for his old friend. At first, Geoff was reluctant to adopt a new companion for Johnny. After several
months, however, he brought a scruffy black-and-white
puppy named Appleseed home from the same shelter where
he'd acquired Johnny.

"It's just like old times," Geoff said. "The dog waits on 10
one side of the kitchen door, the cat on the other. One of
them pounces; then they're off to the races. Then after a
while, they curl up together and fall asleep. It's nice to see
that continuity."

DISCUSSION QUESTIONS: "Frankie and Johnny"

1. When Johnny was adopted by Geoff Watson, how did Frankie
adapt to the kitten?
2. When Frankie was thirteen, what physical problems did he
develop?
3. What did Geoff initially believe was the reason Frankie wasn't
losing weight even though he seemed to be eating less?
4. What did Geoff discover Johnny had been doing with the cat
food?
5. When Frankie died, what did Geoff get from the same shelter
where he had found Johnny?
6. How is the relationship between Johnny and Appleseed "just like
old times"?

WRITING OPTIONS

Collaborate with Peers

1. Over the past few years, stores specializing in pet products and toys have become very popular. Working with one or two classmates, share your knowledge of unusual pet products now available. Then write your own paragraph or short essay on the most popular products and toys for dogs and cats. Include specifics on how useful or beneficial each item is for the pet's well-being.

Connecting with the Author's Ideas

2. Surya Drummond says of her cat's compassion for a wounded dog, "I've never seen a cat . . . behave so tenderly toward another creature." Write about a time when you saw an animal show kindness or compassion toward an animal or a human.

Other Options

3. If you own a cat and a dog, describe either the behavioral differences between these two pets or write about the unusual bond that has developed between these two animals.
4. If caring for your pet or pets involves more responsibilities and expenses than you expected, describe each responsibility and expense as specifically as possible.
5. Based on your experiences as a pet owner, describe your greatest aggravations as well as your greatest joys.
6. Not everyone is a suitable pet owner. In a paragraph or short essay, explain why.

A Healing Touch

Bill Holton

Years ago, Connie Gates found an Australian shepherd puppy wandering lost in a cemetery. Ironically, "Annie" is now a certified therapy pet, helping the living cope with the debilitating effects of strokes and traumas. As her owner states, "I'm privileged to watch Annie bring a bit of light into somebody's darkness."

Words You May Need to Know

endearing (para. 1)	lovable
waif (1)	stray animal
contrary to (2)	in opposition to
hail from (2)	come from
dub (2)	name
rehabilitation (3)	the process of restoring to good health
lustrous (3)	shiny
trauma (4)	violent injury
CEO (4)	chief executive officer
salutary (4)	healthy, favorable
vividly (5)	distinctly
hunched (5)	bent
drawn (5)	exhausted
glazed (5)	glassy
tentatively (5)	unsurely, hesitantly

After Connie Gates found an Australian shepherd 1 puppy wandering lost in a Huntsville, Alabama, cemetery, she spent several days trying to locate its owner. When that failed, the high school business teacher found the endearing waif a new home. As she prepared to take the dog to its new owner, she realized it was already too late. *I can't give you away*, Connie realized. *I've fallen in love with you.*

2   That was nine years ago, and today, Connie and the dog she named Annie are still best of friends. Loving, loyal, and attentive, Annie is a fine example of her breed—which, contrary to its name, did not originate in Australia. Annie's ancestors hail from the Basque region of Spain. In the late 1800s, Basque sheep herders began immigrating to the United States and Australia, bringing with them the little dog that American breeders would one day dub the Australian shepherd.

3   Aussies, as they're often called, perform well at search-and-rescue work and make accomplished guide dogs for the blind. Others, like Annie, serve as certified therapy pets. Three or four times a month, Annie and Connie call on the Health South Rehabilitation Hospital of North Alabama, where they visit with patients, often assisting with their physical therapy. When Connie says, "Go visit," Annie slowly approaches and sits at the patient's feet. Few can resist running their fingers through Annie's lustrous coat. Others ask for a kiss, and Annie is always happy to oblige.

4   In the physical therapy room, stroke survivors and head trauma patients enjoy their exercises more and push harder when they exercise with Annie, according to Rod Moss, CEO and chief administrator of Health South Rehabilitation. "Studies have demonstrated that patients require less medication after a pet therapy visit, and that the salutary effects can last long after the animal has gone," Moss says. "Annie also helps our patients feel less anxious and more like they're at home."

5   Connie vividly recalls one stroke victim named Jean whom she first encountered sitting hunched and drawn in a wheelchair. Jean's eyes were glazed and unfocused, and she had not reacted to anyone during her stay at the hospital. Gently, Connie took Jean's hand and placed it on top of Annie's head. After a few moments, Jean began to tentatively stroke Annie's fur. When another patient called out to Annie, the dog trotted over to say hello but soon returned, nuzzling

Jean's hand back into perfect petting position. Later, when it was time to leave, Jean gazed straight into Annie's gentle brown eyes and softly said, "Come back to see me, Annie." Annie did just that.

"I'm privileged to watch Annie bring a bit of light into 6 somebody's darkness," says Connie of the therapy sessions. "She and I both get back much more than we give."

DISCUSSION QUESTIONS

1. Where did Connie Gates find Annie, and why did she change her mind about finding a new home for the animal?
2. Ironically, the Australian shepherd breed is not originally from Australia. Explain.
3. What tasks do Australian shepherds, or "Aussies," perform well?
4. Annie serves as a "certified therapy pet." What does this title mean?
5. How does Annie help motivate stroke survivors and head-trauma patients to work harder on their physical therapy?
6. What was remarkable about Jean's response to Annie?

WRITING OPTIONS

Collaborate with Peers

1. Pet visits have a positive effect on patients in a rehabilitation hospital. Working with a partner or group, discuss other places where the presence of a pet might have a positive impact. You can discuss both visiting pets and resident pets. Then, write your own paragraph or short essay on the subject.

Connecting with the Author's Ideas

2. Annie is described as "loving, loyal, and attentive." If you are a pet owner, write a short essay examining how these adjectives apply (or do *not* apply) to your pet. If you do not own a pet, you can interview a classmate or acquaintance to see how those adjectives apply to his or her pet.

Other Options

3. The author, Bill Holton, states that Connie is an Australian shepherd, a breed that "performs well at search-and-rescue work" and "makes accomplished guide dogs for the blind." Schedule an interview with someone who works for an organization that relies on specially trained dogs (i.e., a police department, fire department, an association for the blind, etc.). Investigate how and where these dogs are found, and ask about some recent triumphs and accomplishments of these animals. Write an essay describing the training required of these dogs, or summarize some of the remarkable experiences or successes you learned about in your investigation.
4. If you or some of your family members were once reluctant to own a pet but now enjoy having a pet in the house, summarize your initial doubts and then describe the reasons you now have a more favorable attitude about pet ownership.

Chapter Twelve

Environmental Champions

"We do not inherit the land from our ancestors; we borrow it from our children."

Native American Proverb

"Now there is one important fact regarding Spaceship Earth, and that is that no instruction book came with it."

R. Buckminster Fuller

Marjory Stoneman Douglas: Patron Saint of the Everglades

Varla Ventura

The first time Marjory Stoneman Douglas saw the Florida Everglades, she was only four years old but knew it was a special place. A renowned author years later, she also become a tireless crusader for protecting Florida's wetlands. At age seventy-eight and nearly blind, she founded Friends of the Everglades, a national organization that now has thousands of members in thirty-eight states.

Words You May Need to Know

habitat (para. 1)	native environment
ventures (1)	enterprises
vowed (1)	promised
unstable (2)	unreliable, unsteady
unmoored (2)	insecure, lost
pursuit (3)	activity
petty (3)	minor, insignificant
merit (3)	value
scruffy (3)	shabby
boom town (3)	rapidly growing town
cub (3)	beginning, inexperienced
opinionated (3)	stubborn
niche (3)	suitable place
unswerving (3)	unchanging
soapbox (3)	platform
ghastly (3)	horrible
roused (4)	awakened, stirred
denizens (4)	inhabitants

extinction (4)	dying out, no longer existing
ecosystem (4)	a system formed by the interaction of a community of organisms with their environment
fetid (5)	stinking
raze (6)	tear down, demolish
going on the stump (6)	making speeches, campaigning
garnered (7)	got, acquired

Although not native to the southernmost state, Marjory 1
Stoneman Douglas took to the Florida Everglades like "a
duck to water," becoming, since 1927, the great champion of
this rare habitat. She was born to lake country, in Minnesota
in 1890, during one of her father's many failed business ventures, which kept the family moving around the country. On
a family vacation to Florida at the age of four, Marjory fell in
love with the Floridian light and vowed to return.

Marjory escaped her unstable home life in the world of 2
books. An extremely bright girl, she was admitted to Wellesley
College when higher education for women was still quite uncommon. Her mother died shortly after her graduation in
1911. Feeling unmoored, she took an unrewarding job at a
department store and shortly thereafter married a much
older man, Kenneth Douglas, who had a habit of writing bad
checks.

Leaving for Florida with her father for his latest busi- 3
ness pursuit seemed like the perfect way to get away
from her petty criminal husband and sad memories. Frank
Stoneman's latest ideas, however, seemed to have more
merit: founding a newspaper in the scruffy boom town of
Miami (the paper went on to become the *Miami Herald*).
Marjory eagerly took a job as a cub reporter. Opinionated,
forward-thinking, and unafraid to share unpopular views,
both Stonemans found their niche in the newspaper trade.
One of the causes they were in unswerving agreement on

was Governor Napoleon Bonaparte Broward's plan to drain the Everglades to put up more houses. Father and daughter used the paper as their soapbox to cry out against this ghastly idea with all their might.

4   Roused to action, Marjory educated herself about the facts surrounding the Everglades issue and discovered many of the denizens of Florida's swampy grassland to be in danger of extinction. The more she learned, the more fascinated she became. When, decades later, she decided to leave the newspaper to write fiction, she often wove the Everglades into her plots. Marjory learned that the Everglades were actually not a swamp, but rather wetlands. In order to be a swamp, the water must be still, whereas the Everglades water flows in a constant movement. Marjory coined the term "river of grass" and in 1947 wrote a book about this precious ecosystem entitled *The Everglades: River of Grass*.

5   More than anything else, Marjory's book helped people to see the Everglades not as a fetid swamp, but as a natural treasure without which Florida might become desert. After the publication of her book, President Harry Truman declared a portion of the Florida wetlands as Everglades National Park. The triumph was short-lived, however. The Army Corps of Engineers began tunneling canals all over the Florida Everglades, installing dams and floodgates. As if that weren't enough, they straightened the course of the Kissimmee River, throwing the delicate ecosystem into complete shock.

6   At the age of seventy-eight, Marjory Stoneman Douglas joined in the fight, stopping bulldozers ready to raze a piece of the Everglades for an immense jetport. Almost blind and armed with little more than a big floppy sun hat and a will of iron, Marjory founded Friends of the Everglades, going on the stump to talk to every Floridian about this rare resource and building the organization member by member to thousands of people in thirty-eight states. "One can do so much by learning, reading, and talking to people," she noted. "Students need to learn all they can about animals and the environment. Most of all, they need to share what they have learned."

Marjory Stoneman Douglas and "Marjory's Army," as 7 her group came to be known, stopped the jetport in its tracks, garnered restrictions on farmers' use of land and chemicals, saw to the removal of the Army's "improvements," and enjoyed the addition of thousands of acres to the Everglades National Park where they could be protected from land-grabbing developers. In 1975 and 1976, Marjory was rewarded for her hard work by being named Conservationist of the Year two years in a row. In 1989, she became the Sierra Club's honorary vice president. Protecting the Everglades became Marjory's life's work, a job she loved. She has never considered retiring and in her 107th year, is still living in the same house she's been in since 1926 and working every day for Friends of the Everglades.

Note: Shortly after this article was originally published, Marjory Stoneman Douglas died in 1998. Her legacy lives on in the hearts of thousands of admirers who care deeply about Florida's precious wetlands.

DISCUSSION QUESTIONS

1. How old was Douglas when she fell in love with the Everglades?
2. What became her escape from an unstable home life?
3. What was her husband's "bad habit"?
4. When Douglas decided to join her father when he left for Florida, what was she leaving behind, and what was her father's new plan?
5. What "ghastly idea" did the governor of Florida propose, and how did Frank Stoneman and Marjory Stoneman Douglas fight it?
6. When Douglas started educating herself about the Everglades, what did she learn about it that became the title of her book in 1947?
7. What did President Truman do after the book was published?
8. Despite Truman's action, what did the Army Corps of Engineers do that upset the ecosystem?

9. What organization did Douglas found, and what was it able to stop?

10. What are some of the accomplishments of "Marjory's Army"?

WRITING OPTIONS

Collaborate with Peers

1. If you live in a region where there is controversy or disagreement about the danger a local plant, landfill, factory, or other business poses to the environment, investigate the nature of the disagreement with two or three of your classmates. You can research articles in your local newspaper and interview people on both sides of the issue. Based on your group's research, write individual summaries of the arguments for or against the continued operation of this business.

Connecting to the Author's Ideas

2. According to author Varla Ventura, Marjory Stoneman Douglas took to the Florida Everglades like "a duck to water." If you have ever held a job that suited your skills and interests perfectly, or if you have ever adjusted well to a new region or city, summarize the reasons you adapted so well to this experience.

Other Options

3. Early in her life, Marjory Stoneman Douglas moved around the country because her father kept failing in business ventures. Based on your own experiences, write an essay about the advantages or disadvantages of moving to a new town or city every few years. If you have lived in one place most of your life, write about the advantages or disadvantages of this experience.

4. Douglas came to see the natural world around her as a treasure. Where other people saw bad-smelling swamp, she saw a river of grass populated by hundreds of creatures. Look closely at your environment and write about one piece of the natural world that you value. It could be as simple as a tree in your yard, a pet, or pigeons on a city street, or as great as a lake or a mountain.

Noah Idechong: Guardian of Paradise

Terry McCarthy

Noah Idechong was the driving force behind the Marine Protection Act of 1994, but he had to convince Palau's fishermen that such protection was vital for their industry's long-term survival. Palau now has over 1,500 species of fish, but a decade ago, they were all threatened by the common practice of "overfishing." Idechong knows that "the law went into effect just in time."

Words You May Need to Know

lurking (para. 1)	lying in wait, hiding
coral (1)	a hard mass made of the skeletons of tiny marine animals
warily (1)	watchfully
reef (2)	a ridge of rocks, sand, or coral at or near the surface of the water
archipelago (2)	group of islands
Micronesia (2)	a large group of islands in the South Pacific
export (4)	sending to other countries for sale
crucially (5)	vitally, importantly
culminated (6)	ended
amid (7)	among, surrounded by
strayed (8)	gone beyond, wandered
confer (8)	consult
vulnerable (8)	capable of being hurt
ecosystem (9)	a system formed by the interaction of a community of plants and animals and their environment

1   Fifty feet below the surface of Ulong Channel off the coast of Palau, Noah Idechong points excitedly at a large fish lurking under a fan coral. It is a brown marbled grouper, quite rare, but a favorite of Chinese restaurants around Asia. It looks back at him warily, not knowing that Idechong is a main reason the fish and many other marine creatures are still alive on Palau's reefs instead of stir-fried on restaurant plates in Hong Kong.

2   Palau is renowned for its marine life. Divers and scientists from around the world fly to this Pacific archipelago 500 miles (800 km) east of the Philippines to view its parrot fish, gobies, damselfish, sharks, turtles, butterfly fish, and stately Napoleon wrasses. The Blue Corner on the western reef is rated one of the world's top dive sites for its abundance of big fish. With 1,387 species at last count, Palau has more fish varieties than any other area of Micronesia. But a decade ago, all this was threatened by fishermen. A short boat from Ulong takes you to another channel that has been almost emptied of fish.

3   "That big grouper under the coral," says Idechong, 47, after he has heaved himself back onto the boat." "If there was still fishing in this area, you would never have seen him—he would have taken off immediately."

4   Palauans have always lived from the sea, but it was not until the mid-'80s that overfishing became a problem. After a half-century as a U.S. territory, Palau was preparing for independence in 1994 and promoting commercial fishing for export as a way of earning a living on its own.

5   "I realized early on that we had no surveys—we didn't even know what we had," says Idechong, who worked for the government's Division of Marine Resources from 1978 to '94. "There was no management program at all. And that scared me." Idechong began studies in 1988—and, crucially, started talking with the local fishermen. By sharing information, Idechong got a picture of what species were in danger, while the fishermen learned how to manage fish stocks for the longer term. "By working with them," he says, "we ended up getting a lot of support."

Idechong's work culminated in the Marine Protection 6 Act of 1994, which banned export of certain species and regulated the fishing for others. "The law went into effect just in time," says Idechong, who drafted it in 1990 but had to wait four years for the political leadership to approve.

Raised in Ngiwal, a fishing village on Palau's largest is- 7 land, Babeldaob, Idechong had his eyes opened to nature's riches only when he left for a year of high school in the U.S. in 1970. He spent that period amid the lakes and forests around Pine City, Minnesota—"one of the best times of my life"—and realized that "wildlife was the field I wanted to be in."

He went to college in Hawaii and then returned to 8 Palau, where he started working for the government. In 1994, he founded the Palau Conservation Society, the archipelago's only homegrown non-governmental organization. He has traveled to Britain, Canada, Italy, the Solomon Islands, and Fiji to study, but Idechong has never strayed too far from his village roots. Every time he begins a conservation project, his first instinct is to confer with the village elders. He is now starting to focus on ways of protecting the dugong (sea cow) and the hawksbill turtle, both of which are vulnerable to fishermen. He is optimistic because two decades of his campaigning have shown the majority of Palauans the logic behind conservation. "I don't think the next generation will eat turtle, for example," he says. His success in preserving Palau's marine life is also beginning to win over other Pacific islands. "The FSM [Federated States of Micronesia] and Pohnpei are planning to follow what we did," he says.

Idechong is not done with his worrying, though. As the 9 government plans to build roads, golf courses, and more hotels to boost tourism, he sees more dangers on the horizon for the country's ecosystem. "Palau right now needs visionaries—people who can say what they want Palau to look like fifty years from now, and what we must do now to make that happen." In other words, people with Idechong's kind of vision.

DISCUSSION QUESTIONS

1. Where is Palau, what is it known for, and why is Blue Corner famous among divers?
2. When did "overfishing" become a problem, and when did Idechong begin studying about species that were in danger of becoming extinct?
3. What were the benefits of Idechong and local fishermen working together? What did the Marine Protection Act of 1994 protect?
4. When and where did Idechong have his "eyes opened to nature's riches"?
5. What organization did Idechong found in 1994?
6. What does Idechong believe are some potential dangers facing Palau, and what does it need "right now"?

WRITING OPTIONS

Collaborate with Peers

1. Noah Idechong says he can see how the emphasis on conservation has changed attitudes. For example, he believes the next generation of Palauans will not eat turtle. With two or three classmates, discuss whether young people today have different attitudes toward nature and conservation than their parents' generation. For example, is the new generation more likely to be vegetarian, to avoid wearing fur, to recycle, to be concerned about clean air? Or have environmental concerns diminished? Use the ideas you gather in that discussion to write about the two generations and their attitudes toward the natural world.

Writing from the Author's Ideas

2. The article states that Idechong is "optimistic because two decades of his campaigning have shown the majority of Palauans the logic behind conservation." If you have ever been involved in a controversial school or local project that gradually gained support and changed people's minds, describe how or why the project became less controversial and more widely accepted over time.

Other Options

3. If you are a member of your school's environment club or local conservation group, summarize the purpose of this organization, its goals, the misconceptions non-members may have of this organization, and the benefits you have derived as a member.

4. According to author Terry McCarthy, Noah Idechong's year of high school in the United States was a turning point for him. Write a short essay describing how visiting or moving to a new city or region changed your outlook or perception about certain issues, customs, or people.

The Story of Kory

Andrea Siedsma

In 1989, nine-year-old Kory Arvizu-Johnson's older sister died of heart disease, a death that may be attributed to "contaminated well water her mother drank during pregnancy." From this tragedy, Kory's environmental activism took root, and she was only nine when she founded Children for a Safe Environment (CSE). Today, Kory is fighting against the dangers that landfills pose for Native American reservations. "True friends are hard to come by when you're in this line of work," she says, but seeing so much injustice "makes me fight harder."

Words You May Need to Know

diva (para. 1)	the principal female singer in an opera, a temperamental person
activism (2)	active involvement
contaminated (2)	polluted, impure
despite (2)	in spite of
launched (3)	began
amphitheater (4)	a circular or oval arena
tarantulas (4)	large, hairy spiders
glowingly (4)	warmly, favorably
styrofoam (5)	a light, durable foam that cannot be easily decomposed
pared down (7)	reduced
landfills (8)	sections of land filled with garbage or other waste

1   On August 14, 1978, in Phoenix, Arizona, an environmental diva was born. Her name: Kory Arvizu-Johnson. Her future: Most likely to succeed in environmental causes. Kory, now twenty-one, gives a voice not only to Mother Nature but also to those who would not otherwise be heard.

And although she's already accomplished much in her lifetime, Kory's work has only just begun.

Her activism dates back to 1989, when her sixteen- 2
year-old sister died of heart disease. The family learned that her death may have been linked to contaminated well water her mother, Teri, drank during pregnancy. Despite their grief, Teri and Kory attended environmental meetings to get the well shut down.

Kory's efforts didn't stop there. Only nine years old at 3
the time, she launched Children for a Safe Environment (CSE), which now has more than 300 members nationwide. CSE, which began by promoting neighborhood recycling, more recently teamed with other environmental groups such as Greenpeace to stop a large waste treatment company from operating three incinerators near Phoenix. Kory, who has spoken to children's and environmental groups across the United States, received a presidential Environmental Youth Award in 1993. During the seventh grade, she became the youngest person to win the Windstar Award, presented by the environmental group created by the late singer/songwriter John Denver. In 1997, Kory became the youngest person ever to win the $100,000 Goldman Environmental Prize; she donated about $30,000 of the prize money to environmental causes.

Kory contributes much more than money to environ- 4
mental causes. At eighteen, she spent five weeks in the Raul Julia Rainforest in Puerto Rico with seven other women, building a bamboo amphitheater. "We would hike eight miles into the forest each day," says Kory. "We had tarantulas landing on our heads. I had 1,036 mosquito bites the day I came home." But Kory's not one to complain, and she speaks glowingly of the whole experience. "It was amazing," she says. "I met really true friends." She adds, "True friends are hard to come by when you're in this line of work. I felt older than a lot of the older kids in school," she says. "I looked at things differently than they did."

Kory says she also learned politics at an early age. Her 5
fourth-grade science project, which featured a styrofoam

cup from a major fast-food chain sticking out of a landfill, was named best in the school. But when she tried to enter a state contest, her project was rejected since the fast-food chain was a sponsor of the event. "I just cried and cried," Kory remembers. "It wasn't fair."

6   Fighting for what you believe isn't always easy, she says. Although she was a cheerleader during high school, she sometimes wasn't too popular among her cheer peers. Some projects of hers, such as putting on a Halloween party for children with AIDS and organizing a blanket-donation program for homeless people, were difficult for others to comprehend.

7   Environmental causes have been a big part of her life, but Kory has made time for other things, such as dancing lessons. She once even held the title of Arizona hula champion. "It seems like I never slow down," says Kory, who also used to volunteer at Children's Hospital. She recently had gall bladder surgery, though, so her schedule has been pared down a bit. She has stepped down as president of the CSE group she founded and is taking a break from her classes at Arizona State University in Tempe, Arizona, where she is studying child psychology. Of course she still keeps busy with correspondence, phone calls, and e-mail, and she's helping out her mother, who also recently had surgery.

8   Kory's latest cause is what she calls environmental racism. One side of her family is of Mexican origin, and the other is Native American/Anglo, and Kory is now working with Indian tribes to fight landfills and other environmentally damaging projects affecting reservations. "I think that's what makes me fight harder," she says about her heritage. "I see so much injustice to minority people."

9   Sometimes, when she thinks about everything that needs to be done, Kory feels almost overwhelmed. "I'm getting tired of being one of the only ones out there," she says. She observes that most people tend to get involved in causes only when they are directly affected, rather than speaking for others.

10   When things get really hectic, she can still rely on her mother for motivation. But Kory knows when to take a

break. Kind of. "I finally said no more interviews and no more pictures until next semester," she says. "But I did a few." Luckily for all of us, she did this one.

DISCUSSION QUESTIONS

1. When did Kory first become active in environmental causes, and what family tragedy sparked her interest?
2. What organization did Kory start when she was nine years old, and what are some of this organization's efforts?
3. What are some of the awards Kory has received for her hard work to save the environment?
4. Describe Kory's fourth-grade science report. Why was she prevented from entering it in a state contest?
5. Kory has learned that "fighting for what you believe in isn't always easy." What are some projects Kory has undertaken that gained little or no support from her peers?
6. According to Kory, when do most people become involved in causes?

WRITING OPTIONS

Collaborating with Peers

1. With two or three classmates, make a list of the most important environmental issues in your community today. They can include issues such as polluted water, dumping of toxic waste, and nuclear waste. List as many as you can. Then write individual paragraphs or a short essay on what you believe are the three most important environmental issues in your community, why they are important, and what should be done to resolve these issues.
2. The organization Kory founded, Children for a Safe Environment (CSE), first concentrated on recycling efforts. If your neighborhood or school participates in a recycling program, investigate when the program started, how beneficial it has been, and whether there any plans for expanding or changing the program. With two or three of your classmates, decide how to research this topic, including whom to interview and what questions to ask. After your group has completed its research, write individual essays to summarize your findings.

Connecting with the Author's Ideas

3. When Kory speaks of her work on behalf of the environment, she says there are times when she feels discouraged. "I'm getting tired of being one of the only ones out there." If you have ever felt alone in your values, in your work for a project, or in your opinion of a controversial issue, write a paragraph or short essay about the experience and what it taught you.

Other Options

4. Kory was deeply affected by her sister's death, but she became actively involved in environmental causes because of this tragedy. If you or someone you know became actively involved in a group or political struggle because of a personal setback or family tragedy, describe the chain of events that led to this activism, and then summarize the goals and accomplishments of the organization itself.
5. If you have always been curious about a children's charity, animal rights organization, or environmental group but have never looked into it, turn this assignment into an opportunity. With the help of your school's librarians or counselors, find out about a group you are curious about. Research its history, goals, functions, and accomplishments. Summarize your findings in an essay about the national headquarters, or a state, local, or school chapter of this organization.

In Helping Save Endangered Species, He Also Saved Himself

Tom Dworetzky

At seventeen, Arthur Bonner was convicted of assault and began serving a four-year prison sentence. Upon release, he found work with the Conservation Corps in California, just happy to be getting a minimal salary. "That's when fate, in the form of a rare, almost extinct native butterfly, changed the young man's life forever."

Words You May Need to Know

notorious (para. 1)	widely but not favorably known
extinct (3)	no longer existing, died out
dunes (4)	sand ridges formed by the wind
ecosystem (4)	a system formed by the interaction of a community of organisms with their environment
habitat (4)	native environment
lepidopterist (5)	an expert in butterflies and moths
amid (8)	among
scrub (8)	an area of low trees and shrubs
revegetation (9)	growing again
diversity (9)	variety
spectrum (9)	range
flora (9)	plants
fauna (9)	animals
flourished (9)	thrived
imperiled (10)	endangered
exclusive (11)	limited

1   Butterflies taught Arthur Bonner how to be free. For years, the twenty-seven-year-old Los Angeles native was, by his own admission, just "rippin' and runnin' the streets" of the city's notorious South Central neighborhood. In and out of trouble with the law, he eventually served a four-year sentence in a California prison for assault.

2   On the November day in 1988 that the bus took him to prison, his first son was born. Not being there, Bonner remembers, was the low point of his then seventeen-year life. "I determined then that when I got out," he says, "I would be a good dad and not run the streets any more."

3   Four years later, Bonner got out of jail and took some advice from his older brother. He joined the Los Angeles Conservation Corps, which pays mostly inner-city youth $4.25 an hour to work on a variety of nature-restoration projects in Southern California. "After four years of working for just 1.5 cents in prison," says Bonner, "I was happy to accept the corps' pay." That's when fate, in the form of a rare, almost extinct, native butterfly, changed the young man's life forever.

4   At the time, the Conservation Corps was sending some of its crews to work on a project initiated by Los Angeles Airport authorities, who were attempting to restore a portion of the El Segundo dunes—the largest remaining coastal dune ecosystem in the Los Angeles area. The goal: to redevelop habitat for an endangered native butterfly species called the El Segundo blue, which numbered only a few hundred at the time.

5   The project was led by Rudi Mattoni, a University of California at Los Angeles (UCLA) geography professor and lepidopterist who was making headway in saving the dunes—the El Segundo blue's last principal habitat. When Bonner joined the effort, Mattoni noticed he was different from most of the other corps workers. "He was really interested and wanted to learn," the butterfly expert recalls.

6   Bonner knew that to keep out of trouble he had to avoid hanging around with most of his old neighborhood friends.

"All I did that first year after joining the corps was go to work and then back home," he remembers. "I stayed inside the house, except to go to the corner store."

The job provided more than just an income for Bonner, 7 who had fallen in love with rare butterflies. "Dealing with these creatures showed me what life really means," he says. "I felt that I was helping to be responsible for something."

In 1994, Mattoni discovered a small population of an- 8 other native California butterfly, the Palos Verdes blue, which was thought to be extinct. The endangered insects were living amid the storage tanks and scrub habitat at the Defense Fuel Support Depot, a U.S. military facility near the Los Angeles port of San Pedro. Armed with a small grant to help save the species, Mattoni hired Bonner to work full time at the site. "Arthur is a decent guy who just had some bad breaks," says the scientist.

Today, utilizing Mattoni's expertise, Bonner serves as the 9 revegetation technician for the UCLA project in the Palos Verdes Peninsula area. "The butterflies of coastal Los Angeles have become symbols for the diversity of life and the struggle for survival," says Mattoni. "We are seeking to reestablish habitat, not just for butterflies but also the full spectrum of flora and fauna that once flourished in this area."

Bonner is responsible for all phases of coastal dune 10 revegetation in the area and for the rearing of captive butterflies for the possible reintroduction into the wild. At a fuel-depot laboratory, he grows food plants for the insects and then transplants the shrubs into the dunes. He also assists with captive breeding of three of the region's most imperiled butterfly species: the Palo Verdes blue, Kino checkerspot, and green hairstreak.

Earlier this year, in honor of their efforts to save en- 11 dangered species, Mattoni and Bonner received a Special Conservation Achievement Award from the National Wildlife Federation. "From a resource standpoint, Rudi's and Arthur's accomplishments have been significant," says U.S. Fish and

Wildlife Service official David Klinger. "From a human stand-point, though, I think Arthur's accomplishments really reach beyond this patch of habitat. He's an example of an individual who is turning his life around. He's demonstrating that natural-resource conservation is not a concern exclusive to the white middle-class community."

12   These days, Bonner is sharing his new sense of worth and freedom with other inner-city kids who come to work at the site through the Conservation Corps and other programs. "I tell kids that it's so important to be out here working in nature," he says. "I'm saving butterflies from extinction, and they're saving me from the streets."

DISCUSSION QUESTIONS

1. In 1988, what was the low point of Arthur Bonner's life?
2. Ironically, how was this low point also a turning point for Bonner?
3. After Bonner was released from jail, what organization did he join, and what project became yet another turning point for him?
4. Who is Rudi Mattoni, and what did he notice about Bonner that was different from the other workers on the endangered butterfly species project?
5. What did working with rare butterflies teach Bonner about life?
6. Who hired Bonner in 1994, and what are Bonner's current job description and responsibilities?
7. Who is David Klinger, and why does he believe Arthur Bonner's achievements extend beyond helping to save rare butterfly species?
8. With whom does Bonner now share "his new sense of freedom"?

WRITING OPTIONS

Collaborating with Peers

1. Arthur Bonner was released from jail as a twenty-one-year-old ex-convict, but he proceeded to turn his life around. He challenged the stereotypes of ex-convicts common in television and

movies. With two or three classmates, discuss the most common stereotypes of ex-convicts portrayed on television and in movies. Then write individual paragraphs or short essays describing how Arthur Bonner challenged those stereotypes.

Connecting to the Author's Ideas

2. Despite Arthur Bonner's conviction and jail sentence, his boss Rudi Mattoni recognized that Bonner "was different from most of the other corps workers" and had potential. If someone in authority once gave you an opportunity or second chance to develop your potential, describe the circumstances that brought you to this person's attention, how he or she affected your life, and what you learned about yourself and others from this experience.

Other Options

3. Arthur Bonner's job working with the Conservation Corps involved more than just a salary for him. If you have held a job that meant more to you than just a paycheck, describe how you first learned about the job, what the interview was like, what your responsibilities included, what you learned about yourself and others, and what the long-term benefits have been for you.
4. As the article implies, a low point in life can also be a turning point for the better. In a short essay, describe one of the low points in your life that convinced you to make changes in your attitude or behavior.

Chapter Thirteen
Community Spirit, Giving Back

"The everyday kindness of the backroads more than makes up for the acts of greed in the headlines."

Charles Kuralt

"From what we get, we can make a living; what we give, however, makes a life."

Arthur Ashe

The Sandwich Man

Meladee McCarty

For over two decades, Michael Christiano has risen at 4:00 A.M. each day to help the homeless before he starts his job as a court officer in New York City. He offers "food, an encouraging smile, and some positive human contact" because it's something he can do "one day and one person at a time."

Words You May Need to Know

grandiose (para. 1)	showy
persevere (1)	maintain a purpose in spite of difficulties or obstacles
stave off (2)	keep off, prevent, delay
makeshift (2)	temporary, created without much preparation
compelled (3)	drove, obliged
unkempt (4)	messy, untidy
amputated (5)	surgically removed
revulsion (5)	disgust
calling (5)	a strong impulse, a vocation
Mayor Koch (9)	Ed Koch, former mayor of New York City
ranks (9)	group
transformed (9)	changed in form, appearance, or character

What would you do if you wanted to make a difference 1
in the world or leave a deposit on a ticket into heaven?
Would you think big and pick the flashiest or most
grandiose of acts? Or would you quietly persevere every day,
doing one personal deed at a time?

Michael Christiano, a New York City court officer, rises 2
every morning at 4 A.M., in good and bad weather, workday
or holiday, and walks into his sandwich shop. No, he doesn't

own a deli; it's really his personal kitchen. In it are the fixings of his famous sandwiches, famous only to those who desperately need them to stave off hunger for the day. By 5:50 A.M., he's making the rounds of the makeshift homeless shelters on Centre and Lafayette Streets, near New York's City Hall. In a short time, he gives out two hundred sandwiches to as many homeless people as he can before beginning his work day in the courthouse.

3   It started twenty years ago with a cup of coffee and a roll for a homeless man named John. Day after day, Michael brought John sandwiches, tea, clothes, and when it was really cold, a resting place in his car while he worked. In the beginning, Michael just wanted to do a good deed. But one day, a voice in his head compelled him to do more. On this cold, winter morning, he asked John if he would like to get cleaned up. It was an empty offer because Michael was sure John would refuse. Unexpectedly, John said, "Are you gonna wash me?"

4   Michael heard an inner voice say, *Put your money where your mouth is.* Looking at the poor man, covered in ragged and smelly clothes, unkempt, hairy, and wild-looking, Michael was afraid. But he also knew that he was looking at a big test of his commitment. So he helped John upstairs to the locker room of the courthouse to begin the work.

5   John's body was a mass of cuts and sores, the result of years of pain and neglect. His right hand had been amputated, and Michael pushed through his own fears and revulsion. He helped John wash, cut his hair, shaved him and shared breakfast with him. "It was at that moment," Michael remembers, "that I *knew* I had a calling, and I believed that I had it within me to do anything."

6   With the idea for his sandwiches born, Michael began his calling. He receives no corporate sponsorship, saying, "I'm not looking for an act of charity that goes in the record books or gets media attention. I just want to do good, day by day, in my small way. Sometimes it comes out of my pocket, sometimes I get help. But this is really something that *I* can do, one day and one person at a time."

"There are days when it's snowing," he says, "and I have   7
a hard time leaving my warm bed and the comfort of my
family to go downtown with sandwiches. But then that voice
in me starts chattering, and I get to it."

And get to it he does. Michael has made two hundred   8
sandwiches every day for the past twenty years. "When I give
out sandwiches," he explains, "I don't simply lay them on a
table for folks to pick up. I look everyone in the eye, shake
their hands, and I offer them my wishes for a good and
hopeful day. Each person is important to me. I don't see
them as 'the homeless,' but as people who need food, an
encouraging smile, and some positive human contact."

"Once Mayor Koch turned up to make the rounds with   9
me. He didn't invite the media; it was just us," says Michael.
But of all Michael's memories, working side-by-side with the
mayor was not as important as working next to someone
else. A man had disappeared from the ranks of the sandwich
takers, and Michael thought about him from time to time.
He hoped the man had moved on to more comfortable conditions. One day, the man showed up, transformed, greeting
Michael clean, warmly clothed, shaven, and carrying sandwiches of his own to hand out.

Michael's daily dose of fresh food, warm handshakes,   10
eye contact and well wishes had given this man the hope
and encouragement he so desperately needed. Being seen
everyday as a person, not as a category, had turned this
man's life around.

The moment needed no dialogue. The two men worked   11
silently, side by side, handing out their sandwiches. It was
another day on the streets of New York, but a day with just a
little more hope.

DISCUSSION QUESTIONS

1. What is Michael Christiano's official job, and what is his unofficial, voluntary job?
2. How early does Christiano get up in the morning, when does he start his "rounds," and how long has he been helping the homeless?

3. The article states that "one day a voice in his head compelled him to do more." Explain.
4. Describe what Christiano did for John and why it was a "big test" of commitment?
5. What does Christiano say is his reason for his good works?
6. How did Christiano's volunteer work give one man in particular some hope?

WRITING OPTIONS

Collaborate with Peers

1. With a classmate or small group, compile a list of extracurricular clubs at your school. Then investigate the types of community service or volunteer service the members undertake. Based on the information compiled and shared by your group, write an individual summary of the various ways specific clubs help others in need.

Connecting with the Author's Ideas

2. Michael Christiani says he just wants "to do good, day by day, in my small way." If someone you know regularly volunteers to help others in need, interview this individual. Find out his or her reasons for helping, why he or she started volunteering, and what the benefits have been. Then write a paragraph or short essay describing this person, his or her background, motives, and good works.
3. Michael Christiani also tries to give each homeless person he meets "some positive human contact." Such contact helps everyone, not just the homeless. It can be as simple as a smile, a greeting, or a "Thank you." It can be a kindness like giving up a bus seat to a pregnant woman or letting someone in a hurry cut into the checkout line at the supermarket. In a paragraph, give examples of the situations in our daily lives when we can provide such "positive human contact."

Other Options

4. Contact a local organization that often relies on volunteers (e.g., a charity, religious group, nursing home, or animal shelter). Write

a paragraph or a short essay about the volunteers at that organization. Describe how they serve the community during holidays and throughout the year.

5. If you had a million dollars to donate to charity, what charity or charities would you give it to? In a paragraph, answer that question and explain your choice(s).

A Circle of Giving

Kate Boren

To help alleviate the plight of the elderly Navajos, Linda Meyers once pledged five hundred dollars from the sale of her artwork. From that simple gift over ten years ago, Linda founded the Adopt-a-Native-Elder (ANE) program, which now claims over five hundred supporters. She was named the 1997 "Citizen of the Year" by the Arizona chapter of the National Association of Social Workers. In her words, "Just to know the elders is a great gift to my life."

Words You May Need to Know

impoverished (para. 1)	poor
elders (1)	older people
convoy (1)	group of vehicles traveling together
reserved (1)	distant, formal
collective (2)	group
mission (2)	task
perplexed (4)	puzzled
octagon-shaped (4)	eight-sided
streamline (5)	to change by simplifying
serene (6)	calm, peaceful
lured (12)	attracted

1   For the last five years, John and Liz Wall have been making the eight-and-a-half-hour drive from their home in Park City, Utah, to the Navajo Reservation in Northern Arizona. As members of the Adopt-a-Native-Elder Program, the Walls help deliver food and other necessities to impoverished Native American elders. But last October, the food run was different. The Walls would get to meet Mae Watchman, the ninety-six-year-old grandmother they had "adopted." Along with boxes of food supplies, the Walls had been

sending photos of their family. As the convoy of fourteen four-wheel-drive vehicles pulled into Pinion, Arizona, in a cloud of red dust, the Walls spotted Mae holding up a picture of their children. Liz Wall introduced herself to Mae and presented a special gift—a turquoise necklace she had bought especially for Mae. The normally reserved Navajo dissolved in tears of joy. *"Nizhoni. Nizhoni. Nizhoni,"* she said, which means "beautiful" in Navajo.

The organization that brought the Walls into Mae's life, 2 Adopt-a-Native-Elder (ANE) is an all-volunteer group with a collective mission to support elderly Navajos in their daily struggle to live in harmony with the earth. "In beauty may I walk" is a Navajo prayer that describes a lifestyle that is difficult for these seniors to maintain—rising with the dawn, herding sheep, achieving spiritual balance and simplicity.

It all started ten years ago when Linda Meyers, an artist 3 in Park City, Utah, attended a small rug sale at a local hotel. It had been organized by a young Navajo named Rose Hulligan, who would return to the reservation with money for weavers and their families. Linda was deeply saddened by the elders' circumstances, and although she didn't have enough cash to buy a rug, she pledged to donate $500 she expected to earn in an upcoming art sale of her own work. From that point on, Linda was hooked. She began speaking publicly about the elders and organized informal collections of food and clothing.

Linda's first visit to the reservation was an eye opener. 4 With the help of translator Grace Smith Yellowhammer, Linda spoke directly with the elders. "Do you need spoons?" she asked. "Yes, one spoon," responded an elder. "What would you like for your birthday?" Linda asked one grandmother. "A six-volt-battery," was her answer. Linda was perplexed, so Grace explained that batteries are used to run lanterns because many hogans (the traditional octagon-shaped Navajo dwellings) do not have electricity—or running water. Some elders travel fifty miles to get fresh water.

It was clearly time to streamline. Linda and Grace, her 5 cofounder, developed a questionnaire so elders could identify their needs: shampoo, blankets, canned vegetables and meat, clothes, paper goods and so on. The elders were asked to describe any skills that might help them earn money. Could they weave rugs or sew? Make silver jewelry? Do beadwork? With this information, Linda could be more effective.

6   Over time, a network of friends and contacts on the reservation grew. Linda came to love and respect sixty-seven-year-old Alice Benally, a serene Navajo grandmother. Alice taught Linda about an important tribal custom known as the Giveaway Circle. In times of crisis, friends and family gather in a circle and donate a valuable belonging that will be sold to raise money for the family in need.

7   One day, Alice took Linda to a Giveaway Circle for a child who had been hit by a car. Linda was shocked when Alice donated some royal-blue velvet that Linda had given her. "That isn't what I bought it for," Linda said through a translator. Can't you please give something else?" Alice paused for a moment before explaining. "You give your very best," she said, "and this is the best I have." Linda understood right away. She was so inspired by the spirit of the custom that she used it as the model for ANE.

8   Operating out of her Park City home, Linda keeps files on hundreds of Navajo elders. Through her, volunteers can "adopt" a grandmother or grandfather by fulfilling his or her "needs list." Volunteers also donate fifty dollars twice a year. Linda and her core team of helpers use the funds to purchase food for semiannual deliveries to towns on the reservations like Pinion, Tsaile, Birdsprings, Teesto, and Big Mountain. Today more than seventy-five people have signed up to adopt elders. And thanks to the work of Jeannie Patton, a regular contributor to the program, a list of more than five hundred supporters receives a quarterly newsletter. For Linda, everyone is part of ANE's circle of giving.

9   Nearly two years after the program began, Linda was approached by an elder who was desperate for money. "Please sell my rug for me," the elder said. After five more

weavers presented their rugs, Linda set out to organize a rug show at a Park City gallery. Local papers picked up the news, and the event was announced in the ANE newsletter.

The sale was a huge success, and the idea took off like 10 wildfire. The rug show has become a much anticipated annual event every November. Navajo weavers are always there to explain how they card and spin the wool for weaving. They also describe the meaning of the intricate rug patterns. "The Yei Bei Chei pattern comes from a winter healing ceremony," says Ella Mae Benally, an organizer based in Pinion and the daughter of an accomplished weaver. "Other designs have to do with nature—lightning, clouds, sun, and water." Recently, Linda was able to produce a full-color catalog of Navajo rugs that can be purchased by mail.

The ANE program draws volunteers from all over the 11 nation. Sandi Bergh of Absecon, New Jersey, was on a skiing trip to Park City when she noticed a poster about ANE in the window of Linda's art gallery on Main Street. Sandi adopted Navajo elder Carol Blackhorse. "Carol is eighty-one years old and still out there riding sheep and horses," Sandi says. Sandi and her companion, Bob Threet, spend two weeks every summer with Carol and her relatives.

The store window display also lured Penny Montague 12 and her husband, Ed Phillips, of Park City. Penny and Ed adopted Ellen Yazzie, a tiny medicine woman who later became very ill. To help pay for healing ceremonies, Penny and Ed sent fabric, deer hides, and blankets. But Ellen was just too sick, and she died. Penny was heartbroken. "I felt like I lost my own grandmother," she says.

For her work, Linda Meyers was named "Citizen of the 13 Year" by the Arizona chapter of the National Association of Social Workers in 1997. The forty-seven-year-old artist and her companion Rodger Williams—who is Navajo—greet the dawn with the traditional offering of sacred cornmeal. Linda describes her own contribution with true Navajo simplicity. "Just to know the elders is a great gift to my life," she says softly.

DISCUSSION QUESTIONS

1. John and Liz Wall are active volunteers in the Adopt-a-Native-Elder (ANE) program. What is this program's mission?
2. What circumstances led to Linda Meyers' idea to help Navajo elders?
3. Describe how Linda's initial visit to the reservation was "an eye opener."
4. Explain the importance of the questionnaire Linda and Grace devised.
5. Who is Alice Benally, and what did she teach Linda?
6. How can program volunteers become eligible to "adopt" a grandmother or grandfather?
7. What has become an eagerly anticipated annual event sponsored by ANE each November?
8. Describe some interesting characteristics of some elders who have been adopted.
9. What do you think are some of the more intriguing or creative aspects of this program?

WRITING OPTIONS

Collaborate with Peers

1. Assume you have been asked by your employer to develop a volunteer outreach program for your town's needy elderly. With two or three of your classmates, develop a plan that incorporates the types of services volunteers would provide as well as the ways volunteers could be recruited. Finally, estimate the operating budget. (Assume that your employer would fund this budget.) Try to be as detailed and realistic as possible. Once you have developed your plan and its budget, write individual essays explaining your plan.

Connecting with the Author's Ideas

2. The author notes that some of the needs of the elders are rather basic: a spoon, a six-volt battery, shampoo, and blankets. If you have worked for a volunteer agency that provides those in need

with basic necessities, describe how you first learned about this association, why you decided to volunteer, and what basic necessities you no longer take for granted.

Other Options

3. The rug show that Linda Meyers organized became an annual event and a successful fund-raising activity. Describe the most creative or effective fund-raising drive you have observed or participated in. It can be a high school fund-raising drive for a sports team or school trip or dance, or it can be a fund-raising drive for a club, community or religious organization. Then devise a fund-raising drive for your own favorite charity or volunteer organization.

4. "A Circle of Giving" describes the lives of elderly Navajos on reservations. Although they face great poverty, their lives are filled with simplicity, natural beauty, and their own generosity. In a paragraph or short essay, describe how you would like to live the last years of your life.

Two Women, Two Lives . . . One Common Spirit

John Grogan

In September 1997, Mother Teresa and Princess Diana, two of the world's most famous women, both died within the same week. In this brief article, columnist John Grogan reminds us that each woman "taught us something about sacrifice and compassion, generosity of spirit, and the worth of human life."

Words You May Need to Know

ironies (para. 1)	unexpected outcomes
ideals (1)	standards
multitudes (2)	great number of people
afforded (2)	supplied to
brethren (2)	fellow human beings
royal trappings (3)	dress and decorations of royalty
creased (3)	wrinkled
self-imposed (3)	chosen by oneself
chaste (3)	sexually pure
embodiment (3)	bodily form
extramarital (3)	outside of marriage
flawed (4)	imperfect
mortal (4)	human being
vulnerability (4)	openness to hurt or temptation
utter (4)	complete
subtle (5)	difficult to perceive
cradling (5)	holding

oddly (5)	strangely
ministering to (5)	caring for
cast-off (5)	abandoned
lepers (5)	people suffering from leprosy, a disease of the skin and nerves
gutter (7)	the home of the poor, of those who live in dirt
cynicism (7)	distrust, lack of belief that people can be good
self-absorption (7)	preoccupation with one's own thoughts, interests, and desires
compassion (8)	deep sympathy and desire to help
allied (8)	allied

First Princess Diana. And now Mother Teresa. It is one 1 of those great ironies of life that these two women who so deeply respected each other—and who, each in her own way, represented the ideals of virtue to millions—would be gone in the same week.

One did not have to be a follower of either to feel the 2 shock and sadness. That Mother Teresa's death came on Friday, even as the world prepared to bury Diana, only increased the sense of loss. Mother Teresa died where she belonged—at home in Calcutta where she had dedicated her life to the poor, the sick and dying. Her greatest gift was not the multitudes she fed and nursed but the dignity she afforded even the least of our brethren.

The glamorous princess, in her jeweled gowns and royal 3 trappings, was so very different from the little nun with the creased face who led a life of self-imposed poverty. Yet they shared common ground. One was chaste and saintly, the very embodiment of goodness, a mother figure to millions. The other, like all of us, was not without sin—an unhappy wife, trapped in a loveless marriage, who took comfort in an extramarital affair.

4   Mother Teresa was our saint on Earth. Diana was our mirror image—a flawed mortal we could all relate to. It was Mother Teresa's selflessness, her utter holiness, that won our admiration; it was Diana's imperfect vulnerability, her utter humanness, that made her all the more dear to our hearts.

5   For all their differences, each was pulled toward those in need: Mother Teresa, whose work with the poor was recognized with the Nobel Peace Prize, in obvious ways; Princess Diana in ways more subtle. Yet the images of the princess cradling unwanted AIDS babies at a time when few others would were oddly similar to those of Mother Teresa ministering to cast-off lepers.

6   Diana's death moved the eighty-seven-year-old Mother Teresa to rise from her sick bed this week to reflect on the Princess: "She helped me to help the poor, and that's the most beautiful thing. She was very much concerned about the poor. That's why she came close to me."

7   One was the saint of the gutter; the other, the people's princess. You didn't need to be a Catholic to love Mother Teresa or British to love Diana. In an age of increasing cynicism and self-absorption, they reminded us of the good in mankind.

8   In their own very different ways, each taught us something about sacrifice and compassion, about generosity of spirit and the worth of human life. And now, as oddly allied in death as they were in life, both are at once gone.

DISCUSSION QUESTIONS

1. According to author John Grogan, what was ironic about the deaths of Princess Diana and Mother Teresa?
2. Where did Mother Teresa die, and what does Grogan believe was her "greatest gift"?
3. What was one basic difference between these two women? What was one similarity?
4. How did Princess Diana's death affect Mother Teresa?
5. What do you think the phrase "the people's princess" implies?

WRITING OPTIONS

Collaborate with Peers

1. With two or three classmates, discuss some famous people whose death affected you. Try to recall how you felt when you learned of the person's death. Consider why you admired each person and what he or she will be remembered for. When you have completed your discussion, write about one famous person whose death had an impact on you.

Connecting to the Author's Words

2. Locate and read some newspaper accounts of Mother Teresa's life. Based on John Grogan's statement that her "greatest gift was not the multitudes she fed and nursed but the dignity she afforded even the least of our brethren," see how many examples you can find from your research that support this statement. Then, in your own words, summarize these examples in a short essay.

3. John Grogan writes that "Diana was our mirror image—a flawed mortal we could all relate to." Find several magazine or newspaper accounts of Diana's life, and make a list of examples that support Grogan's statement. Summarize these points in a short essay.

Other Options

4. Based on the article, select three traits from either Mother Teresa or Princess Diana, and describe how a person you know and admire reflects these traits.

The Music Man

Sean Piccoli

After his wife died, eighty-year-old Gil Spence found himself searching for a purpose. To the delight of South Florida nursing home residents, he found it in his record collection. Playing his records and conducting sing-alongs, he knows he has found a calling. "I don't charge for this," he says. "It's therapy for me, too."

Words You May Need to Know

hand truck (para. 1)	a small frame on wheels for carrying loads
stereo console (1)	equipment for playing records and cassettes
strapping (2)	tall and robust
trundles (2)	rolls
cueing up (2)	following up on
jovial (3)	hearty
gravelly (3)	grating, harsh
node (3)	a mass of tissue
rec-room (4)	recreation room
USO (5)	United Services Organization, a group that helps members of the armed forces
exultant (5)	joyful
amplifier (7)	a device that magnifies sound
access (8)	ability to use
inventory (8)	equipment on a list, or the making of a list of objects
reel-to-reel deck (12)	an old form of tape recorder and player

Prohibition (9)	the period from 1920 to 1933 when the sale of alcoholic beverages in America was forbidden
music-obsessed (9)	preoccupied with music
bug (9)	craze, obsession
abiding (10)	continuing, unchanging
acquiring (10)	getting for oneself
bounty (13)	abundance, generous supply
incredibly (13)	unbelievably
obscure (13)	not well known
Alzheimer's disease (14)	a brain disease that leads to confusion or memory loss
subdued (15)	quiet
medley (15)	music that combines a mixture of songs
standards (15)	old, favorite songs
lyric (16)	words to a song
literally (17)	actually, really

Gil Spence, retiree, cracks himself up every time he 1
says, "I got nowhere to go and nothing to do, and all day to
do it when I get there." But he's running late. On a recent
Friday afternoon, Spence, 80, rolls a hand truck through
the front door of Mariner Health, a nursing home in his
Boynton Beach, Florida, neighborhood. Strapped to the cart
are an old stereo console and a milk crate holding two
speakers, wiring, and a dozen albums.

Spence, a strapping man with combed-back whitish 2
hair, trundles everything past the reception desk and stops
in a windowed recreation room. He moves the gear onto a
table and, with the residents arriving by wheelchair and on

foot, plugs in. A cassette goes into the console. Records come out of the milk crate. Spence is cueing up a request made the previous Friday by one Mariner resident for "America's Sweethearts," Golden Age duo Nelson Eddy and Jeanette MacDonald. But he opens, as always, with the cassette tape of "Happy Birthday to You" because there's always a good chance it's somebody's birthday.

3   Spence may be the world's oldest mobile diskjockey, but he is new to the field. He started in the spring, volunteering his time and his record collection at nursing homes, about a year after his wife, Jean, died following a long illness. "When she passed away, I was lost," says Spence, his voice a jovial but gravelly scrape—he had throat surgery to remove a node. "I didn't have anyone to grind up pills for . . . didn't have anyone to care for except myself." Now he has audiences every week at a handful of nursing homes in Palm Beach County.

4   About twenty residents are gathered to listen at Mariner. The rec-room group includes Wayne Vosburg, who tells a visitor, "I'm the last Vosburg there is." Esther Dunn, seventy-nine, rolls her eyes at certain songs and says, "Oh! This is one of my favorites." Rachel Lent, ninety-six, wonders, "Why is this so loud?"

5   Lent gets shushed by a couple of other residents. Spence lets Side 1 of the "America's Sweethearts" collection play straight through: "Ah! Sweet Mystery of Life (The Dream Melody)," "Rosalie," "Farewell to Dreams," "Ciribiribin," and "Stout-Hearted Men" drift by like moments at a USO dance. The couple's bluebird voices are scuffed by a smattering of needle-to-vinyl pops. But they're as exultant as ever singing like wartime recruiters, "Give me some men/Who are stout-hearted men."

6   Jackie Trimble, seventy-four, wheels into the room about twenty minutes after the program she requested has started. Those are her songs Spence is playing. Trimble is late, but pleased to see the DJ. "He's been here about four weeks, and I've been here every time," she says. "I'm really surprised he remembered me."

Spence has trouble forgetting things. He walks around 7 with the contents of a 3,200-album collection knocking around inside his head—which might have more storage space than his house. The Spence home interior looks like a collision between a flea market and a repair shop. Albums not shelved have taken over tabletops. Stereo equipment is labeled with numbers so he can keep the wiring scheme straight. A hand-written sign in the bedroom reads, "DON'T TURN ON TUNER #4 OR AMPLIFIER #4 IF RECEIVER #1 IS ON."

Spence appears to have quick access to every piece of 8 inventory. A breezy Latin song is playing on an old reel-to-reel deck in his living room. "What's that?" Spence is asked. "Los Norteamericanos," he says without looking up, "a band I heard in Tijuana."

Spence, a self-described "World War I baby" born in 9 Michigan in 1920, got early exposure to all kinds of music at the bars in Wisconsin that his parents ran after Prohibition. But he wasn't particularly music-obsessed. He first learned electronics as an Army radio engineer sent to North Africa during World War II. Spence came to South Florida afterward and tended bar in these parts for most of his life. He caught the record bug in his thirties. George Gershwin albums were among the first he bought. He calls a 1942 recording of Gershwin's "Rhapsody in Blue" by pianist Oscar Levant "my pride and joy."

Jean Spence—whom Gil Spence married, divorced, and 10 married again—had worked hard to keep her husband's abiding hobbies from taking over the place. "My wife was the neat one," he says. She beat back shelves crammed with vinyl albums, singles, cassette tapes and eight-tracks; hundreds of hours of reel-to-reel tapes; turntables, speakers, tape decks, amplifiers, and owner's manuals that Spence has spent decades acquiring.

He passed his first several months as a widower, he 11 says, "just sitting [at home] looking at the stars and watching the baseball game." Meanwhile, the house was going to hell. Everything was spilling out. Spence had to get organized. So he set himself a task: catalog every piece of music he owned and transfer some of the vinyl recordings to tape—for backup, he reasoned, in case anything ever happened to the albums. It would give him, in his own words, "something to do."

12 He began taping records reel-to-reel, an old method but ideal for him because he had miles of blank tape on five- and seven-inch spools, and a working reel-to-reel deck. He filled spiral-bound notebooks with names of albums and artists: Crosby, Lombardo, Gershwin, Belafonte, Sinatra, Krupa, Caruso, and on and on.

13 Somewhere along the inventory process, Spence got an idea: Why not share this bounty with some people who would appreciate it? "He found us," says Donna Verrow, until recently the activities director at Mariner Health. The nursing home agreed to a trial run. Spence played for a group of residents in June and went over well enough to be invited back once a week. "Some of the residents have really bonded with him," says Verrow. "They shoot the breeze and talk about these incredibly obscure songs that I just have no idea."

14 That engagement led to others; he plays two or three days a week now. His newest client is an Alzheimer's Community Care Center in West Palm Beach. Going in, he says, he was nervous and wondered if people stricken with Alzheimer's would even respond to music. "It went beautifully," Spence says. "Good thing I brought a lot of dance stuff: The employees were dancing with the patients. Everybody was up and having a good time."

15 A good time looks more subdued at a nursing home. Some residents doze through the recital. Most listen quietly. Spence has moved from America's Sweethearts to recordings of "Dancing in the Dark" and "Cheek to Cheek," followed by a Mitch Miller medley of standards. Spence hands out copies of a lyric sheet so Mariner residents can sing along. A few voices in the room pick up the verses of "Bicycle Built for Two."

16 Spence likes to save the sing-along for last. The program has run almost two hours this afternoon. He typically

winds up a visit by collecting the lyric sheets; they tend to disappear if he doesn't. "Those old people are really collectors," says Spence. "They'll collect anything." But he hasn't made the rounds yet. "You want to stay?" he asks nobody in particular. "I'll keep playing." He spins a Guy Lombardo tune.

"He'll just stay there till they kick him out, literally," 17 says Trimble, chuckling. "I think he's lonely, too, and enjoys being here."

Spence will tell you as much: "I don't charge for this; it's 18 therapy for me, too."

DISCUSSION QUESTIONS

1. Gil Spence is described as possibly "the world's oldest mobile disk jockey." What does he carry on his nursing home visits?
2. When did Spence start volunteering to play his records at nursing homes?
3. The author Sean Piccoli states that Spence actually "has trouble forgetting things" (rather than remembering things). Explain what this play on words means.
4. How was Spence exposed to music when he was young?
5. How did Jean Spence prevent her husband's hobbies from taking over their house?
6. After his wife died, how did Spence try to "get organized"?
7. How did people who had Alzheimer's disease respond to Spence's music?
8. Why does Spence enjoy his trips to nursing homes?

WRITING OPTIONS

Collaborate with Peers

1. With two or three classmates, compile a list of various stereotypical assumptions some teenagers have of the elderly and vice-versa. Then work individually on this assignment: Select one stereotypical assumption from each list and describe how a person you know does not fit the stereotype. Be as specific as possible.

Connecting with the Author's Ideas

2. The author, Sean Piccoli, says that Spence has "the contents of a 3,200-album collection knocking around inside his head." Piccoli is referring to Spence's knowledge of music from the mid-twentieth century. If you or someone you know is an expert in some area (for example: television shows, basketball, hip-hop music, fashion, science fiction movies, and so forth), write about the person and his or her expertise.

Other Options

3. Although Spence could technically be labeled as "elderly," what are some of his traits that are not usually associated with people in their eighties? Summarize these traits and provide examples of them.

4. Spence's wife had to work hard to prevent his hobbies from taking over the house. If you or a family member has a hobby that is literally taking over parts of your home, describe the hobby and explain when it started, what others find unusual about it, how well others tolerate it, and the benefits the hobbyist derives from it.

5. Spence began inventorying his vast record collection for easy reference. If you are a music lover and could save only your five favorite songs, describe why each song is so valuable to you, and then predict why the next generation would enjoy the songs also.

Each Day Is a Lifetime

Judith Viorst

Judith Viorst, a bestselling author, volunteers weekly at a local hospice. In her words, "When somebody says to me, 'It must be depressing to volunteer in a hospice,' I try to explain why being allowed to do the small things I do is an honor and a privilege and, no, not depressing."

Words You May Need to Know

mavens (para. 2)	experts
hospice (2)	a nursing home for the dying
informing philosophy (3)	dominant belief
unstinting (3)	unlimited
drastic (3)	severe
futile (3)	useless
interventions (3)	interferences
measure (3)	amount
reek (4)	smell strongly and unpleasantly
pomposity (4)	showiness, self-importance
siblings (5)	brothers and sisters
lyrics (5)	words of the song
perched (5)	sat, rested
masses (5)	heaps
mentors (6)	trusted teachers, advisors
elect (6)	choose
strive (6)	try hard
profound (7)	deep
astonishing (7)	amazing

I remember trying to keep my voice from shaking as I ex- 1
plained to the nurse at the hospital that my mother, my dying

mother, was in pain. "You don't know her," I said. "You don't understand that she's someone who never cries. So if she's crying now, she must really be in hell—and you have to give her more medication *this minute.*" The nurse consulted her chart and said that my mother was due for another shot—in an hour. There was, though I pleaded and hollered, no appeal. In places that go by the book, the dying do not get to go gently into the night. My mother, age 62, did not go gently.

2   For a decade after her death I accepted, as hateful fact, that dying—the process of dying—had to be fitted into the rules and routines of a hospital. I also accepted as fact that on every issue, not just the issue of pain relief, the medical mavens had the final word. But then I heard about hospice care and became a weekly hospice volunteer. On Monday mornings for the past seven years, I've worked at Hospice of Washington, near my home in Washington, D.C. I have learned, in these seven years, that people needn't die the way my mother died. I've learned, as well, that there can be meaningful life at the end of life, that each day is a lifetime.

3   "Each day is a lifetime" is the informing philosophy of hospice, which offers comfort care, exquisite attention to special needs, and—yes—unstinting pain and symptom relief to people who (in most instances) have only six or fewer months left to live. Patients in hospice care, whether at home or in an inpatient facility, do not have their lives dragged out by a series of drastic and futile medical interventions, nor do they end their days hooked up to some machine. Treated by people instead of technology, they're given all possible ease of body and spirit. They're allowed a full measure of choice and dignity. For though the dying are dying, they may want butter but, please, no syrup on their pancakes. They may want their water ice cold, but without the ice. They may want to have this light off and that light on, their curtains drawn, another blanket. They may want to have more medication *this minute.*

4   By taking some control, by making choices, and by having their choices count, they are still counted among the living. And so when somebody says to me, "It must be

depressing to volunteer in a hospice," I try to explain why being allowed to do the small things I do is an honor and a privilege, and no, not depressing. I also try to explain—but where are the words that do not reek of pomposity?—that what I get from the dying is far greater than what the dying get from me.

What do we do? We sit together. We watch daytime TV 5 together, commenting on the weirdnesses we see. Sometimes I read them their favorite psalms from the Bible. Sometimes I read from a book of poetry. Sometimes we discuss their families and friends, their work, or how they met their spouses, or what they believe the Afterlife will be. Sometimes they speak of the illness that brought them to this place. Sometimes we just hold hands, and we don't say anything. I have sat in a hospice garden with a woman who named twelve tulips, one for each of her siblings, and dared me to commit them to memory. I have sung, in my not-so-great voice, "Down in the Valley" and "My Bonnie Lies Over the Ocean," and watched a silent old man mouth the lyrics with me. I have perched on the bed of a woman who gaily pored over masses of catalogs searching for something terrific in which to be buried. I have helped patients eat breakfast, helped change their diapers, helped make their beds, and respectfully helped wrap and tag their dead bodies. We volunteers need do only what we're comfortable doing. But we do need to feel fairly comfortable with death.

My mentors have been the nurses who elect to do this 6 work, nurses whose compassionate regard for the men and women in their care—and for their families (hospice also helps families)—brings me to my knees with admiration. *They* would have known who my mother was. They strive to know each man and woman there, from what will ease his suffering to whether she prefers cranberry juice to orange. They also know when to back off and respect a person's privacy, and when they ought to reach out to weep with someone or to offer a wordless embrace.

They know how to pay attention. They have taught me 7 to pay attention. And I find that by paying attention to what each of these one-of-a-kind human beings is and needs, we two—the dying sooner, the dying later—can fashion moments of profound connection and astonishing sweetness. "I went to the hospice to die," said one hospice patient, "and I lived." I went to the hospice to give, and I received.

DISCUSSION QUESTIONS

1. What does author Judith Viorst mean when she states that there was "no appeal" when she insisted that her mother needed more pain medication immediately?
2. What has Viorst learned about the differences between a hospital and a hospice regarding how each one treats a terminally ill patient?
3. How are the terminally ill still "counted among the living" in a hospice?
4. What does Viorst try to explain to those who feel that "volunteering in a hospice must be depressing"?
5. Who have become mentors for Viorst?
6. According to Viorst, what is the importance of "paying attention"?

WRITING OPTIONS

Collaborating with Peers

1. Viorst says that the sentence, "Each day is a lifetime," is the main belief of the hospice movement. Working with two or three classmates, discuss what this sentence means to those who work or live in a hospice. Then discuss how the sentence can also be a motto for other people. Write individual paragraphs or short essays based on your discussion.

Connecting with the Author's Ideas

2. The author regrets that she didn't know about hospice during her mother's last days; she learned only later that "people needn't die the way my mother died." She finds her volunteer work at a hospice very fulfilling now. If you are now a volunteer worker for an

organization you wish you had known about sooner, describe what your duties involve, what benefits you derive from your work, and how the organization could have helped you or someone you know if you had known about it earlier.

Other Options

3. Unfortunately, some hospitals and nursing homes are understaffed, and patients are not always treated as individuals. If you or someone you know has been treated poorly by an uncaring staff or bureaucracy, explain the effects of such treatment and how the treatment could have been more humane.

From the Heart

Richard Jerome, Beth Karlin, Peter Carlin,
Thomas Fields-Meyer, Alec Foege, and
Samantha Miller

In 1998, People *magazine profiled various generous and compassionate individuals from different walks of life. As the magazine noted, "Giving more than their share and finding joy in the gift, nine ordinary Americans make themselves unassuming symbols of the spirit of charity."*

Note: In this reading, discussion questions will accompany each brief selection. Writing options related to this reading are located after the final selection.

A Bootblack Saves His Tips for Sick Kids

Words You May Need to Know

bootblack (see title)	a person whose occupation is shining shoes
pediatric gastroenterology (1)	the study of children's diseases of the stomach
humanitarian (1)	a person who works to improve the welfare of mankind
developmentally disabled (2)	slow in mental development
telethon (2)	a fund-raising program on television
uncommon (3)	unusual
unshod (3)	with their shoes off
spiffs (3)	cleans
participants (3)	those who participate, members
pediatric endocrinologist (3)	a physician who specializes in children's diseases of the spleen
Andrew Carnegie (4)	a wealthy steel manufacturer

siblings (4)	brothers and sisters
clientele (4)	customers
beaming (6)	smiling happily

Dr. Samuel A. Kocoshis, director of pediatric gastroen- 1
terology at Children's Hospital of Pittsburgh, rests a foot on
a gray metal box and watches Albert Lexie work his magic,
spreading black polish then furiously buffing his client's
loafer. "Albert's work is as important as any doctor's," says
Kocoshis. "Albert is a true humanitarian."

Kocoshis doesn't exaggerate. Over the past seventeen 2
years, Lexie, who is developmentally disabled, has donated
more than $40,000 to the Children's Hospital Free Care
Fund, which helps pay medical costs for the needy—all from
tips on his two-dollar shines. He got the idea just before
Christmas 1979, when he saw a telethon for the hospital
on TV. "I said, 'I can do that; I can give money for the children,'" recalls Lexie, fifty-six, who earns about $9000 a year.
Working in and around his hometown of Monessen,
Pennsylvania, he saved $730 by the next telethon. "Then a
friend asked me, do I want to see where I give my money,"
Lexie recalls. "He took me to Children's Hospital, and someone says, 'Do you want to shine shoes here?' 'Oh, yes,' I said."

Lexie has been servicing hospital staffers on Thursdays 3
and Tuesdays ever since, working the halls like a doctor on
rounds; it's not uncommon to find distinguished physicians
sitting at meetings unshod while Lexie spiffs leather in
the next room. Thirteen years ago, he started Albert's Shoe
Shine Club, where participants get a free shine for every five
he punches on their membership cards. And he gives a prize—
say, free lunch at the cafeteria—to the month's top tipper. "I
thought I'd never win, so I started bringing in shoes twice a
week," says April's champ, Dr. Thomas Foley, Jr., sixty-one, a
pediatric endocrinologist. "I also bring in my wife's shoes."

Like another of Pittsburgh's big givers—Andrew 4
Carnegie—Lexie grew up poor. Abandoned by their father,
he and his three siblings were raised by their mother, Nellie,
on public assistance in a Monessen housing project. "Our

mother did everything for him," says Lexie's sister Kathy Cooper, forty-nine. "Albert grew up in a time when if someone in your family was slow, you kept him almost like in a corner." Still, Lexie made it to high school in special classes, and though he never graduated, he learned to read and write. He found his calling when he saw some boys making shoe-shine boxes in shop class. "I said, 'That's what I want to do,'" says Lexie, who made his own box, then went door-to-door, building a clientele.

5   More independent since Nellie's death in 1978, he rents a one-room apartment, cooks and cleans for himself and likes playing gospel tapes. He cherishes his monthly visits with the hospital's patients. "Last year the kids made a big birthday card for Albert," says staffer Mary Diesing. "He was so happy, he started crying."

6   "They're my kids," Lexie says, beaming. "They like me."

DISCUSSION QUESTIONS

1. What does Albert Lexie do, and how much money has he donated over the years to the Children's Hospital Free Care Fund?
2. Where did Lexie get the idea for donating to this fund?
3. What club did Lexie start, and what are some of the incentives for participants to be good tippers?
4. What did some of the children at the hospital make for Lexie that made him cry with happiness?

An Ex-Slave's Son Takes Affirmative Action

Words You May Need to Know

alma mater (para. 2)	old school
endowing (2)	giving funding for
abolition (2)	elimination
affirmative action (2)	an effort made to admit members of minorities to college

dynamic (4)   energetic and forceful

fathom (4)   thoroughly understand

Crispus Attucks Wright was deeply moved when he re- 1
turned last summer to the University of Southern California
Law School. Sixty years ago, his was the only black face in
the law school. But his strongest impression last year, he
says, "was that I saw African Americans *there.* I woke up the
next morning and knew where my donation would go."

Wright, eighty-four, a retired Beverly Hills lawyer, has 2
given two million dollars to his alma mater, endowing
scholarships not only for minority students but for students who pledge to use their degrees to serve minority
communities. In a small way he hopes to soften the impact
of California's abolition of affirmative action in public
college admissions. "USC has done an excellent job of re-
cruiting qualified minority students," he says. "I wanted to
encourage that."

Wright is the son of a former slave, Warner Wright Sr., 3
who was born on a Louisiana plantation and was freed when
he was eight; he put himself through a college founded for
ex-slaves and built a career as a high school principal in
Alexandria, Louisiana. Warner died when Crispus was only
six, but Wright followed his father's example, sometimes
working three jobs at once to pay his way through USC's law
school.

"Crispus is a dynamic man. He has a sparkle and a 4
smile that's just amazing," says USC law student Stephen
Perry, twenty-three, who gets $23,000 a year from the
Wright Scholarship Endowment. "I can't fathom the amount
of money he has given away." Says Wright: "It's the joy of my
life to be able to give."

DISCUSSION QUESTIONS

1. Sixty years ago, why was Crispus Wright unique at the University
of Southern California Law School?

2. How much money has Wright given to this university, and what scholarships has he made possible?

3. What is admirable about Wright's father's background, and how did he set an example for his son?

A Teacher Enriches His Beloved Alma Mater

Words You May Need to Know

frugality (para. 1)	thriftiness
haute cuisine (1)	fine cooking
splurging (1)	spending money extravagantly, on expensive purchases
amass (2)	accumulate
AT&T (2)	American Telephone and Telegraph
blue-chip stocks (2)	high-priced stocks
socked away (2)	put into savings
USO (3)	United Services Organization, a group that helps members of the armed forces
revues (3)	theatrical entertainments
philanthropist (4)	a person who donates to needy persons, causes, or institutions
Rockefeller, Vanderbilt (4)	families with great wealth

1   A drama instructor at Miami Beach Senior High School for thirty-two years, Jay Jensen has raised frugality to an art form. He clips coupons from the Sunday paper, prefers Denny's to haute cuisine, takes public transportation, and shares a 950-square foot, one-bedroom apartment with his ninety-three-year-old mother, Billie. "I don't know what splurging means," says Jensen, sixty-seven. "I'm not a fussy eater, and you can wear only so much clothing."

All of which is fortunate for the University of Miami, 2 where Jensen earned a bachelor's degree in 1954. This April, Jensen gave $500,000 to the university's School of Education to endow scholarships, raising the sum of his gifts to his alma mater to nearly three million dollars—not bad for a retired teacher who had never made more than $46,000 a year. How did he amass his fortune? "I still don't understand it myself," he says with a laugh, explaining that in 1960 he got ten shares of AT&T from his mother and just kept buying blue-chip stocks. Now he has close to five milion dollars socked away.

A self-described conservative investor, Jensen longed to 3 be in show business when he was growing up in Newark, New Jersey, the son of a jewelry designer. The closest he got to stardom, though, was when he and a St. Petersburg Junior College pal, future star Carroll Baker, teamed up as dancing partners at USO revues in the early '50s. "He was so outrageous, I always thought he would be successful," says Baker.

As it turned out, Jensen found his success first in the 4 classroom, where he taught and inspired Andy Garcia—for which, the actor has said, he "will always be thankful"—and later as a philanthropist. "We come into this world with nothing," says Jensen, "and I don't care who you are—a Rockefeller, a Vanderbilt—we're all going to go out with nothing. This way I'm leaving my mark, and generations to come will benefit."

DISCUSSION QUESTIONS

1. How does Jay Jensen keep his living expenses to a minimum, and how much money has he accumulated since 1960? How much money did he give to the University of Miami's School of Education?

2. What subject did Jensen teach, and what future professional actor did he inspire?

3. What is Jensen's philosophy about life?

"God's Helper" Delivers His Bounty

Words You May Need to Know

bounty (see title)	generous gifts
honor (para. 2)	accept
pleas (2)	appeals
doled out (2)	given out in small quantities
Albert Schweitzer (2)	a doctor and missionary in Africa who won the Nobel Peace Prize
Martin Luther King, Jr. (2)	a minister and civil rights leader who won the Nobel Peace Prize
recipients (2)	receivers
bedridden (3)	confined to her bed
donors (3)	a person who gives or donates
stipend (3)	regular payment
augment (3)	increase

1   They were hardly standard mailing addresses. "The Man Who Gives Away Money," read one envelope. Another was sent to "God's Helper." And yet, over the years, each letter found its way to the Richmond, Virginia, home of Thomas Cannon.

2   Cannon, seventy-three, doesn't honor pleas for cash. Rather, he finds unsuspecting strangers and surprises them with checks of up to one thousand dollars. Since 1972, the retired postal worker, whose salary never climbed above $32,000 a year, has doled out about $102,000. His generosity arises in part from his humble origins. After his father, a Richmond transit worker, died when Cannon was three, his mother moved the family to his grandmother's wooden shack in rural Virginia. Following time in the Navy, he

returned to Richmond, where he married Princetta Cooper, now seventy-one. Unhappy sorting mail at the post office, he fed his spiritual hunger by reading Albert Schweitzer and Martin Luther King, Jr. and came to feel that he had a mission to improve the world. "I might have been chosen because I was the sort of person who could withstand ridicule," he says. The recipients of Cannon's good will include a wheelchair marathoner who lost his legs in Vietnam, eight Chesapeake, Virginia, kids who pulled a horse out of a marsh, and a group building a Hindu temple. He once gave a blind street beggar a thousand dollars accompanied by a brief note: "Please buy your dog a steak."

Remarkably, he was giving so generously while living in 3 a slum area. To make matters worse, Princetta, who is blind, suffered two strokes that have left her bedridden since 1990. Cannon's good deeds were rewarded, though, in 1995, when real estate developer Gary Fenchuk raised $45,000 from donors to buy Cannon a new home, then began providing a monthly stipend to augment his pension. Of course, Cannon has often put the money to other purposes. Once, after accepting a Christmas check for $2,300, he handed out that amount in fifty-dollar bills to strangers on a bus. "When it comes time to depart," he says, "I'll have the satisfaction of having tried to make a more peaceful world."

DISCUSSION QUESTIONS

1. What does Thomas Cannon do that is so unusual?
2. Since 1972, how much money has Cannon given away, and what is his annual salary as a postal worker?
3. Where did Cannon's spirit of generosity come from? Explain.
4. Despite Cannon's giving so much money away, how extravagantly does he live?
5. How have others benefited from Cannon's gifts?
6. How does Cannon justify his unusual habit of giving away so much of his money?

A Woman's Gift Is Music to Baltimore's Ears

Words You May Need to Know

ne'er-do-well (para. 1)	slang term for a person constantly in trouble
ventures (para. 1)	business undertakings in which loss is risked in the hope of profit
con artist (1)	a swindler, a deceiver
gullible (1)	easily deceived
plucky (2)	brave
debacle (2)	sudden collapse
fiasco (2)	complete failure
the Depression (2)	the economic crisis and period of low business activity, widespread unemployment, and poverty in the United States, beginning in 1929 and continuing through the 1930s
siblings (3)	brothers and sisters
paramount (3)	most important

1   By 1993, retired Baltimore social worker Jean Harnish had lost her life savings—and gone $20,000 in debt—supporting a ne'er-do-well former client in can't-miss business ventures. "I thought with enough help he could get his life going," says Harnish. "But he was a con artist, and I was gullible."

2   Lesser mortals might have lost faith. Not the plucky Harnish, eighty-three. Since recovering from the financial debacle, which left her living for a brief time in a homeless shelter, Harnish has pledged $15,000 a year for three years—half the $30,000 she receives annually from Social Security and her pension—to Baltimore's Peabody Conservatory of Music. "I wouldn't have given this money if there had not been this big fiasco in my life," says Harnish, who regularly attends concerts at the Conservatory, just three blocks from her $310-a-month efficiency apartment, To pay off the $20,000 dollars in debts to friends, Harnish sold her car,

gave up nights at the opera and stopped traveling. "I grew up in the Depression," she says. "I know how to live simply."

A native of Palmyra, Pennsylvania, Harnish and her two [3] siblings were raised by their father, a school principal, and their mother, who directed a church choir. After earning a degree from Bryn Mawr in 1947, Harnish moved to Baltimore, where she counseled troubled families before retiring five years ago. "She is known for giving wise advice," says Ellen Barnum, a Peabody graduate student and friend, "She is so full of life and eager to share the things she loves." Among which, music is paramount.

"People say I should travel or do this or that," says [4] Harnish. "But I'm doing what I want. I want the music to go on after I'm gone."

How to Make Kids Smile? Pay for Their Braces

Words You May Need to Know

coveted (para. 1)	strongly desired
alas (1)	sadly, unfortunately
snaggletooth (1)	someone who has a tooth growing out beyond or apart from others
ordeal (2)	severe experience
subsidize (2)	pay for
affiliated (3)	associated
facial disfigurements (3)	scars, blemishes, or other conditions that spoil the appearance of the face
orthodontia (4)	braces or other devices that correct irregular teeth

Growing up in Chicago during the Depression, Virginia [1] Brown coveted one thing above all else: her older sister Marjorie's braces. Alas, her parents couldn't afford to fix both girls' teeth. When a grade school classmate called Virginia "snaggletooth," she was crushed. "I don't think I smiled from that moment on," recalls Brown, now seventy-two.

2   Not, at least, until she turned sixteen and finally got her longed-for braces. Determined to spare others the same ordeal, Brown has donated $130,000 to the University of Missouri–Kansas City's dental school to pay for braces for forty-eight needy children. The Kansas City resident has also started a program with local orthodontists to subsidize treatment for thirty kids a year. "When you need braces," she says, "you need them now, not when you can afford them."

3   This isn't the first time Brown has given money away. In the mid-'80s, she and her second husband, oilman Maurice L. Brown, gave hundreds of thousand of dollars to UMKC and affiliated hospitals to help patients with facial disfigurements. And in 1992, three years after her husband's death from sinus cancer, Brown donated a dental wing to a clinic at the University of Kansas. It was then that she hit on the idea of braces, which cost about $2,750 per child.

4   "Almost nobody gives money for orthodontia," says Brown, a grandmother of six. "To feel good about yourself is so important. There are so many other things that knock you down in life."

DISCUSSION QUESTIONS

1. When Virginia Brown was young, what did she want "above all else"?

2. How old was Brown when she got her wish, and why has she donated $130,000 to the University of Missouri–Kansas City's dental school?

3. Who benefits from the yearly program Brown started with local orthodontists?

4. When did Brown get the idea regarding braces for children whose families couldn't afford them? Why does she feel providing orthodontia is so important for children?

A Delaware Family Gives Till It Hurts

Words You May Need to Know

browse (para. 1)	look through
valedictorian (1)	the student, usually the one with the highest academic ranking, who delivers the farewell speech at a graduation ceremony
revere (1)	respect, honor
latter (2)	the second mentioned of two (The first mentioned is the *former.*)
literacy advocate (2)	a person who promotes the importance of reading and writing skills for all
modest (2)	not showy or extremely expensive
wryly (3)	sarcastically

At times, growing up in Wilmington, Delaware, Josh 1
Arthur didn't completely understand his parents' kind-
nesses to strangers. He and his sixteen-year-old sister Emily
had to browse through the discount ranks at Marshall's
while friends shopped at Macy's. Then, after graduating as
Concord High School's 1997 valedictorian and wrestling
captain, he had to give up his dream of studying at Stanford
and attend the University of North Carolina, which offered a
$10,000 scholarship and lower tuition. Yet Josh, nineteen,
has come to revere his parents. "I was disappointed," he
says. "But giving away the money instead of paying for my
education was the right decision."

Sam and Judy Arthur donate forty percent of their 2
income, or forty thousand dollars a year, to six charities,
including their Brandywine Valley Baptist Church and Food
for the Hungry. On Judgment Day, explains Sam, forty-eight,
"I could say that I had a really nice automobile or beach
house, or I could say I tried to make a difference in people's

lives." Choosing the latter, Sam, a DuPont chemist, and Judy, fifty, a paid literacy advocate, drive a 1984 VW Rabbit and a 1989 VW Fox and live in a modest three-bedroom house. But having splurged recently on a CD player and a VCR, says Sam, "we're part of the twentieth century now."

3   Raised on a farm in North Manchester, Indiana, Sam was already giving away ten percent of his one dollar weekly allowance when he was eight. "From an early age, I wanted to do what I thought was pleasing to God," he says. His one regret is that he hasn't found a way to donate a full half of his income. "I didn't realize children would be so expensive," he says wryly.

4   Still, he hopes he has given Josh and Emily more than just a roof over their heads. "I've always thought that if they were concerned with the welfare of others, they would be happy," he says. Josh understands. "Their giving has really blessed them," he says. "If I had the money today, I would probably do the same thing."

DISCUSSION QUESTIONS

1. When Josh Arthur was a child, what did his parents do which was difficult for him to understand?
2. How large a percentage of their income do Sam and Judy Arthur donate to charities each year? What is Sam's explanation for giving away so much of their income?
3. What purchase does the couple consider "splurging"?
4. How does Sam Arthur hope his children have benefited from his habit of giving? Does Josh have a different view of his parents' charitable giving than he did as a child?

In a Bleak Place, a Kind Presence

Words You May Need to Know

bleak (see title)	hopeless, depressing
lurking (para. 1)	lying in wait, wandering quietly but watchfully

amid (1)	among
intimidating (1)	frightening
impose (2)	thrust oneself on others
corporal (2)	low-level officer
bouncer (2)	a person hired at a bar, to throw out disorderly persons
vowed (3)	pledged, promised
prominence (4)	fame

Lurking amid the darkened pawn shops of a garbage-strewn street in downtown Norfolk, Virginia, Don Stephenson cuts an intimidating profile. But to the neighborhood's homeless, his six-foot, three-hundred-pound figure is reassuring. One night a week, Stephenson, thirty-six, parks his Lincoln Town Car by the Greyhound bus station and distributes free food and cash to all who ask. "I don't want to see anyone hungry," he says. "I take it personally." 1

In 1991, Stephenson was homeless himself for a spell after the grandparents with whom he lived died and a cousin inherited their property. "I always had a lot of pride," he says. "I didn't want to impose." A former Army corporal working as a poorly paid nightclub bouncer, Stephenson eventually landed a seven-dollars-an-hour job as a janitor at a local power plant. But his time on the streets left an impression. "I didn't know where my next meal was coming from," he says. "It was rough." 2

Within months he was promoted to crane operator—and vowed to give others a lift. By putting in overtime, Stephenson earned enough to dole out fifty to one hundred dollars every week, mostly on street corners, in fives and tens. "When you try to do God's will," he says, "things will happen." 3

One thing that happened was that Stephenson, by then promoted again, to boiler mechanic, got a write-up last year in *The Virginian-Pilot*. He used his newfound prominence to organize a clothing drive and a Thanksgiving feast for three hundred of Norfolk's neediest. "They want to know 4 that people really care," he says. "I understand because I've been there."

DISCUSSION QUESTIONS

1. What does Don Stephenson do one night a week in downtown Norfolk, Virginia?
2. What are some of the low-paying jobs Stephenson has held?
3. What is Stephenson's current job, and how much money does he give away each week to those in need?
4. What is Stephenson's motivation for helping the homeless, and what does he say about Norfolk's neediest individuals?

WRITING OPTIONS

Collaborate with Peers

1. The profiles in "From the Heart" include people who don't make much money but manage to give to the needy anyway. With two or three classmates, brainstorm ways that you, despite a tight budget, could set aside a little money each week (loose change, savings from supermarket coupons, and so forth) to contribute to charity. Then write individual paragraphs or short essays on three ways to save a little for charity.

Connecting with the Author's Ideas

2. One of the people profiled, Crispus Wright, says, "It's the joy of my life to be able to give." Write about a time when you felt good because you gave to someone. You may have given a tangible gift, like a birthday present or flowers on Mother's Day, or you may have given an intangible one, like the gift of time or special attention. Describe the gift and how you felt when you gave it.

Other Options

3. Review the brief tales of generous giving, and then select one individual who impressed you the most. In a paragraph or short

essay, summarize the reasons for your choice. Arrange your supporting details in emphatic order (least to most important).

4. Parents mentioned in various accounts significantly influenced their children's values and attitudes. Select two individuals whose parents (or parent) greatly affected them, and summarize the extent of this positive parental influence.

5. We often assume that people who give away thousands of dollars must be wealthy. However, several profiles in this article contradict this stereotypical assumption. Do you feel that any of these generous individuals is behaving irrationally? In a short essay, defend your view as specifically and logically as you can.

6. If you suddenly found yourself able to donate thousands of dollars to a variety of charitable causes, how would you determine which charities would make the most efficient use of your gift? Would you research how the money would be distributed? Would you interview anyone? In a short essay, describe the steps you would follow to select the most suitable charities for your generous donations.

CREDITS

Matt Schudel, "Finding the Key" by Matt Schudel. Copyright © 1998. Reprinted by permission of *the Sun Sentinel.*

Robert Huer, "Sammy Sosa: Homerun Hitter With Heart" by Robert Huer. Reprinted from *Américas,* a bi-monthly magazine published by the General Secretariat of the Organization of American States in English and Spanish.

Elizabeth Berg, "My Heroes," by Elizabeth Berg. Copyright © 1992 by Elizabeth Berg. First appeared in *Parents.* Reprinted by permission of International Creative Management Inc.

Roger Rosenblatt, "The Man in the Water" by Roger Rosenblatt. Copyright © 1982 Time, Inc. Reprinted by permission.

Tamika Simmons, "Beyond the Call" by Tamika Simmons. Copyright © 1998. Reprinted by permission of *the Sun Sentinel.*

Mike Mayo, "New Yorkers Comfort the Heroes" by Michael Mayo. Copyright © 2001. Reprinted by permission of *the Sun Sentinel.*

Andy Friedberg, "A Real Survivor" by Andy Friedberg. Copyright © 2000. Reprinted by permission of *the Sun Sentinel.*

Susan Straight, "The Heroism of Day to Day Dads" by Susan Straight. Copyright © 1998 by Susan Straight. Reprinted by permission of the Richard Parks Agency. First published in *Family Circle* magazine.

Colin Pero, "Winning for Zola" by Colin Pero. Reprinted with permission from the January 1999 *Reader's Digest.* Copyright © 1999 by The Reader's Digest Assn., Inc.

Suzanne Chazin, "No Turning Back: The Singer Named Jewel" by Suzanne Chazin. Reprinted with permission from the January

PHOTO CREDITS